The Life and Times of Victoria Architect
P. LEONARD JAMES
FRAIC, MAIBC

With researched lists of his commissions and those of his partners:
Hubert Savage, ARIBA, MAIBC and Douglas James, MAIBC

Rosemary James Cross, BA

Dear Brutus Publishing
Victoria, BC

Copyright © 2005 Rosemary James Cross – Dear Brutus Publishing

All rights reserved. No part of this publication may be reproduced or transmitted in any form or by any means, electronic or mechanical, including photocopy, recording, or any information storage and retrieval system, without permission in writing from the author.

Library and Archives Canada Cataloguing in Publication

Cross, Rosemary James, 1924-
    The life and times of Victoria architect P. Leonard James / Rosemary James Cross.
Includes bibliographical references and index.
ISBN 0-9737259-0-7
    1. James, P. Leonard, 1878-1970. 2. Architects—British Columbia—Biography. 3. Architecture—British Columbia—Victoria—20th century. I. Title.
NA749.J34C76 2005   720'.92   C2005-901962-X

Book design and layout: Jim Bisakowski, Desktop Publishing Ltd.
                              desktoppublishing@shaw.ca
                              bookpublishingservices.com

Printed in Canada

Dear Brutus Publishing
349 Linden Ave.
Victoria, BC   V8V 4G1
250-384-2461
dbrutus@shaw.ca

Acknowledgments

Much of the information comes from The British Columbia Archives, The City of Victoria Archives, The Esquimalt Archives, The Saanich Archives, The Archives of the Anglican Diocese of British Columbia, The Cowichan Valley Museum and Archives and The Edmonton City Archives.

Thanks to supportive family members; the Canadian Authors' Association and many others for information, especially Jennifer Nell Barr, Stuart Stark, Donald Luxton, R.W. Siddall, Dr. Nick Russell, Mary Doody Jones, Dr. William Muir, Colin Barr, and in particular to Judith Andersen, Nick and Sharon Russell, R.W. Baxter, and Janet Stevens, who worked with the Victoria Heritage Foundation team cataloguing the City of Victoria's residential and neighbourhood building plans, and researched from the City of Victoria Downtown Heritage Registry by Foundation Group Designs, 1989, and revised in 1996.

Thanks to Dr. Larry McCann for the map he compiled and to Ole Heggen of the Department of Geography, University of Victoria.

Introduction

Percy Leonard James was my father. He practised architecture in Canada for over 45 years. I am not attempting an architectural treatise of his work, but am telling his life story as I know and have researched it. I hope this history evokes many memories and that my account of his personal and working life stories offers an enlightening and amusing view of the life and times of the architect Percy Leonard James.

Many anecdotes are from his childhood and my own. The changes that have occurred in everyday living since Victorian times fascinated us both. My parents lived for over fifty years in our comfortable family home in Oak Bay. It had window-seats and many nooks and crannies where things could be stored, creating a family archive rich in Canadiana.

The lists of buildings are an important part of this book. They include work not only of my father, but also of his partners, his brother Douglas James and Hubert Savage. The excellent work of his partners has been recorded less fully and I expect these lists will help many people who are interested in architectural heritage and local history. What a lot of buildings there are to consider!

Foreword
by Pamela Charlesworth, FRAIC

'Architecture is the way a certain period of time expresses itself'
Mies Van der Rohe

Rosemary James Cross has cast her father, Percy Leonard James, as the centerpiece of the story of a time when Victoria's rich architectural legacy was emerging.

She weaves a very personal story of a family, in which she was an only child, into the cultural, economic and political fabric of an era of this unfolding capital of Canada's most western province. Her father's work was not only a reflection of where he had come from, having been in practice in England prior to coming to Canada in 1906, but also was an indicator of where Victoria wished to go and how it wished to be perceived.. It was fashioned for the time but, as we now know, ageless in it's contribution to the quality and character of what is clearly, the rich architectural legacy we enjoy today.

Working on his own or in collaboration with his brother, Douglas James, Hubert Savage, K.B. Spurgin and others, including, on a number of occasions with the volatile and talented Francis Rattenbury, his works include major public and commercial buildings, the CPR Steamship Terminal, Royal Jubilee Hospital, the Crystal Garden and the Federal Building. They include grand mansions, as well as modest urban residences including those that spoke of changing times in the International or West Coast vernacular. His regular visits to the British Isles no doubt contributed to his knowledge of and insight into the wide range of architectural movements in the world as he continued to search for expressions to convey the changing times in Victoria and beyond.

The collection of his drawings, together with the extensive photographs of his work, most, thankfully still standing, and a well-researched listing of his projects, provide a very complete outline for those interested in pursuing a serious architectural study. For those of us within the profession, it allows us to relive the times of those we knew only from a distance, through their work, as we continue to search for expression within our period of time. For those that simply want, through this additional knowledge, to know and better understand the Victoria around them it is an "enjoyable read" that brings to life the social 'mores' of our not too distant past, through the story of a family whose father left such a lasting legacy to the city we know and enjoy today.

Foreword
by Geoffrey Castle, BA, MTA, FRGS

As an archivist with the B.C. Archives and Records Service it was always with a feeling of pride that I responded to public requests to see the plans and particulars of eminent British Columbia architects. One of them, Percy Leonard James, was of special interest to me as we both hailed from London, England. Imagine my delight when James's daughter Rosemary James Cross, an artist in her own right, asked me if I would like to write the foreword to her book which not only describes the architect and his work but also focuses on his role as a warm, loving husband and father.

From 1908, James worked on some 200 commissions, nearly half of which were for new construction work. For more than 40 years, James displayed a willingness and ability to design in a number of idioms which included Arts and Crafts, Tudor Revival, Georgian Revival, Chalet, Ranch style, International and Moderne. The style he appears to have favoured most – English Arts and Crafts – was popularized by William Morris and came to North America in the 1890s.

While the majority of James's commissions were in Oak Bay, there were nearly as many in the City of Victoria. Apart from Vancouver Island, others were for clients at Kelowna, Grand Forks and Lake Louise. It is gratifying to find today so many of this architect's structures still standing which undoubtedly is a reflection of the quality of materials and labour demanded.

James, like many of his contemporaries – Samuel Maclure, Francis Rattenbury, Thomas Sorby, Hubert Savage and Ridgway Wilson – was influenced by the work of British architect C.F.A. Voysey. With his first rate professional training, ability to correctly interpret his clients needs, and his likeable ways, it was small wonder those clients included Dr. J.D. Helmcken, R.H.B. Ker, Judge P.S. Lampman, J.A. Sayward, Captain Hobart Molson and Norman Yarrow.

Rosemary James Cross is to be congratulated on writing this book which was no easy task balancing objectivity and the inevitable bias. The inclusion of her father's sketches, working drawings, family photographs and recent photographs of some of James's commissions, together with a comprehensive bibliography and extensive lists of commissions, are unexpected and welcome bonuses.

I have no hesitation in recommending this book to a broad spectrum of readers who appreciate architecture, biography, history, or an interesting story.

Prologue

I can picture him at the opening on September 5th, 1952, of his last major work, the Victoria Federal Building and Post Office, as he waited at the entrance doors to meet and be congratulated by Prime Minister Louis St. Laurent. A thin six-footer, Percy Leonard James stood to one side of the dais with the sun shining on his bald pate, the picture of a reserved English gentleman. Quite a crowd had gathered. While the different levels of government representatives had their say, the architect found himself reflecting on his life's work.

… There was a lot to recall since his early training in England: the many hospitals he had helped design there before the First World War; his move to Canada and his first jobs in Edmonton before coming West to Victoria; his many partnerships, including the short-lived alliance with the bombastic, ill-fated Rattenbury. He thought with satisfaction of all the buildings he had designed around Victoria on Vancouver Island and beyond: the Royal Jubilee Hospital; two Colwood golf clubhouses; the Crystal Garden; the many fine residences and smaller comfortable homes; and of his contributions to the formation of the national and provincial Institutes of his profession. He considered how fortunate he had been to have had two strong women guiding his life and fortunes: first his mother, whose iron determination had helped shape his early life; and then his elegant wife whose own determination had out-matched his mother's and whose love, support and sense of humour had supplied unfailing strength to his life and career. His thoughts wandered to the office and his treasured library of technical books, many now outdated.

His young partner, Robert Siddall, newly-graduated from the University of Manitoba School of Architecture, had eyed some of these books in positive amazement - "Electricity" was the simple title of one of the oldest books, and "History of Architecture on the Comparative Method," Banister-Fletcher's beautifully illustrated Victorian tome, which had been presented to him by his first boss, A. Saxon Snell, when he left the London firm in 1906. Architects had relied upon this classic source book for many years, but with the rise of the International Style and new methods of construction it had become a relic.

It was well-past time for him to leave the profession he had chosen nearly sixty years ago…

Then it was his turn to shake the hand of the Prime Minister and be congratulated on this commission, his last major building.

James had intended to take retirement at age 69, but his architectural colleagues had insisted he take on this Federal Building and Post Office as a fitting culmination to his more than 45 years of practice in Canada. He felt relief that the building had come to a successful completion and he could now take a well-earned retirement. But more than that, he felt great satisfaction in this building that represented the climax of his art and his long years of practice in Victoria. He was glad to have undertaken this one last task. The building, his crowning achievement, stood firm behind him. It represented him.

And it would do so, in a way that he never expected, into the 21st century.

CONTENTS

Illustrations viii

CHAPTER ONE
Early Days 1

CHAPTER TWO
Pulling Up Stakes 15

CHAPTER THREE
First Jobs In Victoria 22

CHAPTER FOUR
James & James 31

CHAPTER FIVE
War and Weddings 43

CHAPTER SIX
Back and Booming 49

CHAPTER SEVEN
What Happened To Douglas 71

CHAPTER EIGHT
Recognizing Style 76

CHAPTER NINE
Family Holidays 87

CHAPTER TEN
Sink or Swim With Rattenbury and the C.P.R. . . . 94

CHAPTER ELEVEN
The James & Savage Partnership 112

CHAPTER TWELVE
A Year Away 134

CHAPTER THIRTEEN
The Practice After 1934 141

CHAPTER FOURTEEN
Glimpses of the Family 157

CHAPTER FIFTEEN
Crowning Glory 162

CHAPTER SIXTEEN
Retirement Years 167

CHAPTER SEVENTEEN
The Legacy 171

Appendix 175
Lists of Commissions 1909 – 1954 by P. Leonard James 175
P. Leonard James Houses Map and Street Address . . 195
Commissions By Douglas James (1888 - 1962) 200
Commissions By Hubert Savage (1884 - 1955) 204
Abreviations Used In Job Lists 212
Bibliography 213
Unpublished Manuscripts: 214
Glossary 215
Index 217

Illustrations

- The James cousins in London c.1900 2
- 1892 Drawings by Percy of soldiers' uniform headgear 5
- City of London on Lord Mayor's show day, c 1900. 5
- Percy's design for a heading in the family magazine (1892) . . 7
- Pencil drawing by P. Leonard James, c. 1900 8
- P. Leonard James in the London office c.1905 9
- Competition drawing of a Suburban House, elevation and section, 1904 10
- The Hatley Park Castle perspective for Samuel Maclure . . 11
- Perspective of J. W. Morris 1912 residence from Prospect Place 12
- 1925 Country Residence for P.W. deP. Taylor, ... 13
  7000 Deerlepe Road, Sooke
- 1927 Country Residence with tower for Hans Hunter, . . . 14
  Thetis Island
- Sketch of the tent home in Edmonton by P. Leonard James . 16
- Royal Alexandra Hospital in Edmonton c. 1909 17
- The 1910 James family home built in 1910 at 2385 Todd Road. 19
- James's first residence commission 1909 for Mrs. John W. Lysle, Esquimalt 25
- Mort Graham's cartoon about payment for this house 26
- Front Elevation for 1910 residence of Judge Galliher, 914 St. Charles Street. 28
- Elevations of 1910 Residence for Duncan Ross, 1560 Rockland Avenue 29
- The 1912 residence for J. W. Morris at 1558 Beach Drive . . 35
- Perspective of the Mexican Experimental Farm 35
- Elevations of 1912 residence for Dr. J.D. Helmcken at 1015 Moss Street 37
- 1910 Oak Bay Municipal Hall. 38
- St. Mary's Anglican Church, Oak Bay circa 1911 39
- The G.H. Edwards 1912 residence 40
- Independent Order of Foresters building 1911 42
- P. Leonard James with his bride 44
- P. Leonard James was awarded this "Invalided from the Service" certificate 46
- 1919 St. Mary's Church Hall, Yale Street and the Memorial Tablet 50
- Soldiers' Settlement Scheme residence for L.P.G. Pearson, 2714 Lincoln Road (1919) 51
- Garden view of the 1920 H.F. Bullen residence, 906 St. Charles Street. 54
- Royal Jubilee Hospital, 1900 Fort Street with views of the Nursery and the Operating Theatre (1925) 57
- 1928 Residence for Judge P.S. Lampman, at 2570 Nottingham Road 58
- 1922 Georgian Revival Residence for Judge P. S. Lampman, 820 Pemberton Road 59

- Projection Room window in the Hans Hunter residence . . . 63
- Opening Day at the 1922 Colwood Golf clubhouse, interior . 64
- Terrace views of the Opening Day crowd 65
- H.H. Boyle's 1921 residence, 1320 Franklin Terrace 67
- P. Leonard James's proposal for the Oak Bay Beach Hotel . . 67
- The unusual eyebrow gable for the 1927 Henry Burt-Smith semi-bungalow 68
- The 1926 residences, #6 and #20 Sylvan Lane, with fireplaces for H.J. Hinton and E.H. Bird 69
- Henry Burt-Smith's 1927 semi-bungalow, 1193 Beach Drive 70
- Douglas James' Cottage, 6392 Lakes Road, Duncan 74
- Douglas James Plan for The Dorset 74
- E.W. Griffiths 1938 Moderne-style residence, 235 Dennison Road, Oak Bay 80
- Dr. T.H. Johns 1940 residence nearly completed with Moderne-style windows 80

Built-In Fittings: (All photos by author unless noted) . . 82
- C.S. Baxter, 1912, sideboard; H.F. Bullen 1920 dining room cupboard; Miss H. Nation, 1923, Pantry built-in cupboards; Mrs. D. R. Ker, 1929, Cupboard

Entryways: 83
- Frank Burrell, 1912; Major W. Garrard, 1927; A.B. Cotton, 1928; J.E. Semmes, 1929

Fireplaces: 84
- Judge Wm. Galliher, 1909, mantelpiece; John W. Morris, 1912, living room; H.F. Bullen, 1920, dining room; A.B. Cotton, 1928. fireplace in bedroom; Mrs. P.S. Lampman, living room 1941; E.A.M. Williams, 1945. living room

Steps & Stairs: 85
- J.W. Morris, 1912; C.L.H. Branson, 1928, Front entrance stair; M. Bell-Irving, 1928 (Photo by present owner); Royal Colwood Golf Club, steps from 18th hole; Forbes-Wilson (Sayward-Wilson], 1930. main stair Dr. T.H. Johns, 1943. Moderne-Style stairway

Windows And Doors 86
- Hans Hunter, 1927; J. W. Morris, 1912; N. A. Yarrow, 1949; M. Bell-Irving, 1928, A.B. Cotton, 1928
- P. Leonard James at Shawnigan Lake with Brutus 93
- CPR 1924 Marine Terminal, Victoria 97
- The Crystal Garden under construction 98
- Crystal Garden promenade 99
- Advertising Pamphlet for the Crystal Garden 100
- Pamphlet centerfold showing swimmers in the Crystal Garden Pool 101
- 1926 Lake Louise Pool unused by 1978 109
- Digby Pines, Nova Scotia pool recently renovated 109
- Costing sheet for the J.E. Semmes 1929 residence 113
- Elevations of M. Bell-Irving 1928 residence, now at 588 Linkleas Avenue 114
- H.C.V. MacDowall 1930 residence, 3065 Uplands Road . . 117
- A.B. Cotton residence 118

- R.H.B. Ker residence, 1524 Shasta Place 1923, Garage 1927 119
- Mrs. D.R. Ker, elevations of 1929 residence at 841 St. Charles Street 120
- Mrs. D. R. Ker terrace, 841 St. Charles Street, Victoria. . . 121
- Recent view of main entrance C.L. Branson residence, 2901 Sea View Road 122
- East view of C.L. Branson residence, *Miramar*, 2901 Seaview Road, Saanich 122
- K.C. Allen's, 1929 residence at 3175 Tarn Place, Oak Bay . 123
- Seafront view of K. C. Allen's 1929 residence 123
- Royal Colwood Golf Club 1930 three views 126
- Elevations of Forbes-Wilson residence as built, 3175 Beach Drive, O.B. 128
- Residence for Capt. W. Hobart Molson, 1663 Rockland Avenue, 1930 130
- Elevations of Capt. Hobart Molson 1930 residence at 1663 Rockland Avenue 131
- P. Leonard James's English sketch of broom cupboard (1934) 137
- P. Leonard James's English sketch of wall-hung handrail (1934) 138
- P. Leonard James's English casement window design (1934) 139
- P. Leonard James's English sketch of 'invisible' shop window (1934) 140
- The Deanery, 1937, 930 Burdett Avenue, Victoria 146
- St. Peter's Anglican Church, Comox, 1939 147
- Mrs. P.S. Lampman's 1941 residence at 925 St. Charles Street is shown in section 148
- Elevations of "Moderne" residence for Dr. T.H. Johns in 1943 at 2753 Somass Drive, Oak Bay 149
- Oak Bay Junior High School, 1951, opposite Epworth Street, Oak Bay 154
- Orchard Gate 1949 country home for N.A. Yarrow at Elk Lake 155
- Post Office and Federal Building at Yates and Government streets, Victoria 163
- The opening of the Federal Building and Post Office, Victoria 164

CHAPTER ONE:

Early Days

Why would the Federal Building and Post Office eventually be named after Percy Leonard James? Would his personal papers stored in the attic of his home and forgotten be important? What sort of man was he? Why did this quiet Englishman come to Canada in the first place? It is perhaps best to start with his childhood, a long time ago now. The bare facts about his mother and father are not only remembered in family lore, but are enlivened with his own words from a memoir called *Early Days* which he wrote after retirement. Then in his seventies, he felt the urge to record his memories of the unrushed, relatively peaceful days and quiet entertainments of the late Victorian era, of days and times now history.

Percy Leonard James was born in 1878 in London, England, a city of wonderful architecture to inspire him through his growing years. He was the first child of architect Samuel James and his wife Hannah Bridle. The family grew to include his sister, Mabel Mary James, (1880) and brothers Harold Victor James, (1884) and Douglas (1887). They formed a closely-knit group, within a larger family group of cousins who became lifelong friends. Victorian society held to strict codes of proper behaviour, which the family observed, attending church twice a day every Sunday. Samuel encouraged the children in artistic and experimental endeavours and held strong beliefs, often contrary to contemporary values.

Group of James cousins in London, Harold in summer uniform, Douglas to his left, and Percy Leonard James second from the end of the line, c 1905
(Photographer unknown - Author's collection)

Samuel worked in London. Both he and Hannah had ancestral roots on the South coast of England, but unfortunately little is known of the families except that Hannah Bridle came from the village of Worth Matravers near Swanage in Dorset, and Samuel had relatives near Sway in neighbouring Hampshire. Once all members of a generation die, it is amazing how little information is left behind. A few stories and fading, often unidentified photographs filter down through various family branches and are not necessarily accessible, if indeed they are kept at all.

Though Londoners by birth and domiciled and schooled in the Highgate and Hampstead areas, the James children spent most of their holidays on the Dorset coast visiting Winspit, Durlston Head and the Tilly Whim caves. The family chose St. Nicholas, the Norman church in Worth Matravers, for the children's christenings.

In *Early Days*, Percy wrote a description of his boyhood, in which he wistfully considered how little family history survived:

> Sometimes I got to wondering what an ordinary boy's life was like in, say, my parents' and grand-parents' early days and wishing they had left some record of them which would have been of interest to compare with my own.

Living on into the early space age, he marvelled at the great technological changes that occurred during his lifetime. He then described the system of horse-drawn trams he saw in operation as a child:

> Tramways held a great fascination for me as a boy. The trams were of different colours, according to where they ran – red, blue, yellow and white. At night they had corresponding coloured lamps. They would stop practically anywhere to pick up or let off passengers, instead of having appointed stopping places as is customary nowadays. I am not defending the old system though; it was decidedly hard on the horses – all that stopping and starting. When they came to a hill a third horse was usually hitched on. These extra horses were in the charge of boys who were very expert at attaching their animal to the moving tramcar and jumping onto the tram step to ride up the hill. They were equally adept, when the tram reached the top, at jumping off and unhitching the horse; then mounting it and returning downhill to meet another tramcar.

Historical records at the London Transport Museum mention the strict regulations in effect for the care of the public transport horses. They worked three-hour hitches, for three days, then had four days off. They were the lucky ones. Many horses laboured long hours and were at the receiving end of whatever cruel or benign temper their masters possessed. Writers of the period actually mention horses dropping dead in their traces.

He recalled the North Metropolitan and London Street Tramways and mentioned that all the tramcars were "double deckers," a few of them still of the early "knife-board" seating (parallel with length of car) though most had seats arranged in the modern way facing the front.

In particular Percy mentioned a transportation "first" he saw when five years old:

> As was the custom in most families of the period, we always had a general servant who lived in the house. Ours was usually a country girl from Dorset. One of the series, Jane Phippard by name, often took us children out in the afternoons, my sister in the "pram" (perambulator) and I walking. One particular afternoon jaunt in 1884 I remember very well, for we were going to see an historical event, none less than the opening of the first steam cable tramway in England. It ran from the well-known Archway Tavern, up Highgate Hill to the "village" of old Highgate.

A large crowd had assembled to see the first cars start on their way; many of them no doubt hopeful of a free ride on the cars – for that was offered this first day. I think it was Jane's idea that we might get a free ride up the hill (she was an enterprising sort of "gal") but alas, each car as it came out filled up quickly with burly policemen, in greatcoats as I remember; so we were all disappointed.

One does wonder where so many "burly policemen in greatcoats" came from. Memory can play tricks with the facts. Perhaps only a couple of policemen stood in front of little Percy and over the years the image of their adult bodies multiplied in his memory. It seems unlikely that some early civic unrest in the peaceful village of Highgate required the immediate presence of all officers from nearby police stations. Could the crowd of men have been members of a uniformed band that would play at the village park later in honour of this Opening Day? And the policemen merely cleared a path for them to catch the trams?

For a family holiday, Samuel and Hannah made arrangements for their maid to bring Percy, then four-and-a-half, and Mabel, two, down to Sway by train. The parents cycled down on their "sociable," quite a rare machine, so called because the riders sat side by side, rather than in tandem. The trip took two full days. What an adventure and welcome change for Hannah, the young mother of two little children! The trip must have been peaceful with scenes of early harvest and the smell of new-mown hay. They saw plenty of horse-drawn traffic in the towns and farmers' carts in the country.

At home, the growing family enjoyed games like "Parchesi" and "Snakes and Ladders." They read *Boy's Own Annuals*. Our family still has two dog-eared volumes, dated 1888 and 1889, where they could read instalments of such tales as *Adrift in the Pacific* by Jules Verne. These inspired the children to put out their own weekly version of this magazine, complete with a fine figurehead page, "To be continued" stories, nature notes, games and quizzes, all handwritten and illustrated by family members in the manner of the *Boy's Own* magazine with ruled borders, columns and by-lines. As a young officer in the merchant marine, brother Harold revived this magazine in 1901, to while away some of his off duty time.

As youngsters, the children and their cousins formed a society, which they called *The Great Wharroo*. Its aims were unclear, but they spent a great deal of time together, engaged in competitions and projects suggested by their parents or occupied in devising complicated cartoons. They used *Wharroo* as a special – perhaps a secret – greeting. (A 1907 postcard to Percy in Edmonton from his brother Harold in Hong Kong contained only the greeting, *Wharroo*.)

> Penny weeklies were numerous and varied at the period. One of them, *The Penny Illustrated Paper*, father took regularly and I looked forward to seeing it each week. England at that time was engaged in fighting in the Sudan and other places, so there were pictures of different battles, drawn from sketches and descriptions of correspondents at the front, for of course there were no photographic illustrations, such as we have

Percy's drawings of soldiers' uniform headgear, 1892
(Author's collection)

architectural office in Gresham Street. They had difficulty just getting there from the Moorgate Underground Station through the crowds that had gathered to see this event. "Penny plain or tuppence coloured," called the street hawkers who sold panoramas of the show. Panoramas, according to my father, were long folding sheets with crudely drawn Life Guards, Beef-eaters, city police, City Marshal and so on, with the Lord Mayor's wonderful gilded coach, bewigged and powdered coachman and footmen thereon and inside a glimpse of the august Lord Mayor himself, supported by his sword-bearer and mace-bearer.

Many of the boys' activities took place out-of-doors. They

City of London on Lord Mayor's show day, c 1904 (Photographer Samuel James, father of P. Leonard James - Author's collection)

today, in periodicals. I was thrilled by the actions of our soldiers – cavalry and infantry – fighting in parade uniforms – scarlet tunics and white helmets (that is, the infantry, of course), for Khaki did not come into general use until much later.

Each November 9th Samuel James took the children to see the Lord Mayor's Show, a stately procession through the City of London. They viewed this spectacle from the windows of his

searched out wild birds' nests and collected some of the eggs. The much-thumbed reference book which helped them learn about their finds, *Common Objects of the Country* by Rev. J.G. Wood, still exists. Percy continued his interest in butterfly hunting into adulthood and kept copious notes of the varieties that he captured. A treasured keepsake is his ventilated metal box with its cork liners for drying butterflies and moths.

Other pastimes mentioned in *Early Days* included top-spinning and driving a hoop along the sidewalk – older boys used an iron hoop with a hook to propel it. Robber and police games were played after dark with parents' permission, using small oil-burning copies of the police "dark lanterns." He referred also to "conkers," the popular boys' game which used horse chestnuts.

As youngsters they fished for tiddlers in Waterlow Park in Highgate and in the Leg-of-Mutton ponds at Hampstead Heath. In their later years they enjoyed playing tennis and attending band concerts in these parks.

The children grew up with animals. Their mother always liked cats and had a terrier called *Tilly* which the children adored. Percy himself kept white mice. When the family moved to Dorset to live, Samuel supervised the careful packing of the mice in a box to be taken on the train with them. In the train the box was put on the overhead luggage rack in their compartment. During the trip Percy climbed up to check on the mice and announced importantly to his younger brothers and sister, "The mice are all right." A nervous woman passenger sitting nearby had to be reassured by his father that the mice were pets and indeed securely packaged for the journey.

Soon after our arrival at Poole father invested in a donkey and neat "governess cart" for general transportation. It fell to my lot to look after the "moke" (donkey), clean the harness and other odds and ends – with the occasional assistance of my young brother and sister. Sometimes I rode Jack bareback through the lanes near home, which was good fun, though he had rather an obstinate nature – not unusual with the breed – and required a good deal of coaxing to set out; but once his head was turned in the homeward direction he would break into a stretch-de-gallop which made it difficult to keep on his back.

His memoir recalls the village atmosphere of the Highgate of his youth. He condemned the sleazy work of the "jerry-builder," who filled in the vacant land and erected rows of small terrace dwellings that gave the area an appearance of shoddy newness.

Mill Lane in Hampstead became the family home in 1884. Percy mentioned that they lived "right opposite the Emmanuel Church." An old church building called "The Emmanuel School" exists today, but their house had been demolished and replaced by an apartment building probably constructed around 1900.

The children constantly changed schools, in order to avoid vaccination which their father, with an interest in homeopathic medicine, distrusted. My father said he changed schools 14 times and wondered that he ever learned anything. He actually escaped vaccination until he joined the army. However he eventually settled in to Dr Haysman's International University School in Hampstead.

On the whole I think I made fairly good progress while I was at Haysman's, managing to keep up with the rest of the form in spite of doing no homework – for father was averse to any of us children studying after school hours and we were excused. Perhaps we were only too willing to comply as it gave us more time for play or hobbies; but I must admit that I have lived to regret it and had I my time over again I should make a strong plea to be allowed to do the homework.

Percy's design for a heading in the family magazine, 1892
(Author's collection)

In hindsight it would seem that the James children had a rich education under their father's care with nature study and collecting, interest in political events, painting, cartooning, writing stories, reporting on happenings that interested them, seaside fishing and boating experience and learning the care of bicycles and animals. Samuel imparted to the children his strong belief in independent thinking and trying out new ideas. This varied childhood established firm building blocks and stable values in their lives. Percy benefitted from the freedom, which allowed him to dream and realize his artistic vision in lieu of rigid homework assignments. He had time, too, to develop greater understanding and far-ranging ideals, to grow and make his own decisions for his future.

Today members of the family still enjoy many of Samuel's delightful watercolours, which show scenes in or near Highgate and along the Dorset coast. Often young Percy accompanied him on sketching trips and learned the use of watercolours. Later the Architectural Division of the Royal Academy recognized Percy's own skill. They accepted a watercolour drawing of a proposed church for Wolverhampton, which is listed in their 1904 catalogue.

Childhood did not linger on in Victorian times, as most professional training began at an earlier age than is the norm nowadays. When 14, Percy left school and became an office boy "at the munificent salary of five shillings a week," at Messrs. Evans and Deacon, Quantity Surveyors at Adelaide Street, Charing Cross, London. Among its commissions the firm supervised on-going maintenance work on Westminster Abbey. Few offices in those days had telephones or typewriters. Appointments were usually arranged by mail or telegram. With five and six deliveries a day, letters posted in the morning would be delivered the same afternoon.

> Giles and myself were employed mainly in copying out specifications in long-hand at the expected rate of four sheets of foolscap an hour, or in squaring and cubing sheets of dimensions of building materials that senior clerks had "taken off" the architects' plans. There were also the daily letters to keep

copies of; this required a good deal of care in damping the paper in the letter book; arranging the hand-written letters with blotting and oiled paper between them; then pressing them in the letter press. Altogether rather a messy process that sometimes led to trouble. But the job I particularly disliked was having to descend to the basement late each afternoon to draw water in jugs, from the only tap on the premises and carry them up three flights of stairs to each room, for the staff to wash their hands in before going home. The "governors" and members of the staff all wore top hats. Giles and I, as office boys, only rated hats of the bowler variety.

Finally in 1894, Percy started on his architectural training. Not yet 16, he was indentured to his uncle, John Elford, Architect, Surveyor and Engineer for the Borough of Poole, Dorset. In this office Percy Leonard James received a very thorough architectural training and a superior understanding of engineering principles, surveying and quantity surveying. A few of his drawings of buildings from this period still exist. Students were sent out to study buildings, to measure and to draw them as part of their training.

In 1899 Percy took first class in his exam and joined the pres-

Pencil drawing by P. Leonard James c. 1904 **(Author's collection)**

tigious firm of A. Saxon Snell in London as junior assistant architect. Known for its innovative sanitary techniques, this firm had a practice that extended far beyond the city. It specialized in hospital and swimming bath construction. In this office, he helped design the swimming baths for Marylebone in London, those in Plaistow and Stratford and the Pierhead Baths in Liverpool. He worked on plans for the Charing Cross Hospital in London and on the Fulham, Marylebone and Willesden Infirmaries, and the Railway Men's Convalescent Home, Herne Bay. All the specialized techniques he learned would stand him in good stead in his Canadian practice.

Many large architectural projects were offered as competitions with one or more top architects judging the best design solutions. Saxon Snell would have established his reputation in competition work. Later, clients came to him and he had no need to enter competitions unless pressure of work allowed. But there was a school competition in which Percy must have had a big part. In fading notes about the firm's entry in the Bexhill Girls School competition, he mentioned that the firm lost out to the man who shared an office with the Assessor (judge) of the competition. His final comment, "It may have been alright," shows his lingering doubt. Then, as now, such judgements can't help but be a little suspect, especially if it is one's own work that has narrowly missed out.

We still have a set of plans for an English country house that may have been done for a competition. Drawn in ink on

P. Leonard James in the London office, c 1905
(Author's collection)

top-quality paper and then coloured with watercolours, these drawings show all the building details and sections. In addition to the main reception rooms and family quarters, they show a kitchen wing with store rooms, larder, scullery and pantries, located down a long corridor from the dining room. Typically the upper classes did not wish to be aware of the bustle of servants or smells from the kitchen. Yet these families did not eat their food half cold, for alcohol burners on the sideboard kept the food warm. There is provision in these plans for a bedroom for the maid, shared if there were two maids, but they did not have the convenience of a bathroom or toilet. Their chamber pot had to be carried down the backstairs and across the courtyard to the outside toilet. The family had the sole use of the one bathroom and separate toilet provided.

When he left Saxon Snell in 1906 to come to Canada, Percy Leonard James had become the chief assistant architect of the firm and well respected by Mr. Snell whose letter of reference stated:

I can confidently recommend him as a first class Assistant with good taste and appreciation in design, and a sound knowledge of construction. He is also a careful and painstaking draughtsman, punctual and businesslike, and has given me complete satisfaction. He leaves me now (and to my great regret) on his own initiative to widen his experience.

A second letter from the chief assistant architect who had been over him, L.E. Godfrey Page, and who had left the firm to set up his own office, commented that James was:

a designer of originality with the knowledge of detail necessary to carry out his ideas in actual work. . . .His knowledge of modern construction, drainage and steel construction on a large scale enables him to take the responsibility of costly and intricate buildings. He is certainly able to act as chief of a large staff.

The firm assured him he would always be welcome back, and just before the First World War he did rejoin the firm briefly.

A Suburban House, elevation and section of a competition drawing, 1904
(Photo by author - Author's collection)

Hatley Park Castle, Colwood. Architect Samuel Maclure asked P. Leonard James to produce this perspective watercolour just after he arrived in Victoria in 1908.
(Private collection - Photo courtesy of owner)

J.W. Morris 1912 residence perspective view from Prospect Place by P. Leonard James (BCA # pdp00576)

1925 Country House for P.W. deP. Taylor, 7000 Deerlepe Road, Sooke, perspective by P. Leonard James (BCA Collection #pdp00579)

1927 Country House for Hans Hunter, Thetis Island, BC, perspective by P. Leonard James (BCA #pdp00578)

CHAPTER TWO
Pulling Up Stakes

As the family matured, many changes occurred. Percy's brother, Harold, left home first, intent on a career at sea. His positions with shipping firms that sailed to Japan and South America always brought him back to his home-port of London and he maintained regular correspondence with his family on these voyages. His letters whetted the appetites of the stay-at-homes to the exciting possibilities opening up worldwide. Eventually the spirit of wanderlust spread to the whole family. Early in 1904, their sister, Mabel Mary, married Everard Groos, son of an old banking family. In 1905, the newly-weds left England for Canada. They settled in Edmonton and reported to London on the desperate need for trained architects in the fast-growing town. In the seven years he worked for Saxon Snell, Percy had risen to the top position outside of a partnership, which might well have been as far as he wished to go with a conservative English firm. He decided to visit his sister and her husband in Edmonton and see for himself what the new opportunities might be. In fact Percy would make substantial contributions to the early building of Edmonton and support the formation of Canadian architectural institutes.

He left Liverpool on the *Victorian* in 1906; in Halifax he joined a group of passengers from his ship heading for Western

Canada by train. Together they decided to buy a supply of food and cook their own meals, a service available in the Colonist cars. They arrived in Edmonton in late April 1906. To their surprise, they found the original part of their hotel constructed of logs. The men already residing at the hotel besieged the new arrivals, trying to buy any spare clothing from them. The booming city, then in early stages of development, suffered shortages in both goods and housing.

In fact, like many others, that summer James made his home in a tent.

Sketch of the tent home in Edmonton by P. Leonard James, 1906
(Author's collection)

In early Edmonton various buildings had been used as theatres or "opera houses" since 1881. In some cases they were rinks, with roof and walls constructed round them, minimum stage allowance and no provision for dressing rooms or storing scenery. These auditoriums had level floors and chairs that could be easily removed, clearing the space for balls and dances. Fires took their toll of these early frame buildings. The best one, which seated 300, burned down in 1906, shortly after his arrival.

The commission to build what Percy referred to as "the first proper theatre" in Edmonton came his way. He always amused his family with tales about this theatre which he designed, but later research shows that Herbert A. Magoon is credited as the architect. However, as a busy man, when Percy arrived armed with his excellent references, Magoon gladly shared his established office and handed the work on the theatre commission to Percy.

The Edmonton Archives produced information on this building. An American, Alexander W. Cameron, wanted his New Edmonton Opera House at 10320 Jasper Avenue to seat 400 people and it had to be completed in record time. He demanded that the plans be prepared and the contract let in 15 days. Percy thought it an almost impossible task, but he accomplished it. The owner continued his drive for speed throughout the construction of the building. The *Edmonton Journal* reported, "The foundations were prepared on September 19th It will open October 11th."

After the opening on October 11th, the *Edmonton Bulletin* reported:

The house though not complete was enclosed and sufficient progress made to guarantee that when finishing touches are put on it will be a very comfortable and commodious one. The stage is large and the gridiron is high enough to allow handling large scenery. The lighting arrangements are good and the acoustic properties of the new house are first-class.

The *Edmonton Journal* of October 12th summed up, "Probably the quickest constructed place of its kind in civilization."

The early theatres offered a great variety of entertainment. Travelling companies brought vaudeville, plays, famous singers and operas. Between times the theatre showed movies. When the movie matinees did not prove much of a draw at the new theatre, the chairs could be cleared out between 2 and 5 in the afternoon and the auditorium used for roller-skating; 150 pairs of rental skates were available.

In his book, *Fallen Empires: The Early Theatres of Edmonton, 1881-1914*, John Orrell described the Opera House, which became known as *The Lyceum*, as "a two-storey iron-clad frame structure. Its flat roof suspended from exposed external trusses, while over the stage soared a great mansard roof to hold flies." Under this soaring roof dressing rooms were also provided. A photograph shows just the front of the building and Jasper Avenue at some stage of early development with streetcar tracks in the middle of the road.

The far-flung James family maintained good correspondence between its members. On June 3rd, Percy's youngest brother, Douglas James, replied to a letter from him in Edmonton, What a strange thing it is that a Hospital Competition should come on so soon after your arrival and certainly I should think you would score in this.

A later article (*Daily Colonist* of May 19th, 1923,) about Percy's appointment as architect for Victoria's Royal Jubilee Hospital referred to the 1906 Edmonton competition and the

Royal Alexandra Hospital, Edmonton. Architects: Magoon, Hopkins and James (Postcard in Author's collection)

fact that he did win a prize for the Strathcona and Royal Alexandra Hospitals in Alberta. He often talked about his work on the Edmonton hospitals and the architects he worked with, but never mentioned himself as one of the partners or a prize winner. A listing in the *1907 Edmonton Henderson's Directory* confirms the partnership: "Magoon, Herbert Alton, PAAA, Edward Colis Hopkins, PAAA and P. Leonard James, PAAA,

Registered Architects." However, in this first mention in the Directory, the Alberta Associaion of Architects is incorrectly identified as the Province of Alberta Architects Association. The AAA was incorporated in 1906, the year when most Canadian provinces formed their associations.

Construction proceeded to completion on the Royal Alexandra Hospital. But though working drawings were completed for the Strathcona Hospital the economy took a turn for the worse in 1907 and some years passed before the building of the second hospital to a newer design.

The youngest James brother, Douglas, followed in his father's and brother's footsteps and became an architect. He took his articled training with L.E. Godfrey Page in London from 1902 to 1905 and then worked as an assistant to John Slater, the vice-president of the Royal Institute of British Architects (RIBA). His studies included a period at the prestigious Royal Academy, and evening classes at Regent Street Polytechnic. His certificate for Architectural Design came from South Kensington Board of Education in 1904. The long tradition of architectural student training by articling with an established architect changed by the end of the decade, as schools of architecture came into being.

While working for John Slater, Douglas began to feel the stirring call to help build the expanding Dominion of the Empire. His announcement that he wanted to go to Canada must have devastated his mother. His sailor brother, Harold, teased Percy on a 1907 postcard from South America:

> What a scoundrel you are luring away another family member. The prairies are apparently gaping for more victims.

Samuel James, already retired for some years and in declining health, had no reason to stay in England, and he and Hannah, decided they should leave the old country and make a home in Canada, where family ties could be resumed. A short letter Harold wrote to Percy in Edmonton before the move is the only record suggesting problems existed between the parents:

> The great movement to Canada was practically settled before I arrived home and I certainly think it will be a jolly good thing for all; the only real objection that I can think of, being that mother and father will again be living together. Of course this would be, by far, the happiest state of affairs provided that the latter would only be a little more reasonable in his habits than formerly.

The stories Mabel and Percy told of the long, cold winters in Edmonton had little appeal. So, Hannah and Samuel emigrated with Douglas in 1907 to Victoria with its much milder climate. Like many other English settlers, they probably thought, "Well, we'll all be in the same country." New arrivals from England often failed to realize the vastness of Canada – Edmonton to Victoria was not an easy London-to-Dorset jaunt!

They broke their train journey and took time for a visit in Edmonton. When they left, Percy took a holiday and joined them on their trip west. After a winter on the prairies, the almost-English weather and the lush growth on the coast enchanted him. He returned to Edmonton just to complete his duties there. A year later he joined his parents and brother in Victoria.

The architect Samuel Maclure interviewed Douglas on his arrival in Victoria. He asked only, "Are you a proper English-trained draughtsman?" before he hired Douglas to work on the Dunsmuir's new home, Hatley Park Castle. Douglas completed 248 working drawings for the building, and twice a week made trips to the castle to supervise the progress of the work. He also had a hand in the design of many of the outbuildings required on the Hatley Park estate. Today some members of the family feel that Douglas, as a fully qualified architect, deserved more credit for the buildings, but he did not have a position of responsibility, having been hired merely as a draughtsman. Maclure took the full responsibility and approved the drawings done by Douglas. As part of his architectural training, Douglas had measured up and studied the construction of *Compton Wynyates*, the great country house that perhaps inspired the design for Hatley Park Castle. Douglas must have been a very knowledgeable assistant to Mr. Maclure.

The James family rented a house on a little point of land in Oak Bay at the bottom of the Oak Bay Avenue steps near Beresford Avenue. Percy called it "a little shootmalong house" – a narrow, two-storey, wooden house – only one room and a staircase wide. Two identical houses sat on that small point. The houses have long since been demolished and today the property is called Haynes Park.

Brother Harold, who had taken a position with the Canadian Australasian Line, joined the family whenever his ship berthed in Vancouver. Soon after he left this line, Harold and a fellow officer formed the James and Jarvis Navigation School in

James family home, 2385 Todd Road, Oak Bay, 1910, with Douglas James, Alys and Hubert Savage in 1912. Many years later the name was corrected to Tod. (Photographer unknown - Author's collection)

Victoria. They also purchased the *Sechelt*, a small vessel for coastal transportation. Hannah must have been delighted to have all her sons with her again and the family discussed where they would like to build their own house and settle down in this most English part of Canada. Their idyllic dream was soon to be shattered when some unexpected and devastating changes occurred.

By 1909 the family decided to settle permanently in Oak Bay. They bought a parcel of meadowland situated on the access road to the oldest house in Oak Bay, the 1852 home of the Hudson's Bay Company's factor John Tod. His house exists today at 2564 Heron Street and has heritage status. The area had good transportation into town with the "Willows" car of the BC Electric Railway. In 1913 the car line to the Uplands was established, providing service even closer to the James residence.

The family chose to name their home at 2385 Tod Road, *Durleston* (with an added "e"), after Durlston Head in Dorset. Originally it stood on almost a whole acre of land. Percy designed it and subdivided the remainder of the property into six small lots called *Laburnum Gardens,* now Tod Place. In 1931 he built the first and, as it turned out, the only cottage of this development and planted laburnum trees along the access road. Perhaps he had in mind a small version of the Hampstead Garden Suburb as designed by Raymond Unwin in 1905 in London. He retained the cottage as a rental property. During the 1940s, the rent increased to 25 dollars a month. Between the wars, the school board needed larger playing fields and bought the three lots nearest Musgrave Street. Sadly, the laburnum trees all died off from lack of sufficient water.

In 1910, the family decided to register the new home solely in the name of Mrs. H. James. Samuel for some time had been unable to take an active part in family plans. On good days he helped his sons plant some of the fruit trees so necessary to complete the garden of the fruit-loving James family. Though barely ever mentioned within the family, Samuel's behaviour had been erratic for years.

Her husband's increasing senility must have been quite a burden for Hannah James. He developed a deep resentment towards his wife. Possibly her determined managing may have finally irritated him too much – the exact sequence of events will never be known. Tempers flared one day as they worked together in the basement. He grabbed the axe off the chopping block and threatened her with it. No serious wound was inflicted but under the rules of the day she had grounds for a serious charge against him. With medical help, she had Samuel James hospitalized for the rest of his days in the Essondale Mental Hospital near Coquitlam on mainland BC. The last mention of him as a resident at 2385 Tod Road is in the 1915 Directory.

Considered a "trusty" by the authorities at Essondale, Samuel wandered freely round the walled grounds to sketch. In the restful atmosphere at the Coquitlam hospital he took up his paints again. He wrote to Percy suggesting homeopathic cures and requesting specific watercolours as he ran low on them. Percy visited him when in Vancouver for the Architectural

Institute of BC (AIBC) meetings, until Samuel's death in 1924. When he felt well enough, Samuel produced some rather grand planning concepts for Vancouver Island and the BC coast. He coloured these schemes by blowing the paint on with a simple blowpipe, a technique popular before the development of the electric airbrush. He produced several different schemes called *Map-Views*. His grandson, Harold Groos had one of these framed and hung in his real estate office in the 1960s.

The family hushed over the whole episode and facts of Samuel's illness. The story of his attack and incarceration only became known a generation later. My mother decided that this part of the family history should not be completely lost and told me after I was grown. Mabel never told her daughter what had happened. My cousins knew there had been some kind of problem with our aging grandfather, but Mabel's sense of decorum did not allow any story to surface that might reflect badly on the family name.

A terrible storm hit Vancouver Island on May 25th, 1911. The *Sechelt* captained by Harold James foundered off Beecher Bay, just beyond the old William Head Quarantine Station, now the prison known as the William Head Institution. There were no survivors. Natives on the shore at the reservation saw his ship go down. Part of the report in the March 25, 1911 the *Daily Colonist* gives an idea of the technology of the time:

When the shock of the thing (the sinking) they had seen passed, the Indian, Harry Charles, started to run over the trail from his house at the rocky point, which marks one entrance of Beecher Bay to the residence of the nearest white settler, about two miles away. He reached the house of Mr. T. Parker, who drives the Rocky Point-Metchosin stage, breathless and told of what he had seen. Mr. Parker saddled a horse and galloped to Mr. Reid's house, where there is a local telephone (strung along the fence posts) which connects with the William Head Quarantine Station. As soon as the news was given to him, Dr. A.T. Watt, superintendent of the Quarantine Station, dispatched a boy, H. Young, in a gasoline launch to carry the news to the city, the telephone line between Victoria and William Head being broken by the storm.

As the first child to leave home and as an amusing and constant letter writer, Harold had always had a special place in Hannah's heart. The entire family sorely missed him.

Soon after the First World War, Everard and Mabel Groos moved to Victoria with their youngsters, Harold, born in 1912 and named after his drowned uncle, Jeanne and David. Over the years the close family ties continued, and the children knew their uncles well.

CHAPTER THREE
First Jobs In Victoria

When Percy Leonard arrived from Edmonton in 1908, his brother Douglas introduced him to his boss, Samuel Maclure, who asked him to produce the coloured perspective of the Dunsmuir's Hatley Park Castle as his first job in Victoria. For some unexplained reason this perspective in its dark fumed-oak frame ended up hanging in the James box room for many years. Most houses of the pre-war period had a catch-all storage room referred to as "the Box Room." Located on the second floor, ours was fitted with shelves on two walls, with room for two chests of drawers and a large table where in later years, my mother cut out patterns and kept her Singer sewing machine.

The friendship that developed between James and Maclure included a shared interest in sketching and watercolours. In 1909 they, with other architects and local artists, including Emily Carr, became founding members of The Island Arts & Crafts Society, which is active to this day. The name was officially changed to The Victoria Sketch Club in 1952 – a name the members had been using since 1926.

Over the years, that Hatley Park Castle perspective which James did for Maclure developed a rather unusual provenance. When the James family home was made into two apartments about 1950, my mother gave the perspective to the Red Cross Superfluity store. James Nesbitt acquired it from the store. After mother died, I consulted Mr. Nesbitt about what should be done with some of the family effects. At one point he said, "I have the best picture Mr. James ever painted." I had no idea to what painting he referred and to refresh my memory he said, "It is of Hatley Park Castle with a group in hunting pink ready to set out on horseback. I got it from the Superfluity Store some years ago." He sounded quite tickled about his fortunate find. Apparently the picture, which the family had stored for so long, was fully appreciated.

Eventually the picture came up for auction in Victoria. The auctioneer gave a history about 'lot Number 7,' the large watercolour of Hatley Park, and the bidding started at $1,500. John Bovey was present and bid on behalf of the BC Archives (BCA), which hoped to buy it. After he reached his limit, two other bidders kept on. Many people wanted Royal Roads Services College to have the painting and the commander had been warned to seek permission from the Royal Military College at Kingston which held the purse strings for heritage items. They gave him permission to go to $2,400, but when that figure was reached the third party kept right on bidding. The auctioneer accepted the three initials of the successful bidder who dodged out the front door before I could reach him. The auction house would not divulge the identity of the buyer.

Some time later at the old North Park Gallery, Fran Willis introduced me to a man who said, "I know where your father's painting is." I was able at last to see the painting again and to take a photograph.

The owner told me that he would eventually donate his Maclure collection to the Maltwood Museum. So the longtime association of the friends, Samuel Maclure and P. Leonard James, has in this roundabout way been preserved and the future of the painting is secure.

In 1908, architect J.C.M. Keith learned of James's extensive background in hospital planning and of his work on the recently completed Edmonton hospital. Keith asked him to assist in the preparation of plans for the up-coming Asylum Hospital competition. A famous architect in New York judged the designs and awarded first place for their design. However, the hospital building was not carried out and Keith became quite annoyed when the project fell through. Such a building would have engendered considerable prestige and publicity. They did, however, receive the promised prize money. That James assisted Keith with the plans for the Essondale Hospital in 1908 has a touch of irony, as by 1916, Samuel James became an inmate of the Male Chronic Wing at Essondale.

The only personal note on their hospital collaboration relates to Keith's fondness for breaking off work for a drink. The hour was not important, but the drink was. He'd always say, "It's ten o'clock, time for a smile," and the pair of them would leave the office for refreshment at a nearby hostelry.

When he set up his own office in 1909 over the old Canadian Pacific Railway Ticket Office on the northwest corner of Government and Fort streets, James used "P. Leonard James" as his professional name. The very first house he designed, *Stonehenge Park* in Esquimalt had two storeys in the English style with hipped roof, 15-paned casement windows and dark-stained siding. Plans for it apparently no longer exist, but a snapshot does, showing James in a straw boater hat, caught by the photographer in front of the newly completed house.

As the architect, James made supervisory visits by streetcar to this site, originally listed on Armit Road with no number. By 1917 Esquimalt issued the first street address numbers and the property became 356 Armit Road. It was later changed to 1179 Munro Street, an address which still identifies it.

When *Stonehenge Park* was under construction, his office was close to the Government-Fort-Douglas-Yates streetcar loop where all the car lines turned round before setting out on their next journey to the suburbs. Even downtown the roads became almost impassable quagmires in wet weather. In the nearby suburbs, dust lay almost a foot deep in summer and choking layers flew up when wagons passed, infiltrating homes and lungs alike. Cars had been on the local market since 1902, but streetcars still offered the most reliable way to get about and new neighbourhoods grew up near the various routes. Water-front lots advertised in Shoal Bay, "only six minutes walk from the Foul Bay car line," cost from $1100 and "inside" lots from $375. In most areas one could see cows pastured in fields between the newly built houses.

A double-ended design, the trams had a motorman's seat and controls at each end. The passenger seats were either hard wooden-slat seats or padded seats with woven-rattan covering. The backs of these seats had handles on the aisle side and could be moved to face either direction. At the end of the line, the motorman caused a crackle of sparks as he changed the trolley on the overhead electric wire. Swinging the seats to face the other direction, he then moved his control handle and fare-box to the opposite end of the car for the return trip to town. Few end-of-line turnarounds existed at that time, but the Uplands No. 9 car had a special turning circle when the line opened; it is still part of the roadway system in the Uplands district, which was designed by the American landscape architects, the Olmsted Brothers

When I started to research *Stonehenge Park* in Esquimalt in March 1983, no plans could be located, and even the name of the first owner seemed in doubt. The best alternative seemed to be to visit the house itself. Former B.C. premier David Barrett and his wife, Shirley, lived there at that time. Both declared that they found the character of the house to be very strong and demanding of its due care. To this end they removed some of the additions made over the years, returning the house more nearly to its original state.

The exterior finish is dark-stained wood on both the board-and-batten above the second floor window-sill level and on the shiplap siding below. The interior fir panelling still glows with its original rich oil stain in the main reception rooms. The dining room and living room areas across the beach side of the house can be separated by sliding doors. Each end of this large space has an identical fireplace. The ground floor den is closed off with a glazed sliding door. It also has a fireplace and is panelled in dark wood.

When the Barretts had some of the firebrick repaired, the tradesman commented, "This could only've been done by a proper English trades-person." Most if not all of the building tradesmen at that time had received their full training in Britain before immigrating to the new country. The house has had a varied career. Three small rooms added across the road-front to make rental space have since been removed, uncovering the original porch. Mrs. Barrett mentioned that the front doors are not original; but they match the style of the doors from the living room onto the seafront garden. The kitchen door appears to be original. Upstairs, a leaded glass door opens onto a small room designed as a sleeping porch, although enclosed with three large windows. A sleeping porch was quite a usual feature for houses of that period when people believed in the health-giving properties of sleeping in an unheated area with access to plenty of fresh air. Casement windows on the seafront side of the second floor have all been replaced with double-glazing.

Mrs. Barrett wondered about the exposed hot water heating pipes noticeable in the main floor rooms. Originally the house had been equipped with a hot air furnace, but an owner found it incapable of heating the windward side of the house when Victoria was having a "good blow." In fact the monster hot air ducts from the basement furnace harboured house moths and dust in the off-season. Around 1930 many families removed the old systems and changed over to hot water radiator systems, which left the newly installed heating pipes to the second floor radiators exposed.

I showed Mrs. Barrett the Mort Graham cartoon published after James's retirement about the gold coins paid for the house. The original owner was an American lady who gave him a couple of sleepless nights. One Saturday she arrived on the boat from Seattle with a payment for the contractor in American twenty-dollar gold pieces. The banks being closed and night depositories not yet invented, James had to take this money home with him. He spent a rather uncomfortable weekend with these unprotected coins which represented payment for the completed portion of the construction. Only at ten o'clock Monday morning was he able to deposit them at the bank.

Mrs. J.W. Lysle residence, Stonehenge Park, 1179 Munro Street, Esquimalt, 1909, with the architect (Photographer unknown - Author's collection BCA #hp68425)

Mort Graham's cartoon, *Daily Colonist*, December 14, 1954 *(Author's collection)*

Getting the correct attributions for such early work with no plans in existence can be baffling. The Esquimalt Archives informed me the plumbing plans had been signed by Mr. A. French and Mrs. E. Manning. They considered them the owners and Mrs. John W. Lysle merely the first tenant. Yet a booklet called *Victoria Architecturally*, published in 1911 by Miss McLean, showed houses designed by P. Leonard James with photographs of Judge Galliher's *Bannavern*, Mrs Lysle's *Stonehenge Park* and a small bungalow for Mrs. Johnson. Perhaps Mrs. Lysle, living in the States, had used local agents to help her during construction.

Durleston, the James family home built in the spring of 1910, has many of the same English Arts & Crafts features as *Stonehenge Park*: hipped roof, two storeys, but shingled on the upper storey with plain roughcast stucco below; similar built-up, square wooden columns supported the porches, and small-paned wooden casement windows with 12 panes were used throughout.

The fireplace, brick with dark-stained wooden brackets and mantel, differed from *Stonehenge Park* only because it was set in an inglenook and had stained glass windows on one side, which borrowed light from the pantry. Like the earlier house, the living room had fir-panelled wainscoting to a high plate rail. The square kitchen was fitted with a half-glazed exterior door, a larder, a pantry, a Welsh sideboard baking-centre with two roll-out pastryboards and four tip-out bins under the cupboards for storage of flour, sugar and other cooking supplies. The large enamel sink had hinged sloping drainer boards on each side. An English-style dish drainer-dryer fashioned with dowel divisions hung on the wall over one side and any drips drained into the sink. That Welsh sideboard baking centre lent itself to making crust for the delicious pheasant pies that the whole family loved. Hannah wasn't above trapping any pheasant that ventured into the new orchard to peck out the recently planted English bluebell bulbs. The bluebells multiplied and each spring the ground under the apple trees resembled a piece of fallen sky.

The heavy oak front door with stained glass panel was replaced later, when the porch was closed in with French doors on both sides for shelter from the north wind. The old oak door stood for many years leaning against the chimney in the basement. The blueprints of the original house are still to be seen at the Oak Bay Building Department. The title on these blueprints is *Cottage at Willows Beach for Mrs. H. James*.

Early city directories recognized the fashion for naming larger houses. They had a section listing house names alphabetically and giving their addresses. In the case of *Durleston* (incorrectly spelled *Durlston*), the address listed as 2385 Todd Road. In those early years not every street had numbering in place. Sometimes houses were just listed as "**ns**" for the North side or "**es**" for the East side of the road.

Some time after my parents became the sole occupants of the Tod Road house, my father extended the original small den to make a decent-sized dining room as my mother enjoyed entertaining at dinner parties. Fitted with built-in shelves, cupboards and window seats, the room doubled as a comfortable library. After I left home they added ground floor bedrooms and made an apartment upstairs, turning the box room into a kitchen.

The largest house designed by James from this period was *Bannavern* at 914 St. Charles Street. The owner, Judge William A. Galliher, wanted a five bedroom mansion complete with a porte-cochère, a grand divided front stair and seven fireplaces all told. A set of blueprints of the original drawings, dated 1909 and signed by the contractor, N. Benneck & Sons, survives for this residence. It was built in the half-timbered Tudor Revival-style with Georgian Revival accents. My criterion for the use of the word "mansion" is the inclusion of a back staircase for the servants.

Judge Galliher, a much admired man, had in his early days earned the nickname "Wild Bill Galliher" during his stint with the Canadian Nile Contingent which went to the relief of Khartoum and General Gordon. Born in Bruce County, Ontario, Galliher was called to the bar in Manitoba, the North West Territories and British Columbia. For ten years he represented East Kootenay in the House of Commons. He came to Victoria in 1909 and in 1910 was appointed to the Appeal Court Bench where he served for 22 years.

Over the years many larger houses have undergone chopping and changing for conversion to apartments, rooming houses or nursing homes. Sometimes the interiors have suffered, with large rooms made into two or more smaller ones, ceilings lowered, fireplaces closed off, and mantels removed and

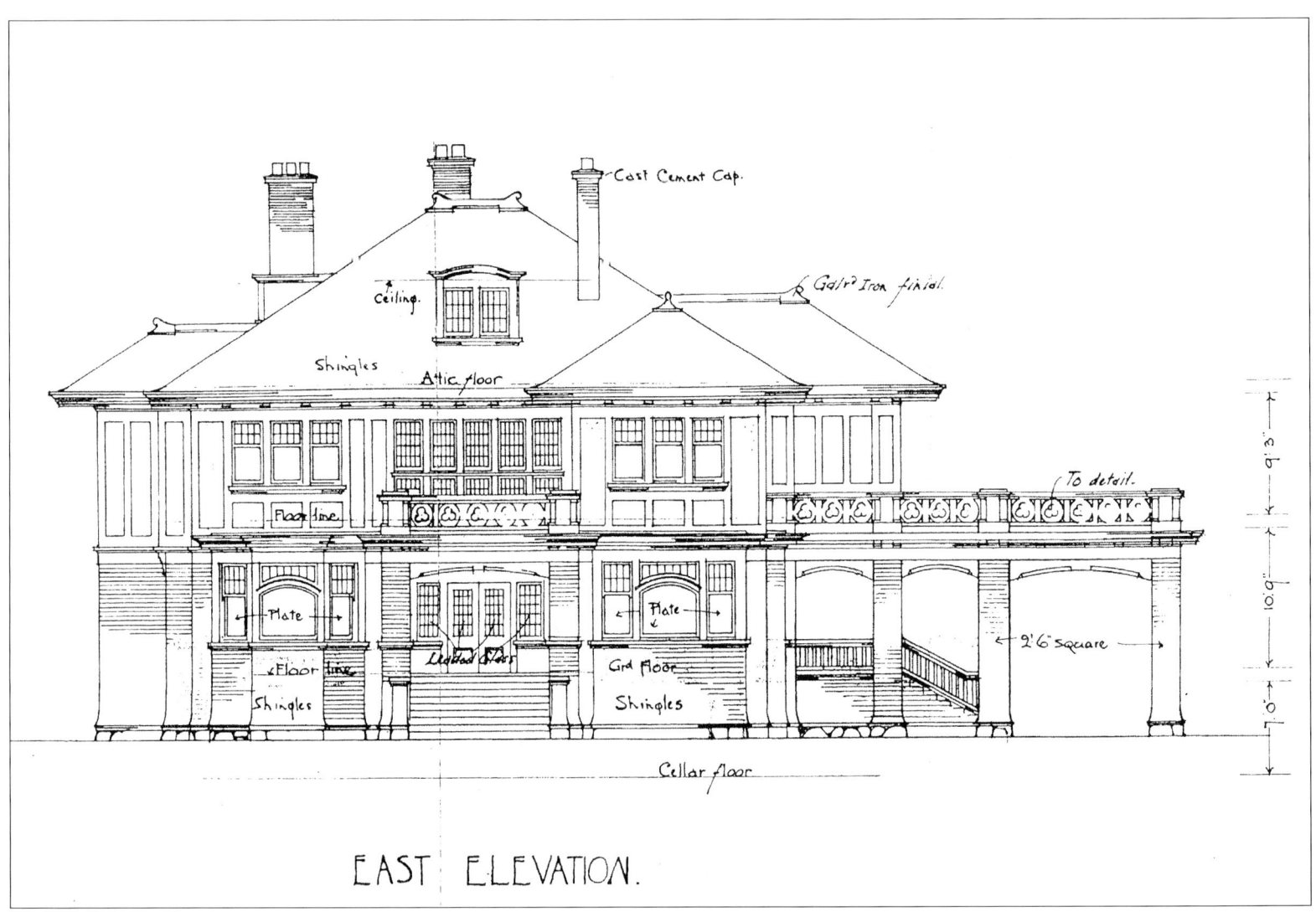

Judge Galliher, 1909, residence, 914 St. Charles Street, Victoria Front Elevation; now condominiums (Courtesy of CVPDD)

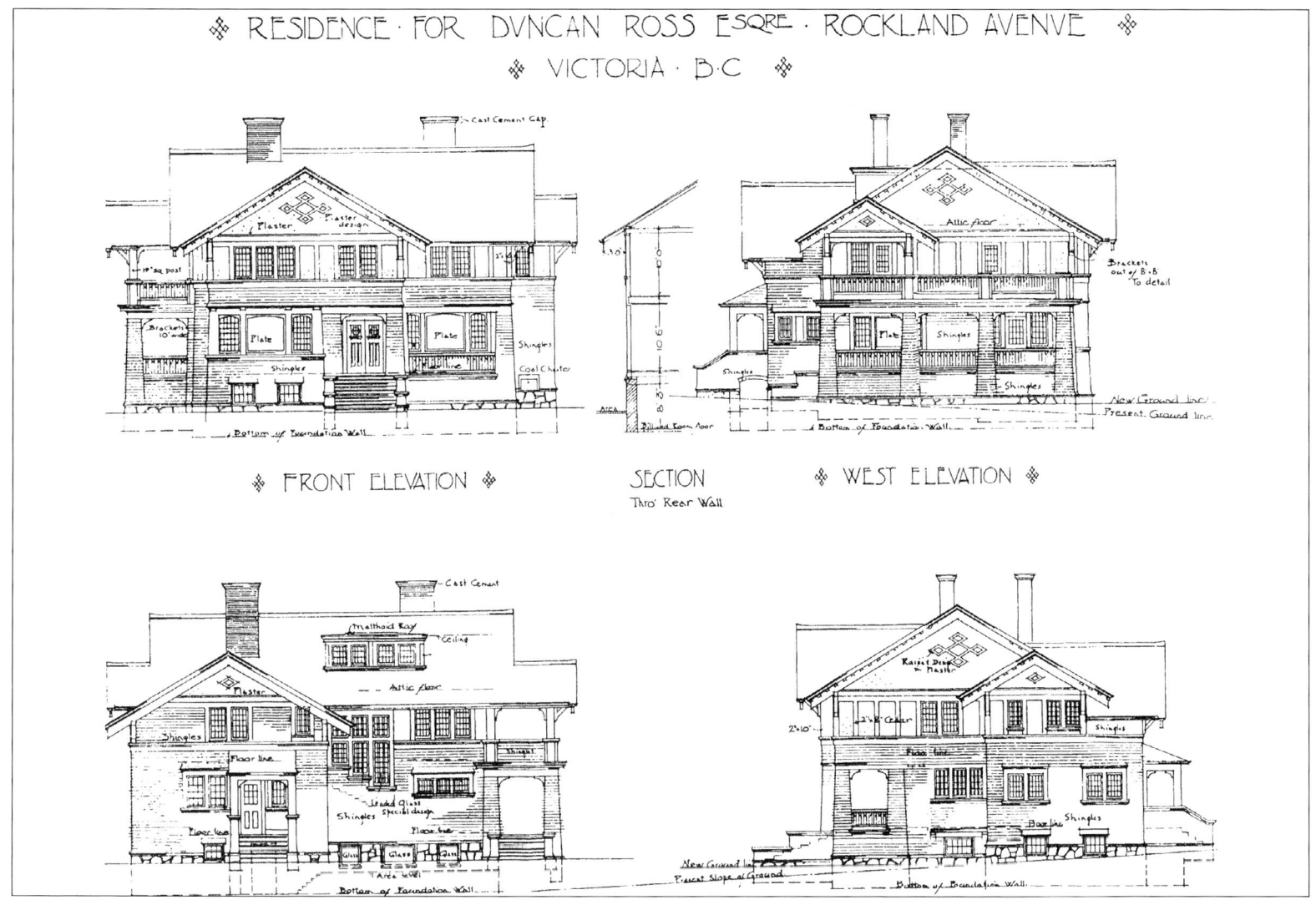

Duncan Ross residence, 1560 Rockland Avenue, Victoria, 1910 Shingle style chalet, with half-timbering and stucco, unusual curved top-rail to major windows (Courtesy of CVPDD)

lost. *Bannavern* had suffered such degradations and looked very shabby in recent years, its future uncertain. However, its mantels had been stored in the large attic and in 1995 they got a new lease on life.

One day that year, I noticed great activity at the house. Demolition? Or renovations? With relief I learned that renovations were in progress. This grand old house would now enter a new phase of its life as up-to-date condominiums. The foreman of the remodelling crew explained the owner's plans for six new sound-proofed condominiums to be fitted into the heritage exterior, four each with one of the original mainfloor rooms retained as living rooms and the other two built into the attic and the basement.

The conservatory, added sometime during the house's history, was removed. Wooden attic casements, rotted by years of neglect, have been replaced with casements of the same design. They are now double-glazed, but on the lower floors the leaded windows are still single glazed. The developer removed all the leaded windows and had them releaded and re-installed at a cost of some $22,000. The mantelpieces, safely stored in the attic, have nearly all been stripped, repainted and re-installed with new fireplace inserts for gas.

Other early jobs have been discovered while the book has been in progress and they are incorporated in the Job List. These include the "Residence for Duncan Ross Esqre" at 1560 Rockland Avenue, a shingled Chalet style with plaster and half-timbering and unusual curved top rails to the main floor front windows. The plans are signed P. Leonard James, ARAIC (BC did not have a proper Institute until 1920.) Another discovery is the two-storey "House for W.S. Drewry Esq" at 727 Linden Avenue. Both of these had a main staircase and a back stair from the kitchen, a popular feature in the days of servants. However only one bathroom and one separate toilet served the five and four bedrooms in these houses. Small finials emphasized the ends of ridges on the hipped roofs of many of the pre-war houses, however with reroofing, these features were not replaced.

CHAPTER FOUR

James & James

Percy and Douglas James formed an architectural partnership in 1910 and undertook many commissions, of which few records remain. However the family has saved the "JAMES & JAMES" metal sign from the partnership's office.

An old *Records* book in my possession gives 1007 Government Street (telephone number, 269) as the James & James office address in early 1912. They had designed an unusual Art Nouveau facade on the Broughton Street side of this building for A. W. Bridgman in 1910. Later in the year 1912, with 23 commissions on hand, they needed more space and moved into a larger office in the newly completed Deans Block, which they had designed at 777 Fort Street. The *Records* book mainly lists jobs and those contractors who borrowed blueprints to figure prices. The book only shows work for 1912 and the names of some contractors. Other early records have been lost, except for a few plans in the *P. Leonard James Collection* at the City of Victoria Archives (CVA).

Commissions of the brothers include the house for J.E. Shenk, a contractor, at 512 Selkirk Avenue, which dates to 1911, but has been demolished, and the house for Francis Hedges at 1327 Arm Street which still stands though the front steps have been changed to accommodate apartments.

In the *Records* book James calculated the cubic-foot cost of early jobs. Smaller houses cost 10, 11 and 12 cents per cubic foot, while houses with several fireplaces cost 14 or 15 cents per cubic foot and large houses with oak flooring as much as 20 or 24 cents per cubic foot. These prices are for 1912 work, but after the war he made some further notes in this book and the values held until 1926 when he stopped making entries. There are no lists showing the jobs undertaken in 1910, 1911, 1913 or 1914. These years may not have been as busy as the boom year of 1912 but there must still have been a number of other buildings commissioned.

Recently, Victoria Heritage Foundation researchers working with the City of Victoria Residential Building Plans have discovered more of the pre-war commissions of the brothers.

James enjoyed the humour of Heath Robinson (1872-1944), an English cartoonist who made fun of machinery and designed highly improbable machines. When it came to dealing with a client's expectation of costs, James jokingly suggested there ought to be a balloon-like Heath Robinson machine to foil overly ambitious clients. The total amount a client wanted to spend on his house would be entered. Then the client would list his requirements and the machine would add these up:

"Yes we need three bedrooms (air was pumped into the balloon for three bedrooms).

One bathroom and a W.C. (another amount was added).

Living room, (this too was added).

Kitchen, (and this).

Oh, and a dining room, of course, (by this time the balloon was getting rather full).

A laundry room in the basement, (more volume added to the balloon).

And, maybe, we should have two bathrooms (enter).

And perhaps a small den, a-n-d –"

"BANG!" The machine would explode when the limit was reached; bringing the client's fantasies back to earth.

Of course the actual process took much longer. Until the contractor figured the job, the owner had only the architect's estimate; his estimate, therefore, was expected to be very accurate, which was the reason James kept careful track of figures. But he could never have foreseen the extremely unfortunate problem that Hubert Savage, his one-time partner, ran into after the Second World War. In 1950, Savage estimated costs for school jobs in Alberni just before the decontrol on building material prices. His estimates were incorporated in the by-law for the school buildings (*Victoria Daily Colonist*, May 9th, 1950.) However the contractors' bids came in after the removal of price controls and were 35% to 63% higher than the architect's estimate. The School Board dismissed Savage as the architect. James and architect Patrick Birley gave professional evidence that won Savage's case against the School Board for wrongful termination of contract.

A local Society of Architects formed in 1891 had lax regulations which allowed various contractors and draughtsmen to claim architectural status. Many people wished to be free of the constraints of "old country" rules in the wide-open West. They resisted attempts to organize a proper institute. As a result, standards within the architectural profession were still poorly regulated in BC when the James brothers arrived in Victoria. Percy Leonard James was a Charter Member in the Architectural Institue of Canada which he had joined when it was formed in 1906 while he practised in Edmonton – "Royal" was added one year later when it became the RAIC. Used to the high standards for architects in England, the lack of professionalism the brothers observed in Victoria amazed them. According to Percy, many of the local practitioners produced very poor drawings. He enjoyed telling of one set of blueprints which he saw, covered with pale lines and scrawly printing, only one line firmly drawn. A note by it said, "Pay no attention to this line."

Working together for the first time, the brothers continued to share the pleasant, teasing relationship of the family. Occasionally they would put a "CLOSED FOR LUNCH" sign on the door and go out to celebrate a contract signed or a drafting job completed, with a drink and the "free" lunch offered by one of the many saloons. But drinking during working hours was not a regular habit of either brother. Restaurants offered good full-course meals for 25 cents. Usually they took different lunch hours so that the office remained open, for they had no secretary and used public stenographers to type specifications. Draughtsmen were hired as needed. After office hours, the brothers spent a nickel for a copy of the evening paper, the *Victoria Times*, to share on the streetcar trip home. However it was at breakfast on Sunday, July 11th 1909, that Douglas exploded, when he saw the article in the *Daily Colonist* "Look at this Percy, someone wants to build a copy of the Parthenon on the hill in Beacon Hill Park. It is to be built with columns of Douglas Fir trees!"

"Well I'm blowed!" said Percy.

"It's the latest scheme to put Victoria on the map," laughed Douglas.

"It'll be easily seen from incoming steamers, if it goes ahead. I suppose the tourists will like it."

The scheme never came to fruition. Instead, some years later a plain, rather English-looking checker pavilion was built. It had windows on all sides to protect the players from the cold winds that sweep over the strait from the Olympic Mountains. It still stands, but in recent, less respectful times the little pavilion has become a victim of vandalism, all its windows now broken and boarded up.

The family took the morning paper, the *Victoria Daily Colonist*, delivered for 50 cents a month. After her sons left for the office, Hannah could study the social pages and check the advertisements for the best prices: oranges -10 cents a dozen; four-pound tins of Crosse & Blackwell's Raspberry Jam – 60 cents; Laundry soap (7 bars) – 25 cents.

At the time, Weiler Brothers advertised a top-of-the-line refrigerator, a three-compartment icebox, for $12.00. The James family kept their icebox with top-loading ice storage on the back porch. It too had three compartments, the bottom one, for the container to catch the melted ice water. The iceman came regularly to replace the ice. He carried the ice on his shoulder from his wagon to the porch. He had big tongs to grip the ice and a heavy sack to protect his shoulder from the cold.

The brothers adorned their office walls with drawings of proposed schemes and winning competition drawings, suitably presented in the fumed-oak frames then so popular. These showed examples of the fine quality of work that could be expected from James & James, Architects. One of the framed drawings on the wall at their office was probably the coloured elevation prepared for the Winnipeg City Hall Competition. Percy had entered the competition soon after arriving in Victoria, but had only placed second. This framed drawing ended up on the wall of our ping-pong room in the basement. By the time I cleared out the house after my parents died, it had disappeared.

A coloured perspective drawing at the BCA shows the "Residence for J.W. Morris," a Tudor Revival mansion built in 1912. It is listed as 1558 Beach Drive, but has a driveway with a porte-cochère through to 1557 Prospect Place. A lovely sitting room with Adam-inspired fireplace and built-in shell-topped shelf alcoves is situated over the porte-cochère. The entrance doors open to a stair hall with stained glass windows, oak balustrade, carved newel posts and fir panelling. Some of its small windows are strongly William Morris in feeling. Built for $25,000 this full two-storey house was converted to apartments many years ago.

Another large house of the period, now turned into apartments, is Dr. J.D. Helmcken's home on Moss Street. It features a Jamesian combination of Tudor Revival and English Arts & Crafts.

Some other early drawings are stored at the BCA. The history of these drawings is unknown and there is no indication whether any of the schemes were carried out. An elevation of a hall the Independent Order of Foresters considered constructing on View Street would have enhanced that site. Two perspective drawings of important but unidentified schemes may have been drawn up at slack times to decorate the office and impress clients.

The family also has a perspective scheme drawn by P. Leonard James in 1909 for the Pacific Government Lands & Concessions Experimental Farm in the Municipality of La Union, District of Montes De Oca, State of Guerrero, Mexico. Rattenbury & James are listed as Joint Architects. This drawing was never stored with my father's architectural papers, but found after he died in a bottom drawer at home. So it remains a mystery.

Oak Bay was home turf to the brothers and the pair contributed several of the early buildings to the municipality:

- On Oak Bay Avenue where the current Municipal Office now stands, they designed a four-room elementary school built in 1910. When the elementary students moved to the new Monterey School, the Oak Bay Avenue school became the first Oak Bay High School. In 1929, the Municipality had a new High School built on Cranmore Road (designed by Spurgin & Semeyn). They continued to use the old building for Manual Training and Domestic Science classes (later to be called Home Economics).

- On the Willows School property just behind the James

J.W. Morris 1912 residence, 1558 Beach Drive, Oak Bay, view in 1913, showing the newly planted garden. Dropped finials were a popular design choice of the time. The original attic dormers have been considerably changed to accommodate apartments. (Photographer unknown - Author's collection)

The Experimental Farm design by Rattenbury & James in Mexico (Author's collection)

family home, they designed a hipped roof wooden building of five classrooms with elongated roof over the entryways at each end. *The Architect, Builder and Engineer* magazine mentions this frame structure as completed in 1913. Meant to be a temporary building, it continued to be used even after the 1920 brick school opened and was not demolished until 1956.

- At the corner of Hampshire Road and Oak Bay Avenue stood the Oak Bay Municipal Hall, which they designed in 1910. The Police Department had its office in the basement. The expanding municipality outgrew the building and it was demolished. Had it been retained it would have fitted in well with the "English" atmosphere Oak Bay has cultivated. Although the building was taken down in 1958, the stair-hall bay window has been saved and built into a home at Prospect Lake.

- James & James designed the first St. Mary's Anglican Church on Elgin Street in Oak Bay. They added the side aisles when required by the growing community.

Madge Wolfenden Hamilton, Assistant BC Archivist for many years, proved an incredible mine of information. She retained her amazing memory through her 98 years and served as a wonderful help to many researchers. Madge told me about a 1931 booklet, *History of St. Mary's Church, Oak Bay, Victoria, BC*, by Percy James, a copy of which is at the BCA. At first I mistakenly thought it was written by my father, for the James family regularly worshipped at St. Mary's. The history mentions the various priests and committees, including the women's committee that carved and presented the reredos to the church. The reredos is now to be found in the new St. Mary's Memorial Chapel:

> Dedicated to soldiers who fell in the Great European War,
> Reredos, St. Mary
> Designer Pierre Boulanger.

The names of the carvers represent many of the early Anglican families, and one can see the carvers had different degrees of skill, some of them producing elaborate work.

> Helen Crease, Mai Gill, Ethel Shallcross, Gertrude Genge,
> Susan Sampson, Jessie Stirling, Edith Hendry.
> xxvi day of November. AD MCMXXV.

The addendum to the booklet mentioned that the James family donated an oak pulpit with memorial tablet to the memory of "the architect, Harold Victor James." The tablet has been saved and is in the new chapel.

> In . loving . memory . of . Harold . Victor . James .
> who . was . drowned .
> Beecher Bay March 24th 1911.

The incorrect mention of "the architect" Harold James would never have been made if my father had been the author of the booklet. Only recently have I learned that another Percy

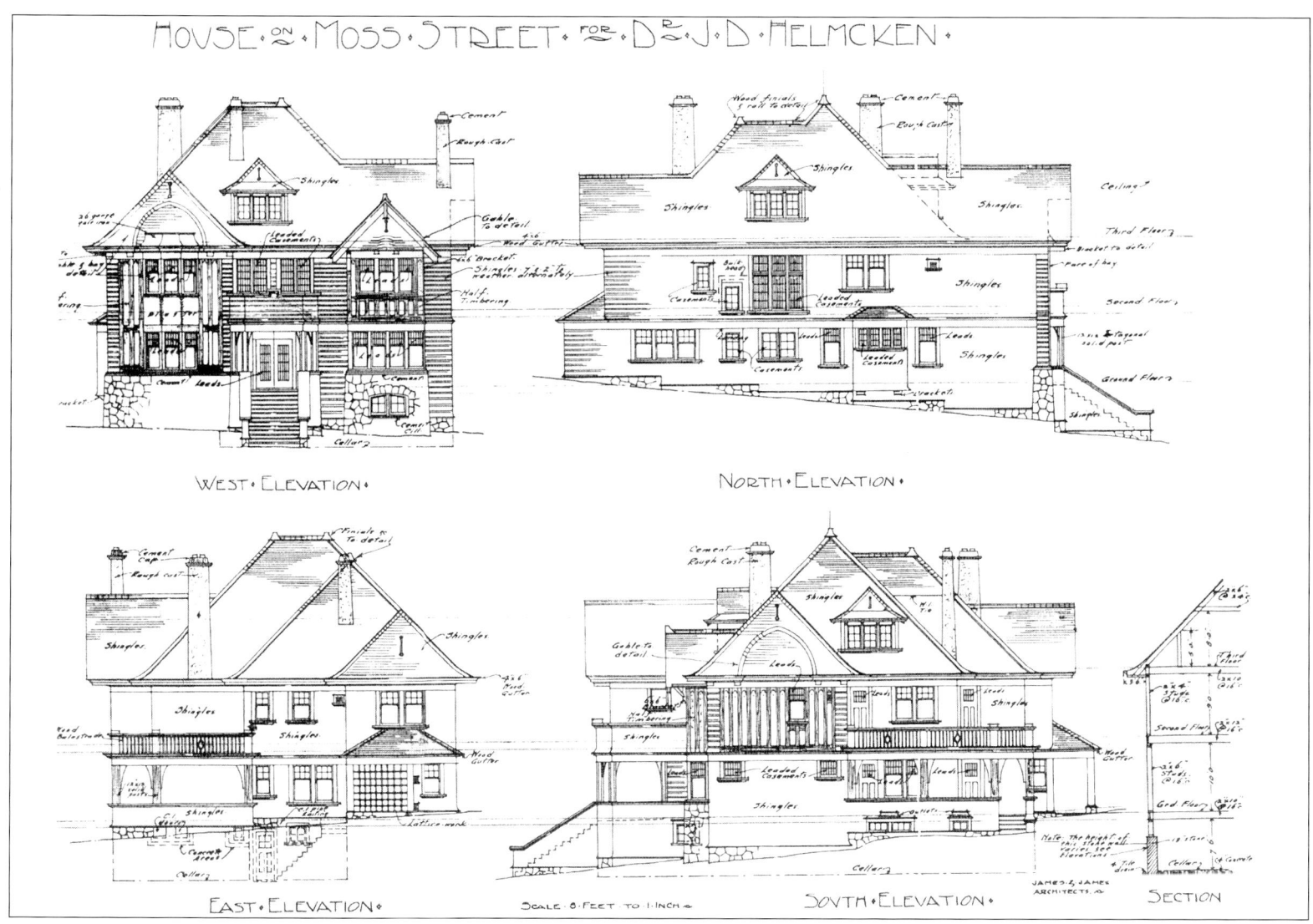

Dr. J.D. Helmcken 1912 residence, 1015 Moss Street, Victoria (Courtesy of CVPDD)

1910 Oak Bay Municipal Hall, Oak Bay Avenue, NW corner of Hampshire Road, c 1950, now demolished (Photo by P.L.James - Author's collection)

James was writing histories at that time. I went to see the Henderson Hall on Yale Street, which P.L. James designed in 1919 as the Church Hall for St. Mary's. The Masonic order bought the hall in 1961 for their meetings. They were sure my father had been a member of their Order. They had a photo, but it was another Percy James who was in the Masonic Order. He was the Percy James who wrote histories and he did not know that one of the James brothers was not an architect.

In 1959 a new church replaced the original St. Mary's designed by James & James and those in charge felt the pulpit donated by the James family in memory of Harold James was unsuitable for the modern building. Such an item is often used in some other location, but there is no record that the memorial pulpit was saved.

The family worshipped at St. Mary's. My father attended services regularly, but my mother only accompanied him at Christmas and Easter. "Ah, Mrs. James, your semi-annual visit," said the archdeacon after a Christmas service. Perhaps a greeting meant to embarrass her. Mother, not chagrined and always forthright, smiled and said, "Yes, Archdeacon, and I expect I shall be here again at Easter."

Information on some James & James houses came from Madge Wolfenden Hamilton's long memory. She knew about the house at Cadboro Bay for Algernon and Letitia Pease, later purchased by Mrs. Alice Maud Robertson of Robertson's Antiques, who called it *Drummadoon*. It has been moved to a nearby site on University of Victoria property and is used as the University Medical Centre with additions at each end. The fenestration and original front door have been retained, but the interior has been changed to suit the Medical Centre. However if a plain modern hall door is opened the original staircase and bannisters to the attic can still be seen. Madge herself lived with her mother in a cottage designed by James & James at 2361 Cranmore Road. But she insisted that Douglas designed it to her own plan.

Madge mentioned, too, the modest little house with jerkinhead gables at Willows Beach, 2422 Esplanade for the Rev. Wm. Barton of St. Mary's, 1913 but no confirming plans exist. Even this modest house had a built-in dining room cupboard fitted with two sets of doors so the cupboards were accessible from the kitchen as well as the dining room. She also knew about the well-documented houses; in some cases, she remembered the contractor for a job.

A style of house called the Chalet-style was often used. The gable ends were usually finished with half-timbering, with a dropped finial at the peak of the roof, and brackets under the wide eaves.

The Herbert S. Lott house at 1220 St. James Street, now Transit Road, is a large Chalet house in the English Arts & Crafts style with half-timbering in the gables. Considered by some researchers to be "a Maclure house," 1220 Transit was designed by James & James. Several sources, Madge included, confirmed their design of the original building in 1912. Many plans from this period, including those for the Lott house, have disappeared from the Oak Bay Building Department files because of fire, flood, or other misadventures. Isla Terry, the

St. Marys Anglican Church, 1701 Elgin Road, Oak Bay, c 1911, under construction with shingle columns, long English Arts & Crafts brackets and Gothic Revival details; now demolished (Author's collection, photographer unknown)

daughter of second owner W.S. Terry, knew that in 1915 her father had arranged for Maclure to add the porte-cochère, enclose a porch and do some interior alterations to the original James & James house.

Oak Bay still has blueprints for another of the Chalet-style houses with half-timbering in the gables, also built in 1912, the "Residence for C.S. Baxter, Esq." In the early years it had the address 2685 Cranmore Road, but is now assigned 1790 Beach Drive. It has been turned into two apartments.

Of the Tudor Revival-style houses which the brothers designed, one of the best, built for G.H.S. Edwards nearly opposite the old Oak Bay Boathouse, has disappeared with few traces beyond a photograph and the contract price of $8,800 in the old *Records* book. The number of bedrooms not mentioned, but there were five fireplaces, four WC's, two baths and four basins.

Before the First World War the James & James partnership designed a number of Tudor Revival residences in Victoria. Stately houses then, they remain so today. Often symmetrical, they reflect the importance of the owners and the confidence of the times. They featured wide bargeboards in the gables, dropped finials, brackets supporting the wide overhanging eaves, and a generous amount of half-timbering with roughcast stucco.

Decorative curved knee braces were frequently used on the vertical panels under the upper floor windows. Plain stucco or shingles were used on the exterior walls of the lower floor. Most architects using the Tudor Revival style chose to restrict the use of half-timbering to the upper floor. The finished effect, while imposing, was not overpowering in the manner of the structural Old-English Tudor, which used the exposed timber construction down to ground level, or if the first storey was stone or brick, then only on the jetted upper storeys. The photo of the demolished 1912 G.H.S. Edwards house is a good example of the Westcoast style of the period. The J.W. Morris house extant at 1558 Beach Drive, also built in

G.H. Edwards 1912 residence, built on Beach Drive, number not located, **(Now demolished - BCA #hp68523)**

1912, is in the same tradition and would have had the half-timbering conservatively stained dark brown or black. It upset James when owners later painted over the half-timbering. He declared it "resulted in the ruination of the design as a whole."

Plumbing arrangements at the time included separate toilets and bathrooms. Such plans allowed maximum use of a minimal set of plumbing. After the war most North American bathrooms contained all three fixtures. An 18-inch mirrored medicine cupboard over the wash basin was the standard size specified then and continued to be used between the wars.

The roughcast-stuccoed Georgian Revival-style home designed for Frank Burrell, manager of Pemberton & Sons, at 1064 Beverley Place has also been converted to apartments. A half-domed porch roof supported by two classical columns and two pilasters protects guests from the weather at the front entry. The house still has the original stuccoed gate piers with wrought iron lamp overhead and a stuccoed garden wall. A summerhouse designed for the original garden has disappeared in the simplified landscaping that now accommodates tenant parking.

The BCA has specifications for this house which include details for the fuel hoist used by the live-in servant who would have loaded wood on the hoist in the basement, raised it to the kitchen and then cooked the family dinner:

> "Construct a wooden fuel hoist size 2'6" x 2'0" from cellar to kitchen, with wire rope running over a grooved wooden wheel operated by an iron crank in cellar."

In the pre-war era, even families of modest means could afford servants, and Chinese servants in particular were much sought after. Accommodation for them was usually a small bedroom and a plain bathroom in the basement. There are even stories that some employers expected their Chinese servant to go to Chinatown to have a bath.

In the early office, many of the working drawings were drawn in ink on linen. When he deemed such drawings need not be kept any longer, James brought them home so they could be soaked. The soaking removed the heavy sizing and the drawing ink (and possibly the only record of a commission). After washing, a piece of very fine linen could be put to a new use. My mother made baby pillowcases, tray cloths and doilies and decorated them with her favourite English embroidery. Nothing was needlessly thrown out. Though recycling had not yet become an issue, thrift was a more universal virtue then.

The James & James partnership designed the Oak Bay Grocery at the corner of Oak Bay Avenue and Monterey Avenue, which served as such for many years. By the mid 1930's this grocery stood opposite a competitor, one of the first chain grocery stores – the Piggly Wiggly. Today the Oak Bay Grocery building is still a focal point on "The Avenue" as the well-known "Blethering Place." Most of the half-timbering is recently added "Tudorizing."

The arrival in Victoria of the English architect, Hubert Savage, and his wife Alys in 1912, revived an old friendship. A photograph taken that year shows the Savages with Douglas James at the James family home on Tod Road. A long-established friendship must have existed between the families, because the Savages stayed with the James family as a break in their long trip to New Zealand, where Savage meant to practise architecture.

AIBC applications indicate that Douglas James and Hubert Savage worked as assistants in the same office in London and attended the Regent Street Polytechnic together. During this visit to Victoria the Savages decided to settle in Victoria and the close relationship between the families continued on both a professional level and a social one. The 1913 City Directory lists Hubert Savage as an architect and his first office as shared space with James & James in the Deans Block at 777 Fort Street.

After the First World War, Savage and James shared office space again and they eventually formed their well-known James and Savage partnership.

By the 1914 recession, James & James had moved to a smaller office on the fourth floor of the Hibben-Bone Block at 1122 Government Street. Early that year Percy left Victoria for a visit to England.

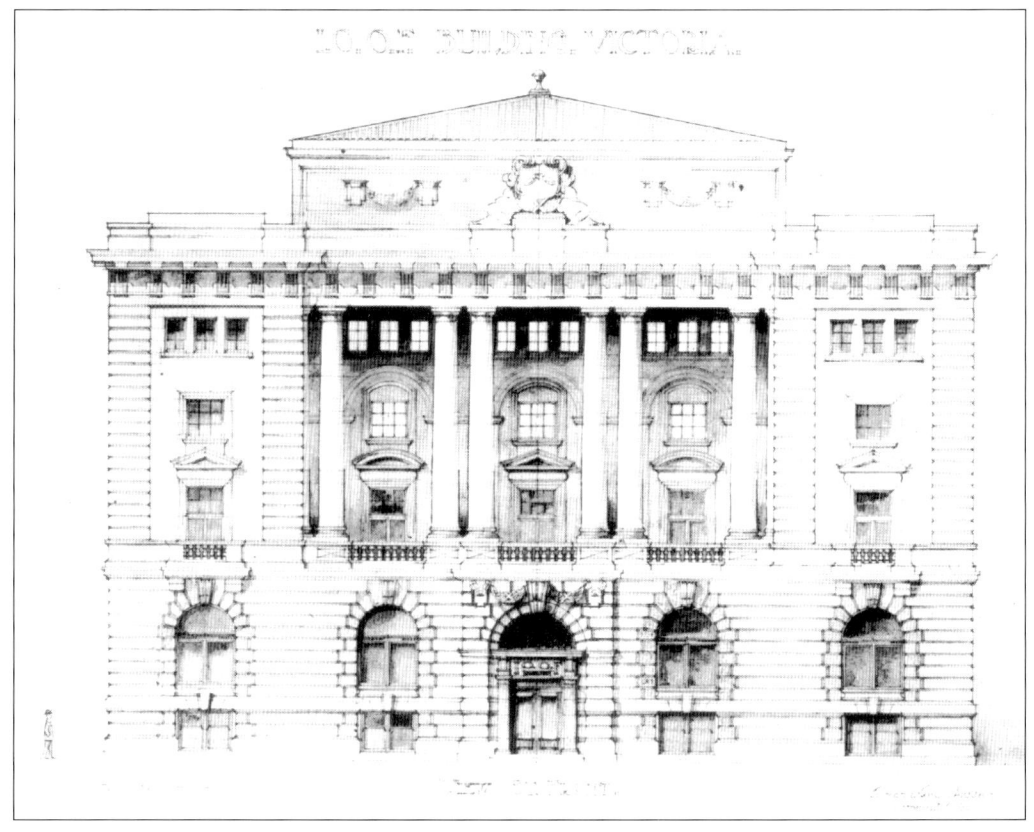

Independent Order of Foresters Building, in Beaux Art style, View Street, Victoria, James & James, Architects 1911, not built (BCA #pdp00577)

CHAPTER FIVE

War and Weddings

The Tod Road property remained the James family home through two generations, from 1910 to 1970. In the early days, when all the brothers lived with their parents, a grass tennis court filled the space between the planting along the front fence line and the house. The fence posts surrounding the court had American Pillar roses growing up them, "Rambler Roses" as they were more commonly called. They had a delicate perfume that gives rise to nostalgic thoughts and can still be found in some gardens today.

The very eligible James brothers, both six feet tall and devastatingly handsome, with the characteristic family looks – black eyebrows, piercing blue eyes, soft brown hair and moustaches – had turned many a female glance over the years. However the busy partner-brothers had little time for social events, though mothers of young ladies contrived invitations to Sunday afternoon teaparties, musical evenings or tennis parties. Always concerned about her cherished sons, Hannah became adept at making slighting remarks about these young women or their family backgrounds and managed to fend off any serious commitments. But the war ended her protection.

The James & James partnership had done well, but in 1914, one of Victoria's recession years, Percy left to rejoin his old firm in London to assist them in the preparation of plans for the East Sussex Hospital at Hastings.

At age 36, far from Hannah's apron strings on the eve of the war, he met a 95-pound willowy ash blond, renowned for her charm and smart clothes. Rose Jesurun Johnston, always called "Molly," no doubt swept P. Leonard James, whom she would always call "Jimmy," off his feet. Schooled in France and trained as a singer by Signor Clerici, she had given concerts in many places, including Bechstein Hall on Wigmore Street in London and a special performance in Lisbon for the President of Portugal, who awarded her a beribboned scroll. Her travels in Spain and France and her childhood years in family situations with a full complement of servants had certainly not prepared her for life in the colonies. Nevertheless, within just one week of meeting each other, they married by registrar, a ceremony kept secret from their families. A year and a half later they had a church service with some family present. The documents for both services still exist. It is interesting to note that Molly claims her age to be 31 on both, despite the passage of 18 months – Edwardian ladies being quite secretive about their ages. Later for her 1934 passport she claimed to have lost another five years.

P. Leonard James with his bride, Rose, who was always known as Molly.
(Photo by Arthur Hailey - Author's collection)

Molly's friends considered her a "social butterfly." Her architect husband charmed them but they warned him, "Well we hope you can survive on boiled eggs and tea – and that **you** know how to boil the water."

Douglas James joined the Canadian army as an officer. While training in Duncan, he was dispatched with his men to rescue a young widow, named "Johnnie" Johnson, during the blizzard of 1916. He and this lively young woman whose relatives started the Butlin Holiday Camps in England, sat on the roof of her house, watching his troup of soldiers dig a way through the giant snow banks. A bare three months later Douglas left to fight in Europe, but he married teasing, chestnut-haired Florence Gertrude Johnson before he left. Their wedding announcement in the *Cowichan-Leader* reflects perhaps as a lark – the importance placed on English background by Duncanites of the period. Though Douglas had lived in Victoria for eight years, his home address is listed as Manor Park, Highgate. (Before moving to Canada, he and his parents had lived in a semi-detached house at #6 Manor Park Road in Highgate, not exactly an English park with acres of trees and long driveways!)

As soon as the East Sussex Hospital reached a stage where Percy could be spared, he joined and trained as an officer with the crack Artists' Rifles Regiment. He transferred to the 12th London Regiment before going to the front in France and Belgium.

A postcard to his wife Molly shows that he went to France in 1916.

> Dearest, Arrived here today. Had letter from Mother, otherwise have received nothing yet. Hope you are well. J.

The late Colonel Michael Allen of the Canadian Scottish Regiment recalled that when he worked, long ago, as a teenage gardening boy at Tod Road, James would chat with him about his lighter wartime experiences. Since he possessed a rather splendid military moustache, his fellow officers teased him about his strong resemblance to Lord Kitchener. In the trenches they warned, "Don't show your head above the parapet, or the Jerrys'll fire with much more rapidity than heretofore."

James also told the story about a special treat sent to him at the front, a canned turkey – probably for Christmas. His batman made an attempt to produce this special hot dinner in the little tin field oven they had in their mess in the trenches. Evidently totally inexperienced with this sort of cooking, the batman put the tin of turkey into the oven without opening, or at least puncturing it. In a short time a tremendous explosion tore the oven apart. Turkey coated the walls and ceiling and was in no shape for eating.

At that time Molly lived with her parents in Finchley. Zeppelins used to arrive silently over the city and drop their bombs. One night she listened to the sound of the bombs falling ever closer and said to her parents, "Let's go to the basement now." They made it in time, but all their dining room windows were broken by the blast of a bomb that fell in a neighbouring garden. One of the Zeppelins, caught in the protective London artillery fire, fell nearby. A ring fashioned from some of the wires in the Zeppelin's framework is the most humble of the family's First World War souvenirs.

By 1917 James had transferred to the Royal Engineer Corps. But he succumbed to rheumatic fever soon after and was sent back to England to recover. He spent the rest of the war stationed at the engineer training camp near Deganwy in North Wales. Photos show him posing with his men by some of the engineering projects. Molly joined him in nearby Conway. When he was demobbed he received a certificate signed by King George V which stated that he "Served with honour and was disabled in the Great War. Invalided from the Service."

In 1919, shortly before returning to Canada, James wrote an article that *The Daily Chronicle,* a London paper, published. In it, he considered the critical shortage of workmen's housing facing the nation in the post-war period, when all factories had been tooled for war production and with building materials in short supply. In his estimation, 500,000 new homes were needed for the industrial classes and he pleaded for:

> A full measure of the much needed reforms in both the broad conception of town planning and the interior arrangements

P.L. James succumbed at the front to rheumatic fever for which there was then no known cure. As a member of the Royal Engineers Territorial Forces, he was awarded this certificate. The illustration by Bernard Partridge, a well-known political artist for Punch magazine. (Author's collection)

of the houses themselves ... For the new industrial class houses to be a real advance on the old order of things which was nothing but a survival of serfdom.

He condemned the jerry-builders for their:

Dreary piles of brick and mortar, the mean streets of terraces ... that disfigure the outskirts of almost any town in Great Britain ... Reform is by no means a new question in this country ... it has long been a recognized shuttlecock in political circles, played by successive governments, discussed in the Press, nibbled at, but never (or with very rare exceptions) seriously tackled. One result of this great apathy on the part of our authorities in the past has been brought to light by the war, for who can deny that the appalling percentage of physically unfit, as disclosed by the recruiting statistics, was largely due to the cramped unhealthy dwellings and tenements in which the majority of our working class people were forced to dwell.

His suggestions to improve workers housing included:

Dispensing with the fireplaces routinely built in every bedroom but never used (though the public thought they supplied ventilation), in favour of decent clothes closets; and supplying a proper inside bathroom with water closet, instead of the tin bath in the scullery and the outhouse.

He started work on a book which was never published about the housing question for the industrial and middle classes. In it he suggested:

Let simplicity be the keynote of the new house exteriors, remembering always that good materials, judiciously chosen and applied, will raise them above the commonplace, a result that can never be attained with any amount of applied decoration or unnecessary 'features.'

A difficult war-bride period awaited Molly when she arrived in Canada after the war. Not only was she coming to her husband's house, but also entering her mother-in-law's domain – a situation where a good bit of conflict was inevitable. The two women had such different backgrounds. Hannah, a strapping countrywoman, never had more than one maid-of-all-work to assist her and, despite all her married years in London, had devoted herself to bringing up her children and so developed little sophistication. With her thorough country understanding of all things domestic, she could not have been impressed by this new daughter-in-law's general lack of useful household knowledge.

Soon after her arrival Molly underwent her first confinement – at home, as English people usually did. She lost the baby, a son. The doctor must have been grossly negligent, as she had a small pelvis and an easy birth could not have been anticipated. Perhaps Hannah argued in favour of the home birth – having children had always been easy for her. A second doctor, called in at the last moment, came down to see Percy, who nervously paced the basement floor.

"Do you want your wife? Or your baby?" asked this doctor.

"My wife, of course," said Percy, overwhelmed with anxiety.

The baby was stillborn after a long struggle during which Molly's hip was displaced. She had to walk on crutches for several months after the birth.

Percy, busy re-establishing his practice, away all day at the office and tired out by evening, did not hear how his mother "did her duty" looking after her unwelcome daughter-in-law. It fell to Hannah to take a lunch tray to Molly while she was confined to bed. Raw-boned and determined, his mother made it her practice to stride in with the tray, plonk it down by the bed and stomp out of the room, without saying so much as one word. Also being a determined woman – her willowy qualities based on firm wiriness – Molly held her tongue. When recovered she visited her husband at his office, as any discussion at home where Hannah might overhear seemed unwise.

"Either she goes, or I go," reported Molly of this visit.

Percy replied, "I will follow you to the ends of the earth, my Darling."

This story came down only in Molly's version, of course, for men didn't relate such intimate tales. This interview resulted in the building of a new small house for his mother that very year, 1919. Although the family owned all those lots next door, it was decided, with some insistence on his wife's part no doubt, to buy a lot within a sensible walking distance on Cadboro Bay Road. Molly became the sole chatelaine of 2385 Tod Road where she lived for the next 51 years.

There is a sequel to the story about the construction of this cottage that Percy and Douglas built for their mother. Douglas's wife, Johnnie, a feisty lady used to the rigours of country living, had suggested the house be built with only a cold water supply, as a hot water tank seemed a needless expense for her husband to have to share. Hannah herself might not have minded, her family in Dorset had always managed without such amenities. However Molly, ever interested in the latest developments, had not been reckoned with. Despite the way her mother-in-law had treated her, she did not consider it right to skimp on supplying hot water for a woman of advancing years.

"She shall have hot water, even if I have to pay for it myself" she announced, sharp of tongue perhaps, but always a fair-minded and considerate person. Thus it came to pass that the other daughter-in-law's suggestion fell by the wayside and the sons agreed to share the $59 extra cost of a hot water tank, a considerable sum in those days. The price is mentioned in the H. James bungalow file at the BCA.

CHAPTER SIX

Back and Booming

After the First World War, though Percy still suffered from the effects of the rheumatic fever contracted in the trenches, he set up his office on July 21st, 1919, shortly after his return to Victoria. Douglas had decided to open a practice in Duncan where he was one of only two architects, so each brother was now on his own. After a first year in which Percy turned his hand to anything that came his way, his practice bloomed. Soon he required several assistants and associates as he worked his way through the major building period of his career. He also became the working partner with Francis Mawson Rattenbury on several commissions undertaken for the CPR, and before the Depression he formed a partnership with Hubert Savage, ARIBA.

Starting out on his own, P. Leonard James kept a diary on the jobs of this first post-war year (1919-20) in the old *Records* book James & James used before the war:

- The Oak Bay Golf Club Building Committee, Oak Bay Golf Club, headed by architect F.M. Rattenbury, asked James to design a clubhouse. He advertised for tenders by August 9th. The committee met to consider the tenders early in September; their budget of $32,000 was to include plumbing, heating and the architect's fee. The prices on construction alone came in at $39,000. The committee considered cutting down considerably, but could not get the price down far enough. By September 19th the Committee decided not to proceed with the work that year and paid James for his work.

- In September he prepared plans for St. Mary's Anglican Church Memorial Hall at 1632 Yale Street in Oak Bay. G.F. Lowe's tender of $4,348 was accepted and the contract prepared. Throughout most of James's career, several contractors submitted prices for a job. The lowest bid was generally accepted and the owner and contractor signed a contract. If the work cost more, it came out of the contractor's pocket. If the owner requested additional items, the contractor would quote a price on the extras. After the architect discussed the extra with the owner, a decision agreeable to all parties would be reached. Work started on September 29th. Four and a half weeks later the trusses were in place. Inauguration of St. Mary's Memorial Hall took place on July 9th, 1920. Lieutenant Governor (Col.) E.G. Prior unveiled the Memorial Tablet with the names of the Oak Bay war dead. This oak wall tablet cost an extra $109.65, plus the cost of fixing it in place.

Above: St. Marys Church Hall, 1600 block, Yale Street, Oak Bay, since 1961 Henderson Hall for the Masonic Order Inset: St. Marys Hall Interior view of pedimented doors and the Memorial Tablet (Photographer unknown – Author's collection)

- In October, architect J.C.M. Keith asked James to assist him with the drawings for his Oaklands School plans. For two and half days of draughting he was paid the going rate of $20.

- On November 21st an announcement appeared in the *Daily Colonist*:

Appointed Superintendent

Mr. P.L. James, a local architect, was appointed superintendent under the housing scheme for Oak Bay by the Council of the Municipality last night. None of the houses have yet been commenced, as the Government has not yet been asked for Oak Bay's allotment.

The Federal Government allotted $25,000 under the Better Housing Act for houses for veterans of the First World War in Oak Bay, as part of the national "Soldiers Settlement Scheme." James approved or made suggestions about plans chosen. The veterans submitted five and six-room house plans with outline specifications and James supervised construction and assured proper practices. Eight men benefited under this scheme: L.P.G. Pearson, M.R. Tredwell, A.H. Charles, E. Waterman,

L.P.G. Pearson, Soldiers Settlement house, 2714 Lincoln Road, Oak Bay, 1919, with the "sore thumb" addition
(Recent photo by author)

Frank H. Mackie, Gunn, Gibson and Shaw. The cost of the houses ranged from $2,900 to $3,400.

The bungalow for Lesley Pearson and his wife, Doris, on Seagull Avenue (now 2714 Lincoln Avenue), was well known to the James family who sometimes had tea there. The house had only two bedrooms, so Mr. Pearson built rooms in the attic as his family grew to include three children. James considered the attic addition a dreadful sore thumb. Remembering his strong feelings about the addition, I visited the Oak Bay Building Department and confirmed that P. Leonard James had designed the bungalow.

- In November, Mr. and Mrs. R. Henderson retained James for interior alterations at their home, *Kenilworth* (since demolished). Afterwards they had plans prepared for a house in Grand Forks for their son, Malcolm, the earliest known of the "wedding present" houses designed by P. Leonard James.

Over the years, several house plans were prepared as wedding gifts from parents. In 1982, I passed through Grand Forks, BC and looking over the valley east of town, I could see a house that might have been designed by James among the mostly gable-roofed houses in that area. The Grand Forks Museum arranged for their retired Director to show me the house where Malcolm Henderson had lived, which was indeed the house I'd spotted. The two-storey English Arts & Crafts house with hipped roof and large eyebrow dormers made a rather rare sight in that small town, although some of the gaunt Doukhobor houses in the West end of town also had hipped roofs.

Invited to see through the house, I found the interior finish disappointing. The carpenter skimped on the stair rail and fireplace mantel materials, instead of following details that would have been supplied – they just did not have the right proportions. The local mill supplied cheap interior doors. The house was built without architectural supervision and for a lesser fee than a fully supervised job.

In 1919, right after the war, a committee worked to form the Architectural Institute of British Columbia (AIBC) This had been fairly well in hand in 1914, but went no further because of the war. James, who had served the earlier Society of Architects as treasurer 1911-13, worked actively on the committee seeking to establish a proper institute and in 1920 the AIBC was constituted. P. Leonard James was a Charter Member and No. 31 on the members' list. Not all the original members were trained architects. The newly formed Institute admitted a few men who had been successfully engaged in building design and construction for a good long period. For instance, Samuel Maclure was trained as an artist. He usually chose English trained architects as assistants and learned about architecture with intensive self-directed studies.

Victoria had the stimulus of a visit from H.R.H. Edward, the Prince of Wales, in 1919. Returned men paraded in their uniforms and a photo shows James in the front row of the veterans lined up on the Legislature lawn. The United Services Organization held a Ball at the Empress Hotel where my parents made a handsome couple: James in white tie, tails and patent leather dancing shoes, and his elegant wife, known for her tiny hands and be-ringed fingers, with one of the shimmering saris her great-grandfather had brought from India draped artistically over her evening dress. It had been a good year and people were optimistic about post-war prosperity.

By 1920 the larger commissions started to come thick and fast. A beautiful Edwardian Classical-style house with a large Palladian window over the porte-cochère was built at 906 St. Charles Street for the Bullen family. F.M. Rattenbury, who had become very friendly with H.F. Bullen when they both lived in the Union Club as bachelors, had discussed ideas for a house design. However Rattenbury handed the responsibility for the working drawings and supervision for Bullen's house, and some other jobs that have not been recorded, over to James. No longer in active architectural practice, he had not bothered to join the newly formed AIBC, but still attracted clients. He placed such work with James, whose work he respected, and took a third of the fee, but Rattenbury's name did not appear on the drawings.

The only existing notes in the BCA file about the Bullen house are hardware prices: "Haddam Colonial" design from Drakes, $69 is noted for the front door hardware with extra escutcheon, letter plate, hood and bell plate. Six sets of French door hardware were ordered at $42 per set – for that time these represent top-of-the-line prices.

Some historical information on the Bullen house came to light recently when a friend confided that she knew Bullen's daughter, Bunty Knoop, very well. When located, Mrs. Knoop confirmed that the family had lived in their large eight-bedroom house for 10 years. Then they had moved to England and rented the house to the Hobart Molsons, who waited at the time for their own P. Leonard James house at 1663 Rockland Avenue to be completed. When the Molsons moved into their new home, the Bullen house was put in the hands of the Royal Trust to find a suitable new tenant.

Meanwhile in England, Mrs. Bullen had been invited by a mutual friend to meet Mr. James A. Wattie, who lived at Haslemere near London. When he heard that Mrs. Bullen had lived in Victoria, he told her that he had plans to move there. "In fact I've been making inquiries through real estate people and they've sent me information about a suitable house. May I show you the photographs they have sent? Perhaps you'll know the house."

It turned out to be the Bullen house and Wattie rented it for some years. He later bought the imposing house at 3125 Beach Drive that was, along with the Molson house, one of James's major works within the James and Savage partnership. P. Leonard James designed it for Mrs. Forbes-Wilson on the waterfront in the Uplands – an unexpected coincidence that both of the Bullen tenants later lived in houses designed by James. Mr. Wattie is remembered for his generosity at Halloween at both those houses, when he gave children who called a dollar each. Of course in those days the children were expected to recite a poem, perform a song, or a dance, for their treats.

Major F.V. Longstaff had bought the house James & James

H.F. Bullen 1920 residence, 906 St. Charles Street, Victoria, Garden view (Photographer unknown - Author's collection - BCA #hp68412)

designed in 1912 for E.H. Harrison on Highland Drive, now 50 King George Terrace. In 1921 Major Longstaff asked James to add a studio with a barrel ceiling and a fireplace of Clayburn brick with library shelving on each side. The alterations included a lavatory and fuel storage by the back door and the installation of gates and piers with the name *Seabank*. In 1931, further additions were carried out.

Major Longstaff wrote two local histories, *Esquimalt Naval Base: History of its Work and Defences,* in 1941 and *H.M.C.S. Naval Barracks* in 1957. He erected a flag pole on his property and the flag was always flown with proper respect under his stewardship. At that period respect for the flag required that it be raised each day near sunrise and lowered at sunset. It was never left out all night, as is the practice even at schools these days.

Do you know why our hospital is called the Royal Jubilee Hospital? One so often just accepts a name and does not question its significance. The original buildings of 1888 were named to celebrate Queen Victoria's Golden Jubilee, which took place in 1887.

Attempts to enlarge the hospital were put on hold over the years of the First World War. After the war, the new building, called the East Wing but later renamed the South Wing, was to be a Soldiers' Memorial Hospital. The Board of Directors even requested some war trophies from City Council. The Board also planned to install a plaque listing BC units, names of the fallen and dates of battles.

On May 5th, 1921 the *Victoria Daily Times* printed the results of the competition for the hospital:

> The choice of Mr. James' name was made from among eight architects who were willing to accept the invitation of the Board to be candidates for the appointment ... Mr. James is a returned man, having served with the infantry and engineers in the front line in France; therefore he feels that he has a particular interest in participating in this memorial project.
>
> While retaining full personal responsibility Mr. James proposes to take as his assistant Major K.B. Spurgin and to employ another returned architect in the office.

The BC Record reported:

> Architect P. Leonard James ... commissioned by the Hospital Board to draw up plans ... It is estimated that the work will run into $300,000. While assuming full responsibility for the designing of the building Mr. James will be assisted by Major K.B. Spurgin as associate architect.

Before the war in 1914, architect Loring Rexford completed construction of the hospital's Laundry Room and Power House. At that time the specifications, now stored among the James papers at the BCA, stipulated that contractors "shall employ only men of British nationality." Immediately after the war the requirement changed and James specified "only returned men to be employed."

The Board of Directors felt that a fitting memorial building, while mainly brick-faced concrete, should have a base course of granite and sandstone cornices; if that proved too expensive, then just sandstone cornices were to be used. Contractors bid on these two options, but prices came in too high. The Parfitts, one of the contracting firms, suggested a third alternative: no stone, just brick faced reinforced concrete and concrete decorative elements. James expected the price to be about $150,000 for this contract, which also included the tar and gravel roof. Parfitts quoted $107,986 and declared it: "A rock bottom cost, a figure that had been tendered only because of the character of the institution." Parfitt Brothers won the construction contract.

In line with standard practice, there were separate contracts for various parts of the work. Luney Brothers did the foundations, steam heating, interior finishing and other features. The plumbing contract went to Thacker & Holt, a firm that caused some problems and was very late completing their part of the work.

By November 1923, with the walls and roof in place, the funds ran low. The hospital put on a campaign requesting financial aid from the public. An appealing photo of some graduate nurses standing outside the windowless structure appeared in the paper. They wore their navy blue capes over their billowing white aprons, and different starched caps, each signifying their training hospital. The architectural firm did their bit and contributed $300. The promotion stated that existing facilities treated 131 patients daily, but the new hospital would have 200 more beds, 57 of which would be private beds.

In her eighth month of pregnancy, Molly was one of the patients in the old Victorian Maternity Pavilion behind the new hospital. I was induced with what she called "stretching and Twilight Sleep," which she described as a horribly long and painful process that ended with a forceps delivery on the 26th of April 1924. James, very concerned, was able to stop in and see her frequently when inspecting the building progress. The doctor suggested any further children should be induced at seven months. However James said, "I'm not going to put my wife through this again. There won't be any more children."

Work on the large hospital commission lasted from 1921 to 1925. Information filed at the BCA covers all phases of the work. There are many photos of both work in progress and rooms ready and equipped for service. The photograph of the nursery with banks of cribs, each with a pretty flounce of dimity-type material, brings a pitying – perhaps a horrified – smile to our antiseptic generation. The general wards, complete with wind-up gramophone to entertain the patients, evoke amused recollections for us "old folk." The steam rooms for bedpans served their purpose until the early 1990s when sweeping renovations took place. Pictured, too, are the pristine operating rooms with the latest gleaming 1920s cabinets and tables. The sunrooms at the south end of each floor had fireplaces, a bed a patient could rest on, comfortable armchairs and a cozy rug on the tile floor. Obviously patients were expected to remain in hospital for longer recuperation than they are today.

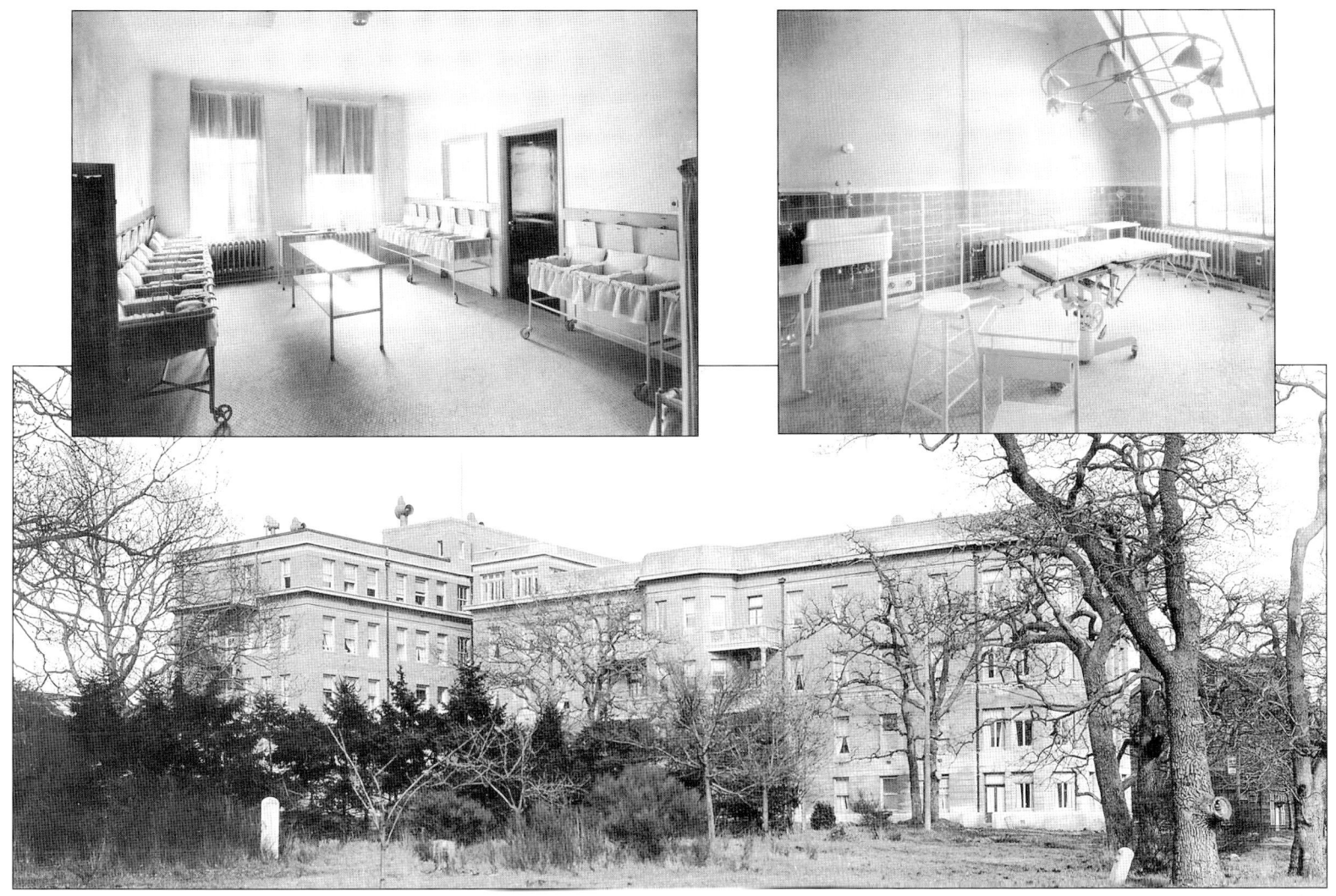

Royal Jubilee Hospital viewed through oak trees, 1900 Fort Street, Victoria, 1925 *(Photo by Edgar Fleming - Author's collection - BCA #68137)* Inset left: Royal Jubilee Hospital Nursery *(Photographer unknown - Author's collection - BCA #hp68155)* Inset right: Royal Jubilee Hospital Operating Theatre *(Photographer unknown - Author's collection - BCA #hp68156)*

A recent visit to the hospital to see if any information existed about the soldiers' memorial plaque that the Board had planned to install was unsuccessful. Probably there just wasn't enough money to carry out this idea.

The interior photos of the 1925 building ready for occupancy interested today's Facilities Planning Department. They found these photos, taken with a large negative camera, very informative. The photos even answered a question about the private rooms, which had puzzled them. Changes over the years had specified other floor finishes in these rooms, which covered the wooden strapping set in the concrete for nailing the original hardwood floors. Recent removal of flooring materials to the concrete level exposed the inset strapping. No specifications exist to confirm the original use of hardwood flooring, however the photographs supplied the answer. It surprised today's resident architect to see exposed pipes in the private room photos. Such piping would normally have been built into the walls at that period. The exposed pipes gave the brand new building the look of an after-thought. When he learned that James had to attend court one afternoon over that contract because the plumbing and heating contractor was two and a half years late completing the work, the resident architect commented, "Ah, things like that happened then too."

In 1922, Judge P.S. Lampman commissioned James to design a house at 820 Pemberton Road. A photograph of this house appeared in the 1930 *Canadian Homes and Gardens First Book of Houses*, published by the McLean Publishing Company Limited, Toronto, titled "A Design for a Garden Setting."

By 1928, the Lampmans decided to move to the Uplands, where they had a second home designed by P. Leonard James, though within the James & Savage partnership. It was built at the end of a trail called Somerset Road, which is now 2570 Nottingham Road. This house is an example of a "butterfly plan" with wings at right angles to one another, on either side of a central core. The Lampmans had fireplaces in the major rooms. The couple obviously expected to make use of these as they also made the rather unusual request that plenty of heat be provided in halls and passages and less in the rooms themselves. Mrs. Lampman had a ground level garden room in the basement.

Judge P.S. Lampman, 1928 residence, 2570 Nottingham Road, Oak Bay
(Photo by H. Knight - Author's collection)

Judge P. S. Lampman, 1922 Georgian Revival Residence, 820 Pemberton Road, Victoria. A view from the lawn was published in Canadian Homes & Gardens, December 1926 (Photographer unknown - Author's collection - BCA #hp68562)

During James's years of practice the carpentry specifications always called for the use of fir. "All lumber to be first quality, free from sap, large or dead knots or other imperfections. All lumber to be sized." Sometimes he specified "Studding to be sized and joists and rafters 'edged' only." In the case of the 1940 house for Mrs. J.I. Cassie when hemlock was first coming into use, he specified "No hemlock to be used."

The 1923 house for Miss H. Nation, who married Robert Henry Brackman Ker, was a "wedding present" given by her father, Major F. Nation. The groom, the son of David Ker, who had established the Brackman & Ker milling business in 1877, was president of the family businesses, which included a flourmill, breweries and an oil company, and was a great philanthropist.

The house, at 1524 Shasta Place, originally had three bedrooms (one with a fireplace), two bathrooms, dining room, living room with a plain tiled fireplace (since replaced with a baroque marble design to the taste of an Italian owner), and a sun porch with French doors and a tiled fireplace that matched the original living room fireplace. A recent owner, on learning the original cost of this residence, $12,126, commented that the property taxes had almost reached that amount!

As the family grew, the Kers had James undertake a large addition. A library with fireplace and unusual arched window, two more bedrooms, a breakfast room, a porch and a sewing room were added in 1929. The Kers liked bay windows. They had one in their new bedroom and altered the window in the existing dining room to a bay. A back stair was added up from the new breakfast room. The original sliding glass cupboard doors have been retained in the pantry. Mrs. Ker took a keen interest in planning the cupboards, insisting that a cupboard to store bridge tables be provided behind some of the library shelving. She also had a very narrow cupboard installed in the small space at the corner of the new master bedroom between the existing chimney and the new hall – perhaps the perfect place to store scarves and jewellery.

The Kers also had James design a summer home at 2274 Arbutus Road on part of the old family property in Gordon Head. It was a simple bungalow suitable for outdoor living. The Kers had two "Sleeping Huts" for visitors, a larger cabin for the "Chinaman's Quarters" and a "Motor Car Shed" that would take four cars, all drawn up by the architect. The family had started the tradition, later adopted by the city, of planting boulevard trees on Victoria streets near where they lived. They continued this interest at the Gordon Head property by planting arbutus trees along Arbutus Road and put up a fence of imported English wattle.

In 1925, Sooke became the site of the imposing country house designed for "P.W.deP. Taylor, Esq." The Taylors had a large piece of property on the cliffs facing the Olympic mountains just north of Whiffen Spit. A visit to the house in the 1980s revealed the private drive which wound through the forest for a good kilometre. The house, called *Deerlepe*, is set well back from the cliff face. There is nowadays considerable encroachment on both sides of the property, where streets and subdivisions have been carved from the woodland. But in the Taylors' time, it must have been a very private retreat in the forest beyond Sooke.

Deerlepe is one of the houses with a spacious "long gallery" hall. It runs from the dining room across the library to the drawing room, with stairs opposite the entry. The space beyond the stairs allowed a later owner to add an elevator. The garage is a separate building, but part of the original design scheme.

The kitchen had not been altered up to the time of my visit: the original broom cupboard, glass-fronted cupboards and sloped drainboards that could be raised for cleaning, had all been retained. The two bedroom fireplaces had coal-burning grates, while the drawing room, library and dining room fireplaces were designed for wood fires.

There is a patio across the seafront of the house, with glass in the screened ends to offer some protection from the breeze. Such screens also protected the porches built in 1929 at 841 St. Charles Street for Mrs. D.R. Ker, and at 2575 Lansdowne Road for Major-General P.E. Thacker.

In 1927 Major W. Garrard commissioned a country home, *Rooks Nest*, on 20 or more acres at Tod Inlet and named it after the Garrard's home near Lambourne in England. He kept his racing yacht on Tod Inlet and had a summer cottage there. He fought in the Boer War, and the First World War. As a crack army sharpshooter he volunteered to use his skill again in WWII if the Japanese arrived.

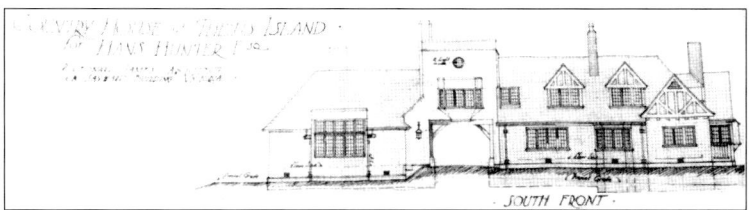

Hans Hunter, 1927 Country House, Thetis Island, front elevation
(Photo by author - Courtesy of SDW)

Garrard bought his large property next to The Butchart Gardens when it was a much smaller operation. The family enjoyed undisturbed rural living there for many years, sleeping on the sleeping porch and being awakened by deer which sometimes came up the steps and nuzzled the sleepers awake. With his family grown Major Garrard eventually found the operation of the house too onerous. He did not want to sell to The Butchart Gardens, but lawyers contrived to make the purchase for them. Much of the Garrard property became the parking lot and behind the work area. The Garrards' English Arts & Crafts-style house designed by P. Leonard James still stands but is hidden from view by a tall hedge at the bottom of the parking lot. It has been used as a staff residence and at present stores The Butchart Gardens archives, but its future is uncertain.

A house that used to be visible from the old island highway near Chemainus is possibly the only house with a tower that James designed. It is situated close to the ferry dock on Thetis Island. Since 1927, it has made a fine view for incoming ferry passengers from Chemainus as they round Daymon Island, but the trees by the highway have grown too large for the house to be seen from Vancouver Island any longer. Capernwray Harbour Bible School now uses the building as one of their international centres of study. The house faces almost due south and sits well back from the beach. The flags of the student countries generally enhance the scene – a veritable Tudor manor on a sandy strand.

Hans Hunter, who lived in Japan, had the house built as a home for his son, whom he wanted to have educated at a private school in Canada, where he would be a boarder. He felt it too great a trek for the boy to return each long holiday to Japan by ship. So he commissioned the house as a home for his son to return to at vacation time, perhaps for weekends too, from Shawnigan Lake School for Boys. He planned to hire a family to manage the farm he envisioned for the Thetis Island property. He expected they would also provide a good home for his son.

Mr. Hunter had been to a well-known public school in England. While in Victoria approving the architectural plans and arranging the construction of the house, he accidentally ran into a former school friend on Government Street. This man, Mr. G.H. Gaitskill, happened to be down on his luck at the time. Hunter suggested that Gaitskill become the caretaker of his farm and, with his wife, provide a comfortable home atmosphere for Hunter's son. The Gaitskill family moved into the house which Hunter himself never occupied. The crash of 1929 ruined Hunter, and he could not continue to pay the Gaitskills for their services. He managed to transfer the ownership of the house to the Gaitskills in lieu of any further payments. It is not known what became of the Hunter boy.

The Gaitskills remained in the house for many years. Many of the island people forgot about Hunter, and thought of Gaitskill as the original owner. Later the house became a centre for several different church groups starting even while Mrs. Gaitskill, who survived her husband, lived there with an elderly amah.

The Capernwray Harbour Bible School's staff did not know P. Leonard James had designed the building. They had quite another story to tell. They directed me to the island historian, Jo Iteah, who repeated the local belief that Mr. Gaitskill's own son, Dudley had designed the house – a young man only 19 at the time. Although he later became quite a famous artist, he hardly possessed the skill to design such a building at that age. The construction of the house was well underway before the Gaitskill family even arrived on the scene. By way of confirmation I sent the School a copy of the perspective drawing of the house signed "P. Leonard James, Architect," from the BCA collection.

The school has successfully altered the interior arrangement from the original farm office and bedrooms to accommodate a large dining area for students. The open driveway under the tower was retained for many years but has now been closed in with French doors to make an entry hall for the students. The original generous 3'4" inch front door is still in place, though its natural fir grain had at one time been obscured with white paint. The large lounge, with its huge bay window, is situated beyond what was the porte-cochère driveway and is used as a general meeting room. The bracketed indirect lighting in this room was possibly added later. A projection room for movies beyond a small bay window at the tower end of the lounge was an unusual feature for a 1927 house. The projection room in the tower has been changed into an office. The end of the room has recently been adapted to provide a new toilet and cupboards and the projection window can no longer be seen.

Jo Iteah, a relation of the Burchell family, which originally owned the property that Hunter acquired, had more information about the property. There had been two earlier houses on the site when the Burchells owned it, both of which burned down.

Mr. Burchell, who had no heirs, sold the land to Hunter on an annuity basis – so much down plus annual payments – which seemed a good plan to ensure his income into old age. Unfortunately Burchell died a year later, so Hunter got the land for a very low price indeed. But even this did not help him when the Depression hit.

Mr. J.A. Sayward, the lumber baron and friend of the Dunsmuirs, financed a golf course on lovely property at Colwood. P. Leonard James designed the first Clubhouse. Photos show the members at the opening tea held in the new Clubhouse in 1922.

Hans Hunter house, Projection Room window (Photo by author, c 1985)

The interior view shows Joseph Sayward posing to the right of the fireplace with other members. His portrait hangs over the granite fireplace. The clubhouse consisted of little more than a big lounge suitable for teas, games and dances, with attractive Chinese lantern style fixtures mounted on the open-trussed ceiling. The members were also photographed on the terrace overlooking the course. You can see some of the men wear tweed suits with vests and plus-fours, others are in dark suits with quite a variety of shirt collars, all with ties and the well-shined shoes then *de rigeur* for gentlemen. The ladies are all fashionably dressed complete with hats. The Saywards pose at the door, with Mrs. Sayward wearing a magnificent fox fur neckpiece. Players' changing-rooms and facilities were situated in the basement below. James bought a skinny 1920s canvas-and- leather golf bag and clubs and took a few lessons from the club pro but he never took seriously to the game. The golf club required further additions and improvements in 1925, 1926 and later. This building met a fate common to many clubhouses – it burnt down – probably a cigarette dropped among the chesterfield cushions

A file at the BCA contains only the specifications for a

Opening Day at the 1922 Colwood Golf Clubhouse (Photo by H.G. Goodenough - Author's collection - BCA#hp68136)

Opening Day at the 1922 Colwood Golf Clubhouse (Photo by H.G. Goodenough - Author's collection - BCA#hp68137)

fair-sized building. They directed the contractor to visit the site "five miles from Victoria, on the **es** (east side) of the highway near Palmer Station" (still a designated stop on the E & N railway on the East side of the Old Island Highway). These directions located an inn designed for Mrs. E. Alexander in 1926. I knew it well since we passed it on the way to the old mile-long Colwood Race Track (the site of which is now part of the Juan de Fuca Recreation Area). Both my parents enjoyed race meets there and we attended as a family. My father teased us saying that my selection of winners by the colours the jockeys wore worked as well as mother's selections based on studying the horses' performances in the *Green Sheet*! As we drove by the building at Palmer Station, we could see the racehorses owned by Mrs. Alexander in the surrounding fields, some days an Alexander horse would be entered in a race. James's inspections of this building may well have been combined with supervisory visits to check the progress of the on-going alterations for the first Colwood clubhouse. The Inn property, now 340 Island Highway, is used as a recreational vehicle and trailer park, the Inn as a clubhouse and apartments. Well-circulated rumours suggest that the inn developed a rather notorious history as a gambling den and brothel. The original owner had allegedly made her money as a Madame in the Klondike. The anecdotes suggest that some of her gold sweetened the Christmas Comforts Fund of the BC Provincial Police, encouraging the police to phone ahead when they planned to raid the inn so that nothing incriminating ever showed up!

Plans for alterations have not, for the most part, been saved, but papers filed at the BCA show an amount of $4,500 for an 'alteration' to a house on Fairfield Terrace undertaken for Mr. H.H. Boyle. The amount suggested a new commission not an alteration the way prices were in the year 1921.

A recent discovery among the plans at Victoria City Hall for houses built after the First World War with funds from the federal government's Soldiers' Settlement Scheme was the house for H.H. Boyle. These records included a very complete file on Boyle's bungalow with a copy of the specification, certificates of payment to the contractor, plans and elevations and a street number on Fairfield Terrace. The street name, Fairfield Terrace, made it hard to find because many of the names have been changed over the years. It is now Franklin Terrace and the house still stands only slightly altered.

On this particular job, despite the inspections that James made early each day on the way to the office, the owner, visiting later in the day, found something that needed attention. A letter from Mr. Boyle states:

> I think the plasterer certainly needs watching. His first coat of plaster is the roughest job I have ever seen and although it can be remedied largely by the second coat – yet in many places it is so rough that it will have to be chipped off which may loosen it from the lath.

James wrote immediately to the general contractor and said that the work must be cemented within 24 hours or the plasterer was off the job. It is unlikely this plasterer was ever again employed on a P. Leonard James job.

Boyle's letter refering to the competent work of "your old plasterer" and to "our man's work," seems to suggest that Mr. Boyle himself may have suggested the man who got the plastering job.

Sometimes James was called upon as expert witness in disputes between an architect and his client. In 1931, architect John J. Honeyman of Vancouver asked him to act on his behalf on the arbitration of extras. "Please don't turn me down. It is a difficult matter to get men of ability, also unquestioned integrity who will arbitrate on the merits of a case entirely regardless of where the axe may fall." James did accept but a settlement was reached.

Eventually he himself had to take a client to court. Asked by hotelier Captain W.C. Merston to undertake the commission to replace an earlier hotel that had burned down, James's design for an Elizabethan-style hotel appeared in the *Daily Colonist* on February 13th 1927. But the owner of the Oak Bay Beach Hotel then went to another architect who possibly cut some corners in the construction or worked for a reduced fee – several of the local architects were not above this kind of rivalry. The plan, filed at the Oak Bay Building Department in April 1928 for the construction, was so similar to James's design that he took the owner to court. He won his case, but neither the record of the court case, nor James's work diary – an important part of the evidence – still exist.

Like the Capernwray School people, not every current owner has been ready to acknowledge James as the architect. "It's a Maclure!" declared one – and at the time I had only a handwritten entry in the old *Record* book – now I have a signed copy of the plans. Another owner declared I had the wrong date and architect, though he couldn't remember the name of the architect. He refused to see the signed and dated plans that have been discovered in City Hall!

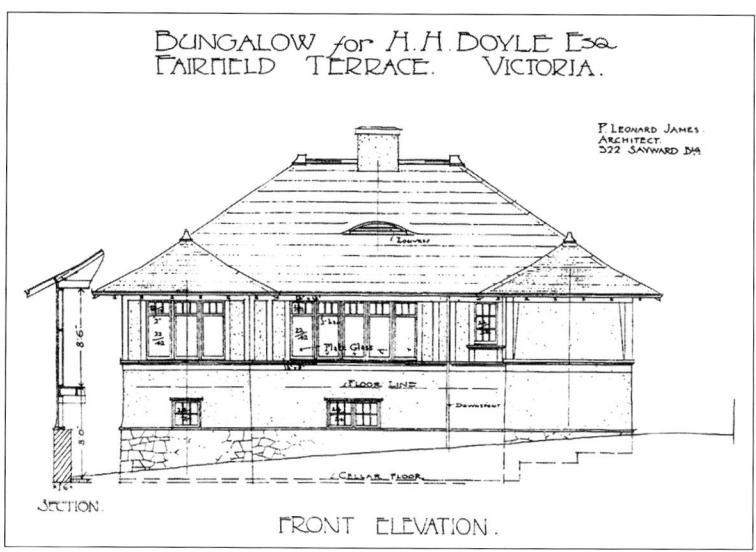

H.H. Boyle, Soldiers Settlement house built on cul-de-sac, now 1320 Franklin Terrace, Victoria, 1921 (Courtesy of CVPDD)

Drawing of the proposed Elizabethan design for the Oak Bay Beach Hotel by P. Leonard James printed in the Daily Colonist, February 13th, 1927, but not built. (Author's collection)

In 1926, another of the "wedding present" houses was built at 20 Sylvan Lane. Mr. E.H. Bird, who planned to live at 6 Sylvan Lane, gave his daughter and son-in-law, H.G. Hinton, the house on the lot adjacent to his own. The houses were built in the same year with rather similar plans. Built in the English Arts & Crafts-style, the houses are compatible but not the same. Only the Hinton house has half-timbering. The front elevations of the two houses are at different angles because of the rocky nature of the sites. Both houses have hooded fireplaces and beamed ceilings.

The drawings of the two hooded fireplaces are on the same sheet of details, which confirms that the same contractor built both houses

One of the delightful smaller English Arts & Crafts semi-bungalows nestles beside the Oak Bay Beach Hotel parking lot. It is a house with an unusual eyebrow eave which can be made out on the elevations. For a while the hotel wanted to demolish this house to increase the size of their parking lot. The Hallmark Society of Victoria became involved in saving the house in the 1980s.

The Burt-Smiths who built at 1193 Beach Drive had very definite ideas. They had done much research on style, on details they wanted in their house and on materials. Eleven pages of handwritten notes given to the architect are filed at the BCA.

"Don't like the present fashion of very low houses, with deeply dug out basements, they look as if they had been sat on," wrote Mr. Burt-Smith some 10 years before ranch houses were even thought of. What kind of low house did he have in mind? An English thatched cottage perhaps! His front door is very little above grade, but the house is a storey and three-quarters and definitely does not look "sat upon."

Some of the other Burt-Smith notes: "A great many electric plugs wanted everywhere . . .Window seat with front sloping back to the floor to avoid kicking . . . Storm windows required for the East and North sides of the house . . . We wonder if fireplaces in the corner of the living room and dining room would be a good idea in case we, or subsequent owners, wish to make

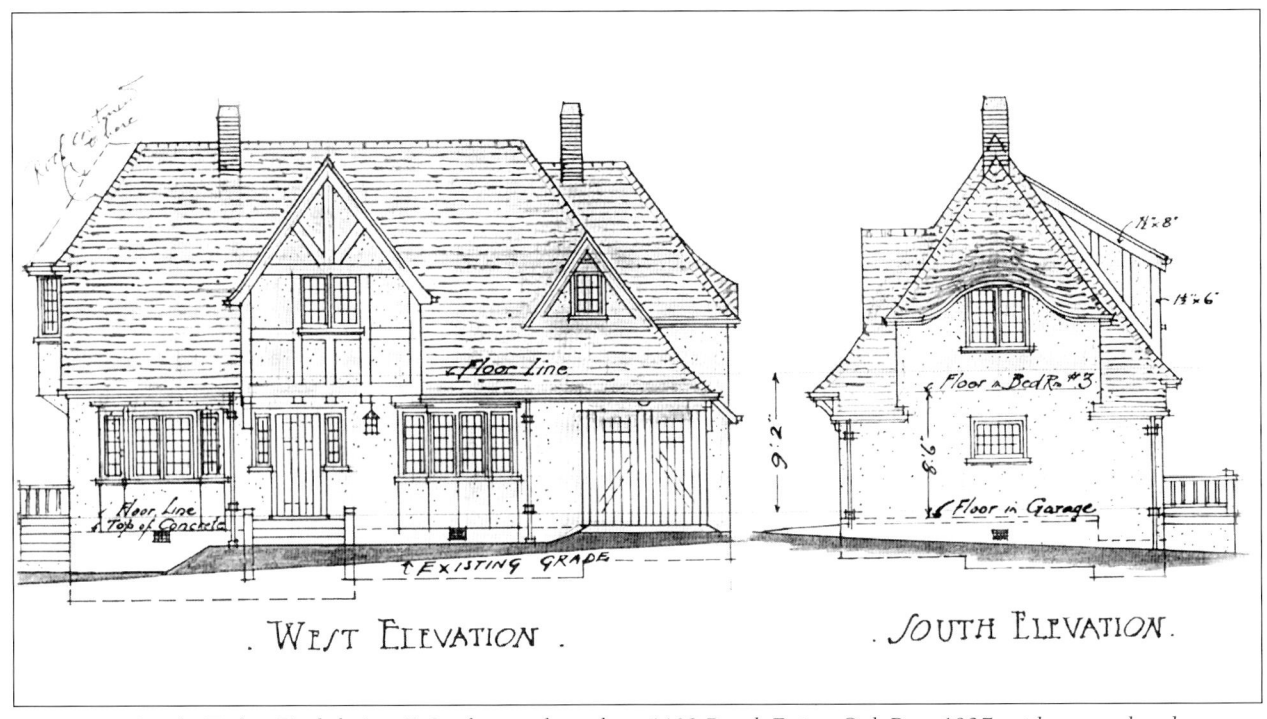

Henry Burt-Smith, Tudor English Art & Crafts semi-bungalow, 1193 Beach Drive, Oak Bay, 1927, with unusual eyebrow gable, the front and side elevations (Photo by author - Courtesy of SDW)

Houses for Hinton and Bird, Gonzales *(Photo by Easthope - BCA #hp685499)* Inset left: E.H. Bird residence, fireplace, 6 Sylvan Lane, Oak Bay, 1926 *(Photo by Easthope - BCA #hp68505)* H.J. Hinton residence, fireplace, 20 Sylvan Lane, Oak Bay, 1926 *(Photo by Easthope - BCA #hp68500)*

one large room of the space."

During the actual planning James steered the Burt-Smiths away from this last consideration. Although the dining room does have a corner fireplace, the staircase entry hall separates the dining room from the living room.

Mr. Burt-Smith made private arrangements to supply many of the materials for his house. This is reflected in the contract price of $5,800, which did not include all the special materials supplied by the owner. The actual price came to well over $11,500. They certainly got an attractive house for their careful considerations. But it sounds like a job that might have driven a few people slightly crazy. Did the contractor get all those special materials delivered on time? Or were there some anxious moments?

Burt-Smith house with Dutch half-hipped roof over an oriel bay window, and marled shingle roof (Photo by architect - Author's collection - BCA# hp68507)

CHAPTER SEVEN

What Happened To Douglas

Douglas James enjoyed a laid-back architectural practice in Duncan for many years. As the Town of Duncan did not keep many of the records such as a larger city would, finding out about his practice came down to research about early building contracts in the *Cowichan-Leader*, which the Cowichan Valley Museum undertook recently. They produced a helpful list of many Douglas James buildings in Duncan

In addition to his architectural practice Douglas built quite a number of houses near Duncan for his own use. He seemed to be searching for the perfect two bedroom house. These included *Stagstones* at1033 Herd Road. On this lovely property at Maple Bay he is believed to have built his first boat, *Radiant*, a 26-foot powered sailboat. In 1924 Douglas and Johnnie moved closer to town to 811 Wharncliffe Road.

About four years later he built a delightful cottage on his Lakes Road property. There he laid down the keel for the *Tang O'Sea*, gradually adding the ribs until the size of this 40-foot cruiser became apparent. After a fire destroyed the cottage, but fortunately, not the boat, he built the house that still stands on the Lakes Road property. A porch with a swept gable protects the front entrance. This house has been enlarged in a sympathetic manner.

After his move to Victoria, he built 1414 Monterey Avenue in 1945. In 1950 he built on Chisholm Trail in Maple Bay. His last home was on Verdier Avenue in Brentwood Bay. The last two houses have either been demolished or so added to that they are unrecognizable.

Douglas James died on September 30th, 1962 at age 73. Many stories of his life and practice have turned up since then to add to those that I already knew.

His grandniece, Elizabeth Turk, and I went to Duncan soon after the 1996 Heritage House Tour. Priscilla Davis, Curator-Manager of the Cowichan Valley Museum, arranged for us to meet the painter who as a young man worked on many of the Douglas James jobs. Claude Green and his wife Edna, delightful, active 90-year olds, served us tea in fine bone-china cups with delicious raisin cake made that morning by Mrs. Green. Several stories came to light that show Douglas's carefree personal style.

Mr. Green volunteered an account of Douglas teasing a well-trained British plasterer on the job for the Huntingdons.

"Come with me, Claude," Douglas winked, "I want a word with our plasterer." They entered the hall where the plasterer stood on his scaffold doing the ceiling.

"Ah," said Douglas to the plasterer, "You know I think I'm going to have to get a plasterer up from Victoria."

"What do you mean?" queried the on-the-job plasterer.

"Well I want to have a specially elegant oval cove run in the living room and I'll have to get a man up from Victoria to carry it out."

The plasterer descended from his scaffolding and came over to confront the pair of them.

"Mr. James," he said in a rather menacing manner, "I can make any conceivable cove that you *can manage* to draw." Claude Green started to laugh and the plasterer realized he was the butt of a friendly joke.

I asked Mr. Green if he remembered Douglas's wife, Johnnie, a rather fiery little woman. Douglas wasn't with her on the day that she took her dog into the old Duncan Post office, and it cocked its leg against a column. When an irate man kicked the dog, Johnnie wrapped her riding whip around his legs.

"Yes, Mr. Ford, the Post Master," laughed Mr. Green almost before I'd finished my sentence. "He actually damaged the dog's jaw and Mrs. James made a real scene about it and threatened to sue him." I was amazed to hear his instant confirmation of my story and to learn the extent of damage to the dog. But it turned out he had more information: "Mrs. James kept after Mr. Ford until she got satisfaction – and that Boston bull was the only dog in Duncan to have a gold tooth."

In the English Arts & Crafts tradition, Douglas insisted on having interior wooden trim finished in black. Mr. Green smiled as he recalled that when he ordered this special black formula, his paint supplier would guffaw and say, "Oh, another 'Birdie' James house." No one seemed to know the origin of the name "Birdie." However, the black finish to interior woodwork has been preserved in most cases.

Mr. Green related some history of the King's Daughters Hospital, which Douglas designed for the Hospital Board. E.W. Lee, one of the two local contractors and the man often used on

Douglas James's jobs, was on the Board. As a member of the Board, however, Lee could not bid on the work. It tickled Mr. Green to report the solution worked out for this knotty problem. Douglas himself undertook the position of contractor and handed in the bid as figured by Lee, under the name of *D. James, Contractor*. With the bid accepted, Douglas became both architect and contractor for the hospital with Lee's crew of workmen undertaking the work. Surely a solution that could only have been made in a small town in "the good old days!"

Mr. Green mentioned the Shawnigan Lake Boys School and Fairbridge Farm as James jobs. Douglas did indeed prepare the plans for the Shawnigan School after a fire in 1926 destroyed the original buildings. But although Mr. Green remembers working for him on the group of buildings at Fairbridge Farm, Douglas did not design it. Major K.B. Spurgin its architect died in 1936 and Douglas took over supervision of the work to its completion. Mr. Green had also prepared a list of various other jobs that he could remember. Thanks to him the list of Douglas's buildings grew to over 30 in number.

From Bill Brown, the son of O.C. Brown, the other Duncan contractor, I learned that a set of plans for a house designed by Douglas James has been saved for over 60 years. Bill and his father constructed the house for H.L. Whittaker at 2159 Quamichan Park Road in 1938. Bill Brown liked the Whittaker house so much that he intended to build a similar house should he ever win a suitable sweepstake, and saved the plans.

His English Arts & Crafts fingerprint shows in the work of Douglas James, and I discovered one more of his houses by looking for his style. The lady who answered my knock on the door at 6899 Norcross Road, Duncan, was the stepdaughter of the original owner and had a blueprint to confirm my find.

That first cottage Douglas built on his property at 6392 Lakes Road had large stone steps and paths semi-covered with thyme, and was surrounded with catnip, heather and Auntie Johnnie's roses. It had diamond-paned, English railway-style windows, which slid down into sockets and were pulled up with leather thongs. Smaller than most of their homes, the cottage had all facilities very neatly planned, much as one would plan galley and bathroom for a boat. Douglas used a photograph of this cottage on his 1944 publication *Carefree Cottages - Plan Book No. 1*. The 12 houses in this book are each illustrated with a plan showing room dimensions, two interior views with furniture in place and a small-scale elevation, all on the one page. Prices for complete one-quarter inch to a foot working drawings including one-inch scale details and specifications varied from $15 to $25 per set. Many books with poor plans by non-professionals were published at the time. He felt his book a good way to get well-planned, simple-to-build, attractive small designs out to the public, who had only to order the working drawings from him. Used to easy-going country life near Duncan, he had unfortunately not considered that the AIBC would not countenance such a procedure. No further volumes of these delightful little house plans appeared. He had to withdraw the books from circulation to retain his AIBC membership.

"The Duncanites," as the family called them, came to Victoria on many a weekend. They lunched at our house and Douglas

Douglas James Cottage, Lakes Road, Duncan, c 1928 (Author's collection)

Below: *Douglas James, The Dorset from Carefree Cottages - Plan Book No.1, c 1932 (Author's collection)*

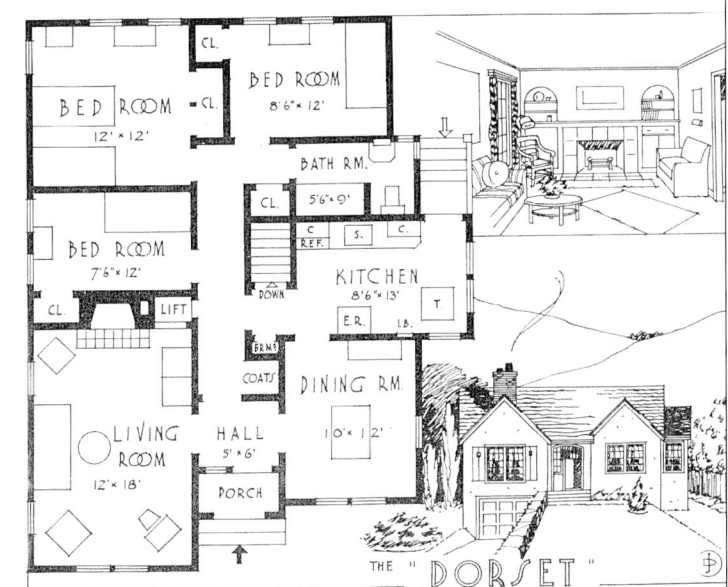

usually brought a bottle of his homemade perry (a cider made from pears) while my father sometimes produced his homemade blackberry wine. These lunches became quite hilarious affairs, each brother trying to outdo the other with puns and stories. But "The Duncanites" were always keen to get back to Duncan before dark. My father teased them with a poem. I remember only a few of the words, "cantering through dear Cobble Hill, we must make Duncan tonight."

Soon the Douglas Jameses planned to live aboard their beautiful *Tang O'Sea*. He had the newly completed cruiser transported down to Maple Bay and launched. Then following their plan, they sold the Lakes Road house and went to live on board at a mooring spot in Victoria.

For my wedding present Douglas gave me the simple coffee table he and Johnnie had used on the *Tang O'Sea*. The piece interested me, not only because he had made it, but because the mahogany wood had been salvaged from the saloon of an old sailing barque when it was dismasted and turned into a barge, a fate suffered by many a sailing ship. Though a modern style, the table nevertheless embraces the romantic dimension of an unknown history at sea.

Douglas made furniture off and on, including our Tod Road dining room chairs, in an Arts & Crafts style. Not the most comfortable of chairs, they creaked quite a bit, probably in need of re-gluing after their 50-odd years of use. I let them go when I sold the family home.

Until its demolition in 2003, the newspapers made many mentions of the old Memorial Arena in Victoria. It may surprise people to learn that Douglas James, in association with Hubert Savage and D.C. Frame, was the designer and working partner for this project. There had been two earlier arenas, both destroyed by fire. My parents, as keen hockey fans, had attended the games at the first arena when the Victoria Cougars won the Stanley Cup in 1925, and had pointed out the site to me on the northeast corner of Cadboro Bay Road and Epworth Street.

When Victoria City Council decided to erect a proper skating arena downtown after the Second World War, they asked four of the top local architects – P.L. James, Douglas James, Hubert Savage, and D.C. Frame – to design it in a partnership, possibly because of limited activity in the building field at the time. My father quickly withdrew from this commission with "too many cooks" – a decision he never regretted.

At the last minute, when the working drawings for Douglas's wooden truss design were completed, an engineer from Vancouver got hold of one of the city aldermen and persuaded him that the City ought to use his patented new concrete barrel-roof design. The alderman convinced the whole Council that this wonderful concrete roof would "put Victoria on the map." The original truss design estimate of cost was $325,000. To Douglas's disgust, the converted City fathers foisted this barrel roof on his design. The heavy concrete barrel supports restricted the sight-lines for a number of seats near the roof, all of which would have had clear views with the truss roof design. The cost for this barrel roof came to a great deal more – $1.2 million.

An article in the *Times Colonist*, on June 28th, 1997 mentioned that this wonderful barrel roof that the City chose in place of the original inexpensive truss design caused serious problems in maintenance and developed cracks within a year of its construction.

In partnership with D.C. Frame, Douglas designed the Imperial Bank using Haddington Island stone and a black granite base. It is sited diagonally across Government Street from the Federal Building and Post Office. The two Moderne buildings are complementary to each other, and honour the English-trained James brothers who designed them.

CHAPTER EIGHT
Recognizing Style

Like other arts, architecture does not remain static but changes as new methods, materials and practitioners rise to prominence and become fashionable. Throughout P. Leonard James's professional life many different stylistic changes evolved.

The public generally recognizes the differences between Tudor, Colonial and modern styles. But do members of the general population know of the fascinating historical backgrounds? Style is more than just the historical differences. It embraces many different attributes including the personal preference of each architect, so that his design choices often include particular details. These personal traits make some architects' work easier to identify than that of others.

Architectural historians have now catalogued the Tudor Revival style, very popular in Victoria before the First World War, as one of several styles under the general heading of English Arts & Crafts. Richard Norman Shaw, a British architect and a master of the Queen Anne Aesthetic Movement, greatly encouraged the Tudor Revival. The style has its roots in the vernacular architecture of the 15th and 16th century when the house skeleton – squared oak timbers and curved tree branches – remained visible, and brick, wattle or plaster filled the spaces between the timbers. In early times the oak weathered to a silver gray.

In Victorian times, with the advent of comfortable travel on the many rail lines that fanned out from London, people started touring the country to see historical sites. Many owners of country houses and sometimes whole towns began to spruce up their buildings. A great number of original Tudor buildings had their woodwork painted black with the newly available bituminous paints and had whitewash applied to begrimed plasterwork. Towns like Chester and Shrewsbury became famous for their "black and white work." However, the half-timbered work of the 19th and 20th century Tudor Revival style is usually purely decorative with boards applied over the building paper that covered the sheathing before the stucco was put on.

In parts of England – Suffolk for one – Tudor houses were often painted pink, perhaps "to fool the eye" that the more expensive brick had been used as infill. Sometimes villages retained the seasoned gray colour of the oak timberwork. These colours were rarely used in Canada. However when houses are being repainted here on the West Coast today, the choice of colours is likely to be much more vibrant than the original Edwardian brown and cream, or the 1920s and '30s black and white. Where shingles are incorporated in the design, as in Dr. J.D Helmcken's house at 1015 Moss Street, they have historical antecedents in the tiles used on walls in earlier periods in England.

Some writers of architectural history in Victoria have suggested that older local architects influenced the work of the James brothers. The popularity of Samuel Maclure's Tudor Revival designs had certainly established a taste in the public mind for this type of building. But fine as the works of Maclure and Rattenbury were, these architects had just adapted the popular Tudor Revival and Arts & Crafts styles, in which the James brothers – and Rattenbury – had been trained in England. It would be closer to the truth to say that the local architects had all been deriving ideas from the work of the foremost English and American architects. They did not copy, but skillfully adapted those ideas to suit local building materials and conditions. *The Studio* magazine and various architectural publications of the time provided excellent sources on the trends currently popular in England and in America.

The other major style was the Classical Revival. Its columns and pilasters, pediments, domes, quoined corners, plain or arched windows – including the famous Palladian window, which combined a central arched window with plain side windows – and fan lights over front doors had preserved and enlarged on early Greco-Roman ideas through the centuries. Variations called "Georgian Revival" and "United Empire Loyalist" in Eastern Canada used symmetry with a balanced number of windows or bays, pilasters and columns. The exterior finish in the West was usually stucco or wood, while stone and brick were used for this type of architecture in many parts of the world.

Charles F.A. Voysey had pioneered a new, plainer English Arts & Crafts style in England from the 1890s. The style had been used frequently by the versatile architect M.H. Baillie Scott, whose range of work before the war also included the older Tudor Revival style. The pre-war Garden City concept of town-planning for middle class and workmen's housing inspired a lighter stucco finish for buildings. After the First World War this much lighter style became popular in Canada. A real shift in ideas took place for many reasons. The war had taken a terrible toll among architects and the craftsmen who could carry out their ideas. The concepts of the English Arts & Crafts Movement now stressed naturalism and protection, perhaps as an antidote to the dreadful confusion the war had created in the minds of people. Much lighter eaves with little overhang and extensive use of stucco, often with little or no half-timbering, became the fashion. Traces of the styles used by Voysey, Baillie Scott and Edwin Lutyens can be seen in the residential work of P. Leonard James.

The practitioners of this new Arts & Crafts-style believed in natural placement of buildings in their environment, so that rather than being imposed on their site, they seemed to have grown there. Symmetry and ostentation were avoided. Features included: wide entrance doors – symbolic of welcome; rough-cast stucco; long sloping roofs – symbolic of protection and family life, which flow down and almost embrace the ground. James's 1930 house for H.C.V. MacDowall at 3065 Uplands Road is a particularly good example of this style.

In the specifications for the roof of the MacDowall house, the wooden shingles were to be treated with several tones of colour before being applied to the roof – this was to give the roof a softer, marled effect that would blend more naturally into the environment than a solid colour. However, Mr. MacDowall considered the contract price too high and this visual nicety was sacrificed. A simple coat of stain applied to the whole roof allowed a saving of $110.00.

Although the larger residences of James's partner, Hubert Savage, are fairly well documented, I became interested in his small houses. These were mostly built in Saanich and sad to say, when the Municipality of Saanich moved into its new quarters in 1965, the Building Department threw out their old plans.

I knew that Savage had designed a number of small houses near his own 1913 house currently numbered 3862 Grange Road in the Marigold area. Some were located nearby, based on their style alone, for he made consistent use of many of the elements mentioned in the chapter on James and Savage, in the construction of his small bungalows. I felt confident that I could find more in Saanich and took to driving and taking walks in many of the areas built up in the '20s and '30s. I did locate several and in most cases the current owners still had the signed contract blueprints to confirm my "find." In the case of 1057 St. David Street, Oak Bay, built in 1938, the owner invited me to come in and go up to the attic. Why? Well there on the roof tie the architect's sign originally used on the job was carefully stored. When I visited Cyril Hume, who wondered about his house, *The Sheiling* at 2525 Beauford Drive, Sidney, my opinion that Savage had designed it, confirmed his own unsubstantiated belief. He had no plans but said that even though his grandmother could not remember the architect's name, she averred that "a proper English architect" had designed the house. Savage, having retained his membership in ARIBA, was more "properly" English than most of the local architects!

Style also played a part in locating some of the houses designed by Douglas James in Duncan, where plans of buildings had never been officially saved. Had Douglas outlived his wife, some certificates and perhaps plans and photographs would have been saved. However Douglas's widow, Johnnie, left everything to the Saxon-Whites, new friends whom she made after his death, and it is unknown if they kept any existing plans or architectural papers. They allowed Percy to take only one memento from his brother's possessions. He chose the painting of the *Glenclova*, a four-masted barque, on which their brother, Harold James, first went to sea – a painting with more meaning for the family than for strangers.

When I wanted to learn more about Douglas's work in Duncan, I had the good fortune to meet Hamish and Daphne Mutter. As a teenager, Hamish, who loved boats, hung around when Douglas built his boat, *Tang O'Sea*, until allowed to assist. They became life-long friends. The Mutters had made a list of some houses and we spent a pleasant day together in the early 1980s going round to see them. As we approached the houses through the trees, I started to recognize the Douglas James houses by their outline and roof style. The current owners welcomed us royally, often with gin and tonic, or tea – my choice as I was driving.

In 1996, the first Heritage House Tour in Duncan included *Stonehaven*, built in 1926 for lumberman Carlton Stone at 3069 Gibbins Road. This building is considered Douglas James's largest Duncan commission. A country home on 14 acres, it has the rustic feeling of a lodge. The client, owner of the Hillcrest Logging Company, requested fireplace mantels be cut from quarter logs, with bark retained on the lower surfaces, and ceiling beams of clear-run timber, not the built-up ones so often used. Rather heavy tiles, imported from Europe, finished the roof, and the main chimney had four flues at angles to one another, an unusual old-country style that Douglas used for a chimney at Hatley Park Castle when he worked for Maclure.

In studying my father's plans and visiting houses he had designed, I noted that he seemed always to be experimenting. In the early 1920s he worked with some transitional ideas, combining elements of Georgian with the feel of the English Arts & Crafts Movement. Judge P.S. Lampman's house, 820 Pemberton Road (1922) and Miss H. Nation's house, 1524 Shasta Place (1923) are examples. This melding of different styles can be noted again later in his 1940s suburban designs. The bungalow at 1549 Despard Avenue for Arthur V. Danby has a low roof and an entryway with a flat Tudor arch, combined with modified quoining created in stucco. The house at 1561 Despard, built for Mr. H. Johnson, has the same low-pitched roof but uses International Style windows.

After his year in England in 1933-34, James designed houses and schools in his interpretation of the International Style. The F.W. Griffiths residence at 235 Dennison Road (1938) and Dr. T.H. Johns' residence at 2753 Somass Drive (1940) are now called "Art Moderne."

Left: E.W. Griffiths, Moderne-style residence, 235 Dennison Road, Oak Bay, 1938 *(Photo by Architect - BCA #hp68122)*

Below: Dr. T.H. Johns, 1940 residence, 2753 Somass Drive, Oak Bay, nearly completed with Moderne-style windows *(Photo by Architect - BCA #hp68549)*

They remain in almost original condition with sympathetic additions, though the original Moderne windows in the Johns house have been changed to plain glass allowing the owners uninterrupted views. The Esquimalt High School Addition (1950) and the Oak Bay Junior High School (1951) use windows which stress horizontal lines. The Oak Bay school does not architecturally disguise the functions of the various parts of the building, but follows the newer dictate of "form follows function," allowing clear differentiation between school shops, auditorium, gymnasium and classroom areas.

In all his work over the years great care was taken in finishing details, in handsome interior spacess, in exteriors that exhibit an elegant plainness and are never overdone. Having been allowed to take photographs in some of the houses, I have come to a greater appreciation of his meticulous attention to small details. While there are ornate cornices and oval ribs on the ceilings of many houses, the small details include the turn of the skirting board on staircases, or the sweep of a long arch under a pantry cupboard relieved with small cutouts in the R.H.B. Ker house.

Fireplaces whether finished with tiles or brick usually had hearths of quarry tile. He used diagonally laid brick either in full herringbone pattern on exterior landings and patios and parts of the elevation of the Jubilee Hospital, or occasionally as a decorative chimney lozenge.

In the case of Jamses's smaller house designs, repeated stylistic details have not been discovered as in the work of Douglas James and Hubert Savage. I have not been able to identify many repeated characteristics of a style in his work, and have not therefore had the fun of exploring and finding buildings, as I did with the work of his partners.

Built-in Fittings

1: C.S. Baxter, 1790 Beach Drive, Oak Bay, 1912. The slightly bowed sideboard has the plain wide Arts and Crafts hardware he often used at this time.

2: Mrs. D.R. Ker, 841 St. Charles Street, Victoria, 1929. Cupboards of this type with a display shelf above enclosed storage shelves or trays for shoes were used under the high roof space of many of the Tudor designed homes. The two panel door on the right was used in houses of this period.

3: Miss H. Nation, who married R.H.B. Ker, 524 Shasta Place, Victoria, 1923. Pantry built-in cupboards had glazed sliding doors. Note that the graceful bows under the cupboards, which concealed lighting for the work surface, have been relieved with circular cutouts.

4: H.F. Bullen, 906 St. Charles Street, Victoria, 1920. Dining room, built-in glass fronted, mirror-backed cupboard. A corner cupboard designed for the elegant octagonal dining room.

Photos by author

Entryways

1: A.B. Cotton, 990 Terrace Avenue, Victoria,1928. Classical style entry.

2: J.E. Semmes, 3155 Beach Drive, Oak Bay,1929. A herringbone brick path leads to the door through the archway in the slightly splay-walled entry gable.

3: C.L.H. Branson, 2901 Sea View Road, Saanich, 1928. The 3'6" inset front door with Arts and Crafts hardware is protected by a flat Tudor arch.

4: Frank Burrell, 1064 Beverley Place, Victoria, 1912. A low stucco wall has piers that support an iron arch, which reflects the shape of the dome over the front door.

5: Major W. Garrard, Tod Inlet, Brentwood Bay, 1927. The massing of the Tudor gable, roofs and triangular ventilator in the top gable give this country home a fitting simplicity.

Photos by author

Fireplaces

1: J.W. Morris, 1558 Beach Drive, Oak Bay, 1912. Living room fireplace with shell-topped shelves.

2: H.F. Bullen, 906 St. Charles Street, Victoria, 1920. Fireplace in the octagonal dining room.

3: E.A.M. Williams, 1915 Crescent Road, Oak Bay, 1945. Living room fireplace. The use of half-round trim was popularized by Frank Lloyd Wright.

4: Judge Wm. Galliher, 914 St. Charles Street, Victoria, 1909. An original mantelpiece re-installed in 1995 condominiums.

5: A.B. Cotton, 990 Terrace Avenue, Victoria, 1928. Arched insert fireplace in bedroom

6: Mrs. P.S. Lampman, 925 St. Charles Street, Victoria, 1941. This arched brick fireplace was used in several houses and is of the type favoured by M.H. Baillie Scott, a Master English Arts & Crafts architect.

Photos by author

Steps & Stairs

1: F. Forbes-Wilson (Sayward-Wilson), 3125 Beach Drive, Oak Bay, 1930. View shows the main stair with its carved and chamfered newel post. The landing door leads to back stairs to the kitchen and servants quarters.

2: Dr. T.H. Johns, 2753 Somass Drive, Oak Bay, 1943. In Moderne-Style, the balusters and newel post, have been replaced with a low plaster wall. The handrail is wall hung.

3: M.M. Bell-Irving, 588 Linkleas Avenue, Oak Bay, 1928. Several houses have newel posts with rather similar tall caps. The alternate plain balusters accentuate the shaped balusters.

4: J.W. Morris, 1558 Beach Drive, Oak Bay, 1912. Striking treatment of the banister to suit a major home design.

5: Royal Colwood Golf Club 1930. After years of neglect, the landscaped half-moon steps in the manner of Edwin Lutyens - top steps cut into the hill, lower ones curved outwards, could still be seen before the Clubhouse was demolished.

6: C.L.H. Branson, 2901 Sea View Road, Saanich, 1928. Front entrance stair - herringbone design brick steps with stone walls.

Photos by author

Windows & Doors

1: Hans Hunter, Thetis Island, 1927. Imposing bay window in the main living room.

2: N.A. Yarrow, 691 Donnington Pl. Saanich, 1949. Patio. *(BCA #hp 68551)*

3: J.W. Morris, 1558 Beach Drive, Oak Bay, 1912. A view-enhancing window.

4: A.B. Cotton, 990 Terrace Avenue, Victoria, 1928, shuttered French doors in Classical style home.

5: While at 572 Linkleas Avenue, Oak Bay, the 1928 M. Bell-Irving home had a herringbone patio outside the French doors. *(Photos by author)*

CHAPTER NINE
Family Holidays

Soon after the First World War, my parents took driving lessons and bought a car, referred to as *The Bluebird*. It had a flat windscreen with a single top-hung wiper blade, canvas roof, wooden spoke wheels, a high running board and a temperature gauge on the front of the engine bonnet. The four doors came without windows then, although some canvas snap-on windows of an early plastic material that rather obscured the view, could be used if required.

For a holiday, "Jimmy and Molly" decided to put their new skills to the test and drive up island as far as the road had been developed. In the early 1920s, the original gravel Malahat was a pretty serious undertaking. A sign near Goldstream announced "Start of Malahat Drive," – there is still one today, but the road has changed. Only one lane wide in places, the original steep grade to the summit required gearing down, usually to the lowest gear. Some cars were believed to have better gear ratios in reverse and there are stories of people who went up the steepest parts backwards. However, another explanation had to do with the underseat gas tanks of early models which had no pumps, and on a steep hill could only deliver the fuel in the reverse position. Speed was not the hazard that it is now!

Arriving in Duncan they visited Douglas and Johnnie to

check up on their recent doings. Douglas had been wounded in the war and received early discharge. Returning to Duncan in 1917, he had to turn his hand to more than architecture to make a living. For a while he cut and sold wood from his wife's property, built a house, made furniture and tinkered with boats and motors. Douglas found it hard to believe that his less mechanical brother and his wife – a most sensible woman despite her giggles and charmingly scatterbrained manner – were going to come through their intended trip unscathed. So he watched with anxious eyes as they headed for Chemainus, Saltair, Lantzville and points north. Their trip took them all the way to Campbell River but they mentioned that the gravel road, maintained locally, was barely passable in some places. They camped on the bank of the Oyster River in a tent.

The trip seemed a great adventure to them, but their tent, which they had borrowed from Douglas, leaked. Percy could never persuade her to camp under canvas again. Molly always liked her creature comforts and even a holiday in a cottage became a torment barely to be tolerated. She laughingly made a point of stating: "The real purpose of a holiday is to make one appreciate home and all its comforts!"

One of their early trips up the island took place while Prohibition was still in effect. My father liked to tell the story of their stopover at a Duncan hotel. When Molly did not feel at all well, he left her resting in the room and went out to see what he could get from the drugstore to settle her stomach. He went to the back of the store where the druggist worked in his dispensary. Leaning over the counter, my father asked in his quiet English voice, "Excuse me. What have you got for a stomach ache?" The druggist gave him a rather strange look and beckoned him into the dispensary, saying,

"Just a minute sir," as he busied himself in the far corner. He poured a tot of something into a small glass which, with another knowing look, he offered to my father. Rather surprised he took the glass, smelled it and quickly drank the contents – a passably good brandy.

"Thank you very much for the drink," he said, "but it is **my wife** who has the upset stomach!" The druggist must have thought him someone desperate for a drink in those Prohibition days. My father always had a good laugh when he told this story.

In 1929, my parents agreed that my mother would take me on the long train and boat trip to Europe to visit her parents, who had retired to Lisbon. There seemed to be many reasons to make the trip. My mother felt that her parents, not in the best of health, should meet their only grandchild before my schooling commenced. And as a "Londoner by adoption," she yearned for a touch of the life she had known in London before she came to Canada. The building boom had filled the family coffers, so it seemed an opportune time to go. After our visit to Lisbon, we would return to London, where many cousins with large houses would welcome us to stay.

As we prepared to leave Victoria in late May, we passed through the Rattenbury and James-designed Marine Terminal building. Polished ticket-wickets lined the large space designed to combine height and an impressive airiness. Father took me over to the glass cases in the centre of the terminal which contained models of the CPR ships for a closer look. Complete in every detail from the passenger railings to the open baggage doors, they even showed the individual boards of the decking. We made our daytime trip to Vancouver on one of the Princess boats. Those Clyde-built ferry boats had all the lines of the bigger ocean liners, two or three funnels, riveted steel construction and those wooden decks, still scrubbed by the crew. My father came to Vancouver with us. My mother, not a good sailor, sat quietly in a sheltered spot on deck, while he undertook to entertain me on the trip. After we had roamed the deck together for a while, we sat and he talked with mother while keeping me busy with a cartoon game which he devised. As well, he made a point of telling me that we were now on a "Little Ship," and how mother and I were soon going to travel in a "Big Train" across Canada. How after five nights on the "Big Train," we would board a "Big Ship" to cross the ocean. Then, when we arrived in England we would get into a "Little Train." His descriptions piqued my five-year old mind. Sure enough, all these changes happened just as he had said they would.

We docked in Vancouver that evening beside the handsome old CPR station at the foot of Granville Street. The cavernous interior of the station gave off strange, rather bewildering, reverberating echoes – whistles, the bustle of Redcaps and their rumbling, heavy-laden baggage carts and the "huff-huff" of the stoked-up steam engine. Father came aboard the train with us and inspected the compartment he had reserved.

"This will be your home for five nights, Nomie (my baby name). It's made up for sleeping now, but in the morning, while you are having breakfast in the dining car, the porter will set up the daytime seats for you." He pointed to the netting on the wall. "See the nice hammock where you can put your treasures and clothes within easy reach during the night." Knowing he would not see us again until early December, he filled the drawn-out minutes before leave-taking with cheerful chat. "And look here. When you pull this down it's your wash basin." He demonstrated the little fold-down basin that emptied itself when folded back up. But he left the discovery that the toilet was noisy, drafty and scary – emptying right onto the track – for my mother to explain. The time for parting hugs finally arrived and mother and I started out on our long journey. In June, we boarded the Cunard liner *Andania*.

Back in Victoria, my father bought a radio, a modern invention he had stubbornly resisted before we left. The airwaves supplied some sound in a house so deadly quiet and lonely after our departure. He became an "Amos and Andy" fan.

By November, mother and I had completed our visit with her parents in Lisbon and returned to London where we stayed with the family of a busy doctor married to a cousin of my mother. There she could leave me with the household staff and attend all the concerts she desired, stocking up on many wonderful performances by top professionals in preparation for the leaner times she would face back in Victoria.

When my father came over to join us in December, he made notes about his first impressions of his dear old England: *LONDON RE-VISITED (1929-1930)*

There are many little differences that strike the returned wanderer after an absence of ten years from "the hub of the Universe."

We [he and fellow ship passengers] entered London by one of the great western highways, having travelled up from our port of disembarkation (Southampton) by motor stage – a method of approach that was not in existence ten years ago; thus, instead of arriving in the orthodox manner at a larger railway terminus, I am suddenly aware that our conveyance is running side-by-side with the familiar red "Generals" (the double-decker buses) of the metropolis and being held up by the London "bobby" at street corners as the exigencies of traffic control demand. It is a new and strange experience to be thus suddenly introduced to the roar and bustle of the crowded thoroughfares, without, so to speak, time to "take breath in the ante-chamber afforded by the railway station," and a rather startling one may it be said.

On its way to town our motor-coach had carried us through some delightful old boroughs that appear to have altered little since I first knew them. The beautiful countryside, here and there clothed with a heavy coating of white frost where the sun had not yet penetrated was a joy to eyes accustomed so long to vast stretches of virgin forests in the West.

My fears that England might have become overcrowded, were allayed by the welcome sight of apparently inexhaustible green meadows, chalk downs and spacious commons on every hand, as our coach bowled along towards its destination. It is true that in places wide arterial roads or "bye-passes" (sic) have been cut to relieve the congestion of the older and narrower highways. I was sad to note that along these new bye-passes large colonies of ugly brick houses are springing up – houses that stand out in horrid contrast to the wayside cottages and manor houses dotted along the older highways. The perpetrators of these new dwellings appear to have a preference for a most bilious yellow "rough cast", as most of them are of this description. In spite of all that has been written and said in recent years of laying out building estates on improved and intelligent lines it would appear that great opportunities have been lost along these arterial roads.

The modern English speculative builder, seemingly, has a sublime contempt for the traditional domestic architecture of the country, surrounded although he is by innumerable fine examples of the genuine styles and disdaining to use the local materials.

When he arrived, I surprised him by hanging back shyly behind my mother, not at first sure that I recognized him. But her enthusiastic welcome soon convinced me that he was indeed "my Daddy." Before long I happily sat on his knee as he told me one of his "Little Jimmy Green" bedtime stories that made me giggle. The main character lived in a hollow oak tree on Cattle Point and had lots of gentle adventures encountering our dog and cats and visiting Willows Beach and other places near home. Unfortunately these stories were never written down, nor repeated, each one simply invented as he went along.

As a youngster my father had enjoyed many pantomimes at Theatre Royal in Drury Lane. In 1894, the theatre acquired its wonderful hydraulic stage. The machinery enabled a large section of the stage to be raised several feet above its regular level, or to be lowered nine feet below it. Some years later they produced the sinking of the *Titanic*. The stage could also tilt from side to side and rock from front to back and tilt, circling slowly. Producers had almost unlimited creative possibilities for spectacular shows. We saw the 1929 pantomime, "Sleeping Beauty," together.

We visited a confusing number of family friends and relations, who all became rather a blur to me. My father would say, "Remember the people with the Scottie dog? Or, the orange cat?" Then I recalled the animals, but only remembered the people vaguely. However I did recall the ones who gave me sixpence as a parting gift!

We returned home together in February 1930. For my father, several very busy years of the James & Savage partnership were ahead.

In 1932 the family took several short holidays either on Vancouver Island or to the Gulf Islands. These family trips seem pretty restrained affairs, but, with prices included, they are delightfully unbelievable today. For instance: a four-day trip to Campbell River in June 1932 included the use of the Mill Bay ferry *Cascade* both ways. My father noted that the 365-mile trip used 17 gallons of gas, so the car delivered 21 miles per gallon. Overnight cabins rented from $1. to $2.50 per night. A bottle of Citronella (mosquito repellent) cost 20 cents. Total costs for the trip: $22.

When passing through Duncan, we always visited but never stayed with Douglas and Johnnie. They lived in a succession of houses designed with only two bedrooms, one used as an office-library. We stayed over at one of the hotels in Duncan or Chemainus. One night at the Tsouhalem Hotel in Duncan, when I slept on a cot in my parent's room, father rigged up a handkerchief to keep the overhead light out of my eyes while my parents read in bed. Hotel lighting was still very basic at that time, just a central bulb hanging on a wire from the ceiling and no bedside table lamps. I woke to the excitement of seeing him teetering round on their bed removing the charred remains of the handkerchief that had started to smoke above the light bulb.

"No harm done," said my father with relief. "All's well that ends well."

In 1936 we motored to the Flying U Ranch at Green Lake in the Cariboo for a stay of one week. My parents planned the trip with me in mind, as I had recently learned to ride at the Carley's stables in the Willows Fairground, just a block from home.

My father kept exhaustive notes for this trip, from July 28th to August 8th. Mentioning mileage, gas consumption and other costs, he noted that he had started out with $125 plus $7.17, presumably the amounts he had in his wallet and pocket change, for a total kitty of $132.17. We crossed from Sidney to Steveston on the old side-loading ferryboat, where return fares cost $11.75 – $5 for the car, plus two-and-a-half passengers.

In those days the trip up the Fraser Canyon on the all-gravel road certainly tested one's nerve. Parts of the road were constructed of wood and hung out over the rushing waters of the river. In other places the road passed across long shale screes that plummeted right down to the river and had no safety railing.

The ranch assigned each of us a horse for the week. We had a comfortable cabin with its own porch and good beds. These were remarkable after the sagging beds usually supplied at beach cabins on Vancouver Island. My mother enjoyed the open rangeland of the Cariboo, as she found coastal forests cramped and depressing. We went to the main ranch house for meals and evening entertainment – dancing every night. There were other families with children and often the parents danced with their offspring. A middle-aged cowhand taught everyone to do the schottische and polka. Dad and I played "Monopoly" – then quite a new game. Each week the ranch staged a round-up, a rodeo and a barbecue for the guests. The stay for the family cost $67.50 and included the use of three horses. On our return trip, we spent a night at the rather posh Sitka Lodge in Ashcroft. The bill came to $4.35 and probably included supper.

Returning to Vancouver Island, we caught the ferry at Steveston by the merest chance. The captain had already ordered the crew to cast off, when, as my father later told friends; "We anxiously raced down the causeway at Steveston honking our horn like Billy-O! To my amazement the crew actually pulled on the ropes to dock again and let us on board. Jolly fortunate, as all I had left was that return ticket!"

At Shawnigan Lake with Brutus, c 1938 (Family photo - Author's collection)

A year later in 1937, we travelled to Portland, Oregon. We made the trip with the Clarksons, Eric the architect, his wife Bea and his father, John C. Clarkson, a retired architect from Yorkshire. Each family drove in their own car and kept pace with one another. We had just purchased our English Flying Standard, a little car that attracted attention every time we stopped for gas in the USA. Eric and "Pa C" shook their heads as my father, besieged by every mechanic on duty, had to open the hood and let them see our four little English cylinders. The purpose of that trip was to see houses designed by Wade Hampton Pipes. He had trained in England with the master architect C.F.A. Voysey and brought his own version of English Arts & Crafts to the Portland area. We drove round an area not unlike the Uplands in Victoria, similarly dotted with lovely houses and flowering rhododendron bushes. Father had always been interested in Voysey who had worked for the London firm, Saxon Snell & Son, some 20 years before he himself joined the firm and he was particularly interested to see Wade Hampton Pipes' interpretations of the English Master Architect.

Each year since my early childhood, our family had spent one or two long weekends at Parksville. Mother loved the warm pools, the safety of the beach for children, the pink shells and sand dollar shells unique to the Pacific coast. After lessons from Mr. and Mrs. Ellison at Victoria's famous Crystal Garden pool, the family felt confident of my swimming ability and rented cottages at nearby Shawnigan Lake. Our St. Bernard dog, Brutus, came with us. One year we even had a family of newly-hatched Bantam chicks and mother hen, that slept together on the enclosed porch in a deep Chinese vegetable basket with a net curtain tied over the top.

Unable to spare time away from the office in these busy years for even a week, let alone a proper holiday, Father used to join us on weekends at Shawnigan. He enjoyed fishing with a hand-line in whatever rowboat came with the cottage. We took turns with the rowing and he taught me to clean my catch.

Friends from Victoria often drove up for a picnic with us. They sat on the dock, toes in the water in really hot weather, drank some of dad's homemade beer and amused my mother with their gossip. Mother hated the dark rooms of those cabins, with their skimpy curtains, but she knew it was as much vacation as she could possibly arrange for her busy husband.

CHAPTER TEN

Sink or Swim With Rattenbury and the C.P.R.

As a youngster I was aware that my father responded with a low growl of annoyance whenever Rattenbury's name was mentioned. Then as he thought of the man's grisly end, his murder being a recent event, he'd add a compassionate, "Poor old Rattenbury" and shake his head! Obviously some bad blood had existed between them.

Francis Mawson Rattenbury – who had begun his architectural career in Victoria in 1892 – had already completed a number of projects for the Canadian Pacific Railway (CPR) before the First World War and was recognized as their architect for projects in their western division. Before the Chamber of Commerce asked him to make suggestions for a hotel near the harbour (The Empress) in Victoria, Rattenbury had supervised various mountain hotels, including Banff Springs Hotel and the early wooden Chateau Lake Louise and had completed a handsome upgrade of the old Hotel Vancouver.

Soon after the First World War, the Chamber of Commerce started to promote the idea, which had been discussed for years, of an amusement centre for Victoria. It seemed expedient to ask Rattenbury, whose reputation was so outstanding, for a design. He had won the competition for the Legislative building just after he'd arrived in Victoria (albeit with the suggestive nom de plume "BC Architect") and completed a great many prestigious buildings, including the Empress Hotel in Victoria. Although considered a genius, his methods of self-aggrandizement annoyed many of his competitors. His scandals, including the misdirecting of marble and a fireplace meant for installation in Government House to his own residence, together with the flaunting of his mistress, shocked many people. However, he enthusiastically sketched a scheme for this amusement centre or Pleasure Palace, which came to be called the Crystal Garden. It certainly was flamboyant: flags flying from towers at each corner; three salt-water swimming pools; a 40-foot fountain which Rattenbury claimed would be illuminated to give the appearance of "a living stream of fire"; an art gallery; an auditorium; and 16 shops around the perimeter of the building. Even a sliding floor to cover the pool area, creating a level convention hall between the two ballrooms, was being considered – altogether a very grandiose concept. In his element, Rattenbury sketched these ideas and helped the Chamber of Commerce sell his wonderful $200,000 idea to business and professional groups. But after the citizens approved this 100,000 square foot scheme, it was discovered to be too large for the available site and much too expensive. And one does wonder how well a sliding-floor mechanism, suspended in the humid salt-laden air above the pools, would have performed.

However, the CPR became interested in taking the project over from the Chamber of Commerce. They sought many inducements: lease of the site for a token dollar a year, no taxation for 20 years and 20 years of free water. Additionally, they expected Rattenbury to continue to work for the cut-rate 4% fee he had accepted for earlier work. The fee under newly established AIBC regulations (incorporated in 1920) should have been a minimum of 6%, or 10% if more than three contracts were involved, as indeed they were in the Crystal Garden. Rattenbury did not maintain an office at this time, nor had he much interest in actively practising architecture; in fact he had not joined the newly formed AIBC. He still attracted clients and had already handed some of these commissions over to James. James did all the working drawings based on a sketch plan devised by Rattenbury and supervised the construction. The two men had also worked on that competition in Mexico mentioned in Chapter Four. As well, a plan for a railway station by Rattenbury, James & James is stored at the BCA.

He approached James who, having assisted in designing so many swimming pools in England, was well qualified to design the pool. Rattenbury and James formed an ill-defined partnership to carry out the development of the Amusement Centre. James would do the working drawings and supervise the project and Rattenbury would continue to rally business support for it and sell the project to the City of Victoria.

All the subsequent drawings were credited to the partnership, "Rattenbury & James." They consisted of drawings to promote the large proposed project and, later, two complete down-sizings of working drawings which had to be undertaken before the Crystal Garden became affordable. Many people eventually felt that the finished building should be attributed to James alone. But the concept was certainly Rattenbury's and as a born entrepreneur, he did undertake selling the idea to Victoria's business people with great energy.

There were lots of innovations for Rattenbury to extol to the residents in his bid to get their support:

- The largest area of glass on the continent.

- The only heated salt-water pool under glass in the world.

- The only 100-yard pool in North America. 75 yards was the longest pool in the USA.

- The largest salt-water pool on the coast.

- Salt-water bathing was itself one of the biggest selling points. English people had long considered sea-bathing bracing and efficacious to their health.

- Therapeutic hot salt-water baths.

- A pool that when empty could be used for conventions, allowing seating on the promenades, bleachers and pool floor for 2,500 guests.

- Fast inflow and outflow: the pool would completely fill with water in 7 hours, and could be emptied in one hour. (When the pool was completed, the initial filling took only five and a half hours).

While the Crystal Garden plans were being developed, the CPR commissioned the partnership to proceed with a new Marine Terminal building at the same reduced fee. Rattenbury must have suggested the design, for it is very similar to his classical temple design for the Bank of Montreal building at Douglas and Yates, a building that had been carried out in stone some years before. James undertook the work and supervision for the Marine Terminal with the 4% fee to be evenly split by the partners. The job proceeded to completion without a hitch during the long and tedious re-workings of the Crystal Garden. The specification for Station and Offices filed at the BCA indicates the architectural firm but has only the seal of the active partner (P. Leonard James) applied to it. At the time Rattenbury had no seal, and was not a member of the AIBC who were pursuing him to join. And finally on August 14th, 1923, he did complete his application form.

James researched cast stone, a new material that had been used by several leading architects in the States, and suggested its use to the CPR when he was satisfied on all points including that it would not "look cementified." He pointed out to Capt. J.W. Troup that the cost to build in stone would be prohibitive, and that to build in brick would produce an insignificant building, unsuitable to be on the harbour in the company of the Empress Hotel and the Legislative Building. His choice made a great saving for the CPR. Only the lower course of the Marine Terminal is real stone. The remainder uses this innovative and affordable cast stone. A sculptor of repute, George Gibson, supervised the decorative details and directed the workmen who produced the cast stone columns in the basement of the new Terminal. The columns were faced with powdered Newcastle Island stone. The Terminal was the largest contract for

CPR Marine Terminal, 170 Belleville Street, Victoria harbour (Photo with 1924 busses - Author's collection - BCA #hp69190)

cast stone in western Canada at the time. Forty years later, James, long retired, expressed his satisfaction at the lasting properties of the material.

James contributed an unusual solution for the foundation of the Crystal Garden, which was built on part of the filled area of the old tidal bay, which ran almost up to the Church of Our Lord at the corner of Humboldt and Blanshard Streets. Instead of the 40-foot piles Rattenbury had used to support the Empress

Crystal Garden under construction (Photographer unknown - BCA#hp68161)

Hotel, James opted for a reinforced concrete raft to support the building. Only the deep end of the pool reached below this two and a half foot thick raft, which floated the whole building on its site.

The newly completed Crystal Garden surpassed all expectations. Palm trees and flowering tropical plants graced the promenade, where wicker tables for afternoon tea were set up. Dancing parties in the evenings used the same tables. The

Crystal Garden promenade *(Photographer unknown - Author's collection - BCA #hp68169)*

building opened on June 8th, 1925 and, in celebration, a week-long carnival was arranged later in the month ending on Dominion Day (July 1st). The American ferries advertised reduced fares and the Port Angeles ferry alone brought 200 cars a day. The Carnival offered a programme of 20 special events including: a Rose Show, Strawberry Festival, Circus, Regatta and a Monster Parade reviewed by the Canadian Governor-General Baron Byng.

A sparkling diver design graced one of the publicity pamphlets. The many services were extolled and a centrefold gave a good view of the pool in action. Ever since the opening the public often referred to this building as the 'Crystal Gardens,' but that is not the correct name.

Who now remembers the neat pockets woven into those wicker tables for hiding bottles of booze from the roving eyes of the commissionaires at the dances? After Prohibition, government liquor stores sold alcohol, but it had to be consumed in private, or, at private parties, not in public places such as the Crystal Garden. The commissionaires, patrolling the area and smiling at the visible collection of soda fountain drinks, occasionally reminded patrons, "Please keep that bottle out of sight, Sir." Pouring of liquor had to be done below tabletop height, not an easy task especially for slightly tipsy patrons. Out of sight, out of mind! During the Second World War, most parties went over to the Empress after the dance and congregated in rented bedrooms in "Guppies Alley." There they finished off their bottles, often carried across the street to the hotel in the very inadequate evening bags of giggling ladies. The name of that area in the hotel changed, depending on the service branch the young men of the party were in. "Guppies" were the young officers-in-training at the Gordon Head Army camp where the University of Victoria is today. The name guppy means a small fish and those in training were very small fish on the military scale.

The use of the Crystal Garden as a convention site probably happened only for the Biennial Convention of the P.E.O. Sisterhood (a secret American

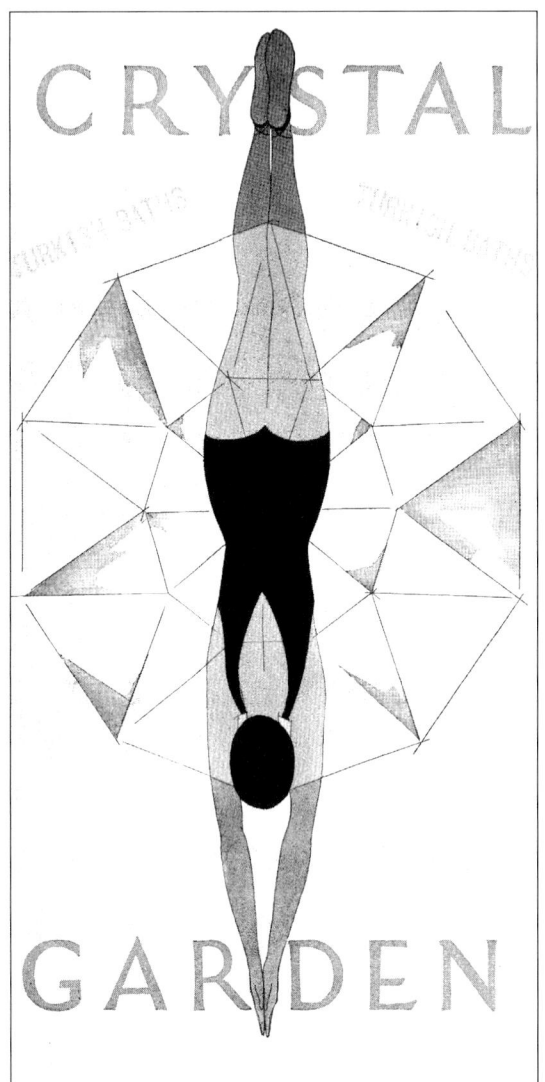

The Crystal Garden pamphlet (Author's collection)

society involved with education for women). 1000 people were accommodated on September 10, 1941, with an access stairway specially built to the floor of the drained pool.

The salt water for the pool filtration plant came through an eight-inch Douglas Fir stave-reinforced pipe that brought the water from near Beacon Hill. The water did not come from the inner harbour, as some writers have suggested, although when necessary the pool could be emptied into the inner harbour. When the wooden intake pipe finally needed repairs after 30 years of service, the decision was made to change over to fresh water.

The completed Crystal Garden left considerable financial imbalance between the partners, with their ill-defined agreement. James had run the office, producing all the drawings for the reduced schemes, and dealt with all the construction, supervision, details and expenses. Though Rattenbury expected an equal share, James considered that the job had been handed over to him and felt justified in asking for an increased amount over the two-thirds fee split he expected. Such a fee agreement had been used for the Bullen residence and other jobs that were handed over to him.

He wrote Rattenbury in a friendly manner:

May 22, 1925
Unfortunately, we started with a big handicap in the matter of fees (for such a building as this) 6% is the minimum rate, but strictly speaking 10% would be correct according to the B.C. Institute as there are more than three Contracts. However 4% was agreed to and that is all we can charge now no doubt. A good deal of responsibility is attached to the carrying out of such a building as this and at least one should expect to make a little money as the outcome. I have to depend entirely on my profession for a livelihood I may say.

I find on looking into the finances of this job that anything less than a three-quarter share from the reduced fees (after all the expenses are paid) would be unremunerative to me.

Shortly after my return from overseas, you will recall, we came to an arrangement that you would receive a third of the commission on any work which you turned over to me. This

Crystal Garden, 713 Douglas Street, Victoria, c 1925, pool in operation. This view taken with a wide angle lens greatly exaggerates the length of the pool. (Centrefold in pamphlet - Author's collection)

was carried out on Bullen's (house) and several other jobs – and as the full commission was charged this was sufficiently remunerative to me. I make an invariable rule of charging the minimum Institute rates myself, or I would soon be out of business, for I find people expect a great deal of detail and supervision of work nowadays. There are also such things as bad debts, etc. to be taken into account.

Trusting you will not feel that I am making an unreasonable proposal with regard to the Crystal Garden fees and that I may have the pleasure of co-operating with you in future work

Yours sincerely,

(This filed second copy is not signed)
In his high-handed hand-written reply of May 28, Rattenbury was not in agreement:

Dear Mr. James.

In answer to yours May 22. In our association together, I have engaged you, on different terms or payment for each work – that I have given to you – In some cases – I have allowed you to take the *whole of the fees*. In other cases – such as the Bullen House which you mention – whilst I planned this house – I allowed you 2/3rd of the fees –

But in the latest building – viz. the CPR Depôt – a building almost as costly as the Crystal Garden – I agreed to give you $1000 for the draughting work &c – this amount being suggested by yourself as a reasonable sum and altho [sic] I planned and designed this Building – you may recall – that I allowed you to put your name on the Plans as Associate Architect – At the time you expressed appreciation of this-

When the idea of the Crystal Garden was first suggested – I spent nearly a year – elaborating the scheme – which has all been achieved – except in minor details – and in Designing the Exterior – also in attending various Public meetings – and later in negotiating with the CPR – all this work would have been gratuitous – had the building not been gone on with.

However it resulted in the CPR engaging me – as Architect for the work. – Nearly all this work was done before – I asked you if you would care to do the draughting work, &c. all as you had done on the CPR Depôt.

But in this case I agreed to give you 1/2 of the fees – viz. about $4000 and you were quite satisfied. Now that the Building is completed –You ask me – if I will give you $6500 and content myself with the balance of $1500.

I certainly think it is a most unreasonable request – and I don't think that you ought to have asked it.

You were quite at liberty to decline the work – and I could have either done it myself – or engaged a Draughtsman – at much less cost to myself. But you were not only satisfied with the terms – but very pleased to get the work – or so you said.

I think you must have made a mistake – in saying that you have received $5795.92 from the CPR – I know only of about $3700 having been paid – if the Bank has cashed a cheque payable to me – without my endorsement – It will be liable for the same – naturally.

Yours very truly,
F.M. Rattenbury "Architect"

James's June 1, reply:

I am sorry your view of our association together does not agree with mine. You speak of having "engaged" me – as though I was just a draughtsman and not an architect in practice.

My idea of our connection is this, viz.; that you having long since retired from practice are nevertheless often consulted about prospective work and are in a position to place such work with an architect in active practice, maintaining an office; the latter being myself in the present case.

I understood that you would receive 1/3rd share of the fees from any job you passed on to me and this appeared a fair basis for our association, provided the full recognized fees were received, such as Bullens [sic] (house) to which you refer.

I take strong exception to the remarks in your letter as to the various things which you have "allowed" me to do. I don't consider there is any question of you allowing me to do this or that. Our arrangement was a business one and I am running my own office.

Altogether I have written nearly 200 letters, issued certificates & orders and carried out the job as only an architectw [sic] with an established office, telephone, stationery etc. could. During this time all correspondence and accounting with the CPR has been attended to by me & instructions received from them direct on all matters pertaining to the building. And this has been no light undertaking I can assure you. I have to straighten out all the difficulties between the different parties concerned – a job you are well out of.

I would like to ask you if you really consider that a half share of 4 per cent commission is an adequate recompense for all this. I cannot afford to run things at a loss even taking into account the privilege of being "allowed" to have my name associated with yours on the plan.

The press added some fuel to the fire of this partnership disagreement when the *Daily Colonist* wrote up the features of the new building in the Sunday pages on June 7th, 1925. With all the self-congratulatory advertisements by the many trades who worked on the building, were photos of all the notables who had approved and furthered the plans for the building. A photo of P. Leonard James was captioned "Building Architect", *but there was no photo of F. M. Rattenbury*. There was also a short article:

P. Leonard James, the architect, has previous experience with swimming pools in the Old Country. However, he has been able to incorporate a number of new ideas in carrying through this work making the bath up-to-date in every respect.

To Rattenbury, so adept at self-promotion, this was too much! He went public with a letter to the editor:

1. Some very erroneous statements have been appearing in one of the daily papers, I have for several days waited to see them corrected – but this has not been done.

2. The whole conception of the building was designed by me – The combination of a salt-water pool in a conservatory of flowers, with promenades and dancing floors – all exactly as carried out in the Crystal Garden – except for size.

3. It was designed and sketched by me – under the eyes of a committee of the Amusement Centre. The Council of the Chamber Of Commerce and other bodies – at many meetings, over a period of months.

4. This can be verified by referring to the descriptions published at that time in the daily papers and also by the gentlemen who were on the committee.

5. On November 15th, 1923, I was appointed sole architect for the Crystal Garden by the CPR. I had the working or constructional drawings made and completed to my designs and instructions and supervision – at my own expense.

6. The completed plans were accepted in November, 1924, by the CPR and I attended at Vancouver the signing of the contract to Luney Bros. Up to this time I was sole architect, but after the signing of the building contract some six months ago, I took P.L. James as associate architect and made him party to the agreement with the CPR, for the general supervision of the building operations under the name of F.M. Rattenbury and P. Leonard James, architects."

Basil Gardom, the C.P.R manager, received a confidential letter dated June 9th 1925 addressed to him at Lake Louise from James.

A further development of l'affaire Rattenbury took place today when I received a 'phone call from the manager of the Imperial Bank (where I have my account when there is anything in it) to go and see him.

He said that F.M.R has been there protesting against the bank having taken my endorsement of the $1822.32 cheque and saying he would hold them responsible.

In order to cover themselves the bank has requested me to leave a sum equivalent to this amount in my account until matters are adjusted between us.

You are aware the cheques are made payable to "F.M. Rattenbury & P. Leonard James" and you remember the subject being mentioned between us, when you advised me that the C.P.R would take my endorsement. It seems but natural and reasonable that they should (and apparently did as the cheques also constitute a receipt). In the same way I have signed certificates, orders and other documents pertaining to the various Contracts without which the work could scarcely have proceeded as it has.

Rattenbury has not approached me himself and if he does I am quite prepared for him and will "stick to my guns" – a course which I am sure you will be behind me in.

I am afraid he didn't get much solace out of the short little paragraph tucked away in the corner of today's "Colonist", in which he was credited with having prepared preliminary sketches. It would have been better if he had kept quiet I think.

With kind regards.
Yours very truly,
P.L. James

Mr. Gardom dealt with the partnership through James alone during the course of the building. He now supported James throughout all the public unpleasantness and asked him to write a confidential letter refuting each of the statements and claims made in Rattenbury's letter. Officials at the BCA thought I should seek the permission of the heirs to quote these confidential letters of 1925. As I am the only heir, there is no problem and I hope that the full letters clarify the fee disagreement.

June 13th, 1925
Dear Mr. Gardom:

Your wire of today's date received. As requested, I append criticism of the paragraphs in Rattenbury's letter. It has been difficult to condense the matter. A great deal more might be said, but I think you can fill in details from your own knowledge.

[In reply to paragraph 1 of Rattenbury's letter]

Presumably he refers to the articles & editorial in last Sunday's "Colonist." Exactly what portions of the statements considered "erroneous" by Mr. Rattenbury I cannot, of course, say. At any rate I personally did not give any information to the newspapers, except in regard to my previous experience in connection with Swimming Pools in the Old Country.

[In reply to paragraph 2]

Four years ago Mr. Rattenbury first showed me a very rough pencil sketch plan of a proposed Amusement Centre Scheme the Victoria Chamber of Commerce had consulted him about. They were endeavouring to promote interest in a municipal Swimming Pool etc. The main features indicated were three large pools, seating, promenades and dancing spaces.

An arrangement existed between us at that time whereby I was to allow him one-third of the fees received from any work

Mr. Rattenbury introduced to my office. He had no office of his own and was not an architect in active practice – in fact he was not a member of the Architectural Institute of British Columbia and therefore not entitled to practise.

He proposed that I should draw up preliminary plans and elevations, saying that he supposed I would like to be the Architect for the building if it materialized. I accepted, having no reason to doubt that our existing arrangement held good. Otherwise I would most certainly have had nothing to do with it, being very busy at the time with the plans of a large hospital building.

During the next two years I prepared several different sets of plans for the Amusement Centre and these were used by the Chamber of Commerce for advertising and promoting interest in the scheme.

[In reply to paragraph 3]

If Mr. Rattenbury did any further designing and sketching I did not see anything of the sketches after the one he showed me at the beginning, already referred to.

[In reply to paragraph 4]

The descriptions published at the time were descriptions of the plans I prepared and these embraced many features I conceived and worked out. Mr. Rattenbury was not paying any of the expenses for the preparations of these plans.

[In reply to paragraph 5]

I have no reason to doubt that Mr. Rattenbury was so appointed at that time. I am not familiar with the early negotiations with the CPR, but I presume that his appointment resulted from the preliminary plans that had been worked out up to this stage. In continuation of the work I had already done, I next prepared the large coloured drawing showing front elevation. This was made extensive use of in connection with the by-law in December, 1923, was signed by the Mayor of Victoria (Mr. R. Hayward) and is part and parcel of the agreement between the CPR and the City of Victoria. The names of F. M. Rattenbury and P. Leonard James appear as architects on this drawing.

The whole of the working drawings, details and specifications were prepared by me and my assistants in my office (with the exception of the reinforced concrete drawings, which I arranged for Mr. David Hardie, Consulting Engineer, Vancouver to undertake – for a fee of $500.)

All drawings and specifications for the purpose of obtaining tenders were completed by the end of July, 1924. The names of F.M. Rattenbury and P. Leonard James, Architects, appear on said drawings under the date. Meanwhile I had paid all expenses; Mr. Rattenbury personally paid nothing towards them.

The whole question of the expenses on the Crystal Garden has yet to be settled between us.

[In reply to paragraph 6]

The plans were finally accepted in November it is true. But in the interval between their completion in July, 1924 and the acceptance of the plans there appeared considerable likelihood of them being rejected by the CPR on account of later estimates far exceeding what Mr. Rattenbury had originally mentioned.

Correspondence and telegrams which passed between us during this period will show how matters stood. Mr. Rattenbury was absent from Victoria for about two months during this critical period.

For Rattenbury to contend that I was not his associate in the preparation of the plans, etc and only appeared on the scene in November 1924, is too ridiculous to need any comment on my part, I think. There is plenty of correspondence between the CPR and "Rattenbury & James" previous to that time, which will serve to show that we were recognized by the former as associated in the Crystal Garden undertaking.

I really think there is nothing to add at present, but as the present position is decidedly unpleasant for me – I can scarcely answer Rattenbury's letter in the press myself without bringing in a whole lot of detail – I will be glad if you see that the position is explained.

Yours very truly,
P.L. James

On receipt of this letter, Mr. Gardom asked Rattenbury to come to his office and went over every one of the points in the above letter. The report of that meeting is that Rattenbury came in like a lion, but after the discussion, left very quietly. The eventual split of the architectural fee was not recorded.

From all the above it seems understandable why my father made a snarly growl whenever his former partner was mentioned.

Terry Reksten's book, *Rattenbury*, contains anecdotes regarding his behaviour. He was far from a lovable character. Most people saw him as a man with an eye to the main chance. People remembered him for the self-serving letter he wrote to the *Daily Colonist* when promoting his steamship venture to transport passengers from Lake Bennett, down the Yukon River to the Klondike gold fields. He declared the hardships of the Chilkoot Pass, "less arduous than a bracing walk along the beachfront at Oak Bay," and that the articles disagreeing with his point of view were probably written by hacks "at so much a line."

There are stories of how the locals ostracized him on the #1 Oak Bay streetcar, moving away from where he sat. Genteel members of the populace shunned him for his rejection of his wife and the flaunting of his mistress, Alma Pakenham. The couple eventually married and moved to England to take up residence in Bournemouth. A young impressionable chauffeur was hired and the tragic story of his besotted love for Alma and eventual murder of Rattenbury is well told in Terry Reksten's book. It is reported that, when Rattenbury and Alma's son came to town, after the 1978 restoration of the Crystal Garden, he was amazed to find Rattenbury now so lionized locally.

Two of the draughtsmen in the office, busy with the Royal Jubilee Hospital and several major residences in addition to the CPR jobs, expressed their feelings that Rattenbury deserved little credit for the Crystal Garden. One was the trained architectural draughtsman, Herbert S. Beckton, the other, R.W. Tomlinson, who trained as a draughtsman in James's office. When the Crystal Garden was being renovated, Tomlinson, then in his 80s, made a point of meeting me. He said he remembered Rattenbury's design as just a sketch on an envelope. He was firm in his opinion that Rattenbury should not get any credit for the Crystal Garden! Tomlinson was just one of many who felt that way at the time. The short paragraph crediting Rattenbury with the preparation of preliminary sketches in the *Daily Colonist* of June 9th, 1925 – which James mentioned in his letter to Gardom – and the original omission of Rattenbury's name in the *Daily Colonist's* supplement about the features of the new building, indicate to me how people felt on the subject.

Of course, the public really did not care, but American visitors do appreciate a *really* **big** name. As a horse-drawn Tally-ho filled with blanket-wrapped tourists passed the renovated Crystal Garden, the driver was heard to say:

"This is our famous Crystal Garden *designed* by Johnny Weismuller." The heads swivelled round for an appreciative look. The only involvement Weismuller – the swimmer and actor – had with the building was his performance at a Swim Gala shortly after its Opening. The commentary was perhaps suitable for tourists who might remember the name Weismuller, but would never have heard of Rattenbury or James. Weismuller, a world-famous champion swimmer, starred as the first Tarzan in the movies. At the Swim Gala, he broke his own record for the 100-yard swim, which might be expected in the more buoyant salt water at the Crystal Garden pool. His manager commented favourably on the 100-yard length of the Crystal Garden pool, mentioning in the *Victoria Daily Times*, August 5th, 1925, that pools in the USA were only 75-yards long.

In the first 20 years of CPR management, there was proper upkeep of the metal and glass roof and condensation did not become a problem. On June 7th, 1925 the *Daily Colonist* reported "Every piece of glass in the roof has its own copper drain to carry away moisture, so that it is free from condensation at all times."

But during the next 20 years that the CPR managed the building, proper maintenance dwindled. Repainting probably covered the copper drains and drips of condensation damaged the ballroom floors. By the time the City inherited the building from the CPR, there were many problems.

After the completion of the Crystal Garden, the CPR wanted still more swimming pools, but apparently had really had their fill of arrogant, overbearing Rattenbury. They retained James alone as the architect to design the outdoor pool at Lake Louise.

In September 1925, he went to Lake Louise to check the site and to establish the placement for the swimming pool. He chose the site between the dining room wing of the Chateau and the lake, parallel with the former and partially set into the slope down to the lake. Around the pool he designed plate-glass walls, which did not interfere with the view from the dining room and hotel, yet shielded bathers from the chilly breeze off the glacier. Steps from the terrace in front of the hotel reached a promenade from which spectators watched the swimmers in the pool. Constructed over the winter under a skeleton wood frame, the Lake Louise Pool opened in 1926.

Above: Digby Pines Hotel, Nova Scotia, pool after recent renovations (Photo by G.W. Cross - Author's collection)
Left: Lake Louise Pool c. 1978. Unused over the intervening years, the pool is now leveled with concrete as a picnic eating area. Broken plate glass has been replaced with bits of fencing. (Photo by author)

The CPR liked the pool so much that they decided to use the design again at the Digby Pines Hotel in Nova Scotia. Disregarding the concept of copyright, they used James's design without permission and without paying to use it. He should have taken them to court. His reason for not doing so is unknown. He may not have been aware of their duplicity until later, when the three CPR pools were illustrated in the *Canadian Homes and Gardens* July, 1933 issue. The article by J.E. Marsh, "In the Swim Across Canada" was published shortly before James closed his office and took the family to England during the Depression.

The pools have different histories. The Lake Louise pool was closed for swimming by 1976. It has been given a concrete floor and converted to an outdoor barbeque area, many of the plate-glass walls units now broken and replaced with low fencing. On the other hand the Digby Pines pool has recently been renovated and is in top shape.

Perhaps there were others who wanted to copy the Crystal Garden pool. When James was 89, he told a visiting relative rather testily that a Seattle concern had wanted to build a similar pool in Seattle, but did not expect to pay to use the plans. In view of his advanced years, I wondered if he was muddled and recalling the CPR's theft of the Lake Louise design for the Digby Pines pool. But on re-reading clippings in my files, I found reference to Gale S. Robinson, chairman of the West Seattle Commercial Club committee. He advocated using the Crystal Garden as a model for a natatorium near Alki Point. So there was a further source of concern and annoyance for James, though in the end, no pool was built. I recall that my father disliked the Americanism "natatorium" and have just discovered the reason.

I spent my married life in various parts of Eastern Canada. In 1978, I returned to live in Victoria and found the Crystal Garden in very sad shape. Naked blackened ribs of the roof reached to the sky, the empty pool was littered with glass and accumulated rubbish. The floor of the old ballroom where I had danced with servicemen during the Second World War was a tangled mess of warped boards. Yet it was heartening to know that it would soon be restored. On the hundredth anniversary of my father's birthday – less one day – a photograph showing the completed restoration appeared in the *Times-Colonist*, December 6, 1978. It symbolized a veritable phoenix to me.

During the restoration several people, having learned that the restaurant in the building was to be called *Rattenbury's*, contacted me. They thought it an unsuitable name to be used in the building because of the unpleasant publicity and disagreement between the partners and that I should complain. I did, but to no avail. Suitable names in the old sense have given away to a more current outlook where a little notoriety and controversy is welcome and possibly good for business!

The Provincial Capital Commission assured me that Mr. James would also be remembered with the Ballroom being named in his honour. Nevertheless, shortly before the opening a full-page article appeared describing all the features of the renovated building. It did not mention the name chosen for the restaurant, but did ask the public to send in suggestions for naming the ballroom. A few people I contacted remembered attending the Flamingo Ballroom, a name that was given to the North ballroom in the 1950's and wanted to use that name for the refurbished South ballroom. I myself had attended the North ballroom with a party of friends and my parents just after my marriage.

It seemed best not to count on the oral assurance that my father's name would be used. Friends rallied round and people wrote letters. One lady in her 90s agreed to write a letter. Later she reported that she had collected 19 names from her bridge club members, who were all old enough to remember Rattenbury and his scandalous doings. The name "James Ballroom" was assured. People joked that it was forever above Rattenbury's, the old enmity still alive in many minds. Others suggested that the restaurant would eventually go out of business. And after several years, it did.

CHAPTER ELEVEN

The James & Savage Partnership

James had already made important contributions in domestic and commercial work during the busy post-war years before he and Hubert Savage started their partnership. The James & Savage name first appeared on the plans for the 1926 Tudor shops for Alfred Carmichael & Company at 716-18 Fort Street, followed in 1927 by the residence for C.H. Carpenter at 2595 Lansdowne Road. Savage and James had shared office space on the sixth floor of the Sayward Building at 1207 Douglas Street for several years, but their partnership came into full effect by mid-summer of 1928.

With their top-quality designs, appropriately sited and constructed with excellent workmanship, the partners rode the crest until the Depression ended all construction. Each partner undertook his own commissions and usually supervised his own jobs.

Even today, realtors may advertise a Savage house as "Designed by P. Leonard James" and vice versa, presumably because of their own personal preference, for the partnership is listed as "James & Savage" on the drawings. The C.H. Carpenter residence at 2595 Lansdowne Road in the Uplands was in fact designed by James. When I offered correct information some years ago to a realtor who advertised the Carpenter house as "by Hubert Savage ," she said, "Oh! Who cares after all this time?" Such a wrong attribution remains in people's memories. Recently an article was written about this house; and even though the owner pointedly stated that it was by James, the article credited only Savage! Such errors become entrenched once published even in a realtor's advertisement. A further possibility for error is in the plans themselves, for the architect's hard-to-read seals were printed above their partnership name, with James's seal to the left of the partnership name and Savage's to the right. It seems people are inclined to stop looking once they have found the seal on the right! The correct attribution should be James & Savage.

With the increasing interest in our built heritage these attributions are important. To this end, Job Lists in the Appendix of this book show as completely as possible which partner designed buildings within the partnership. The City of Victoria Archives (CVA) has James and Savage plans stored in separate collections. Other information comes from the BC Archives (BCA) and from blueprints still in present owners' possession, from newspaper accounts and from oral sources which are credited in the Job Lists of each partner.

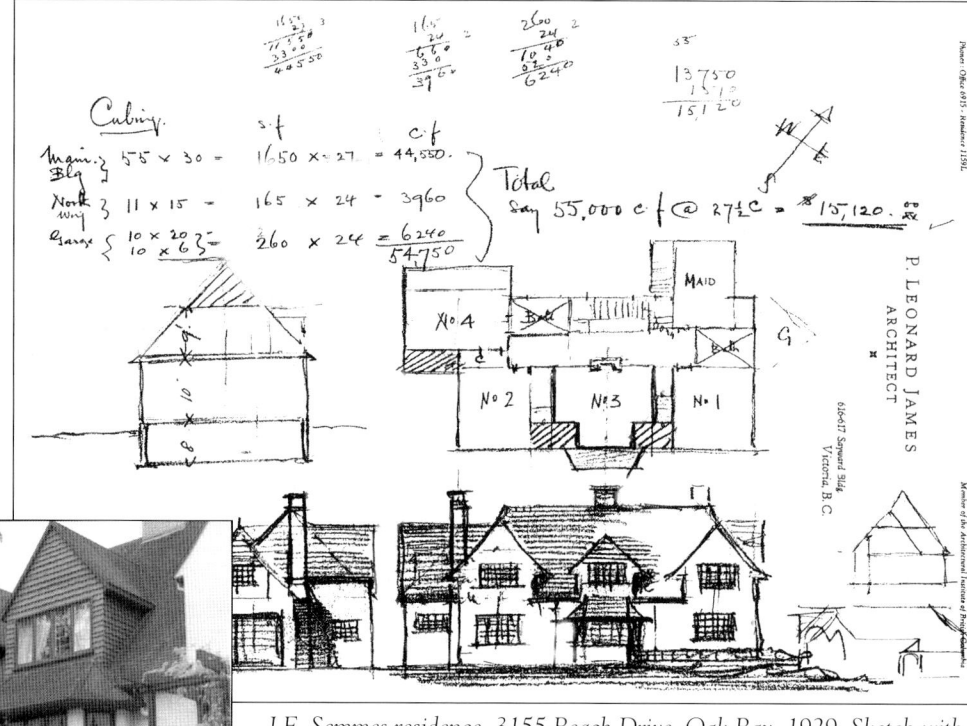

J.E. Semmes residence, 3155 Beach Drive, Oak Bay, 1929, Sketch with cost calculations of $15,000 for the proposed plan. Note final Contract price with extras for sea wall, tennis court and swimming pool came to $20,000. (BCA MS 502).
Insert of the gable c. 1985 *(Photo by author)*

The Royal Architectural Institute of Canada recognized James's pre-eminence in the profession. His election to the College of Fellows of the RAIC took place in 1931. As the only

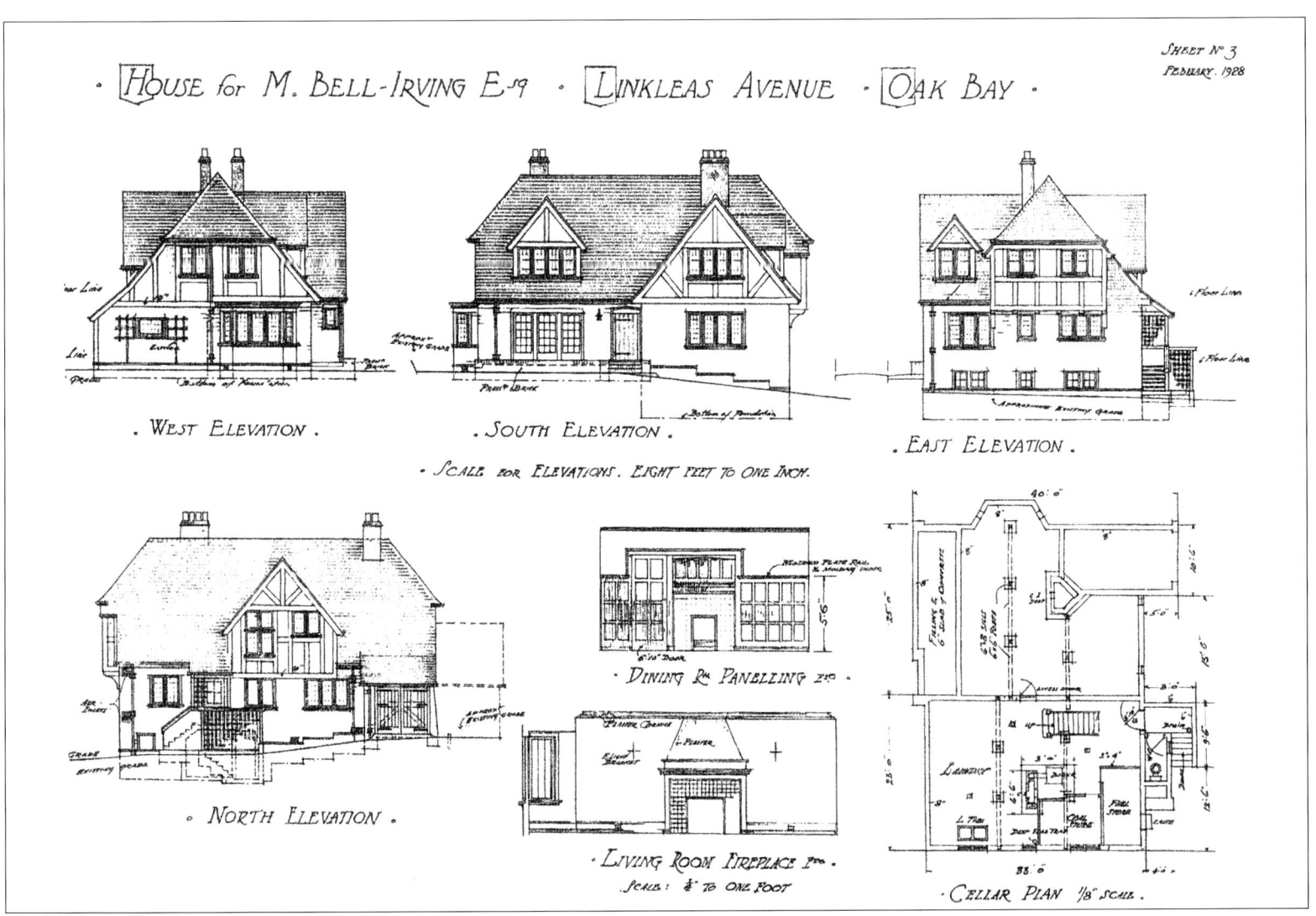

M. Bell-Irving Esq., residence, 572 Linkleas Avenue, Oak Bay, 1928 sheet of elevations with details of two of the four fireplaces (Elevations courtesy of current owners)

architect to hold this honour in BC for over 16 years, he encouraged other deserving BC architects to consider being elected. Firms in Vancouver felt it old-fashioned and rather pooh-poohed it. Eventually he persuaded John Y. McCarter to accept this professional honour and gradually others followed suit. College of Fellows members met annually to consider possible changes in architectural practice. They received red satin "dog collars" which they wore with evening dress at RAIC conventions and balls.

Savage always retained his membership as an Associate of the Royal Institute of British Architects (ARIBA), which gave his work a special cachet that is recognized to this day. The members of the firm were a prestigious pair.

As a small child, I noted the special "dry" smell of the James & Savage office on the top floor of the Sayward Building. The smell included a mixture of India ink, pencil shavings redolent of cedar, various blueprints, papers, tracing linens and the smell of soap from the damp linen roller towel that hung by the sink.

During the '30s, my mother and I shopped together on Saturday mornings, ending up at the office to meet my father in time to drive home with him at one o'clock. Offices closed early on Saturdays as a standard practice between the wars, while stores took Wednesday afternoon for early-closing.

At different times a student worked on the extra drawing board in the outer office. One early trainee, R.W. Tomlinson, proved very adept at the work. He was a family man and when the CPR advertised a permanent position for a trained draughtsman, James recommended him for this position which came with a pension programme, something not available to a regular architectural draughtsman. According to his obituary, marine draughtsman Tomlinson designed docks at the CPR terminal in Victoria and the interior arrangements for every ship built by the CPR between 1925 and 1963, 11 in all. Freddie Pease, of the family for whom James & James had designed a residence and probably the jam factory overlooking Cadboro Bay, was another of the early students. Clive Campbell, a student who continued his studies and became BC's Provincial Architect, died before I returned to Victoria in 1978, but I did contact his son, who completed architectural studies at university. Fittingly enough, this young architect designed the compatible addition to the old James family home on Tod Road for the Cobham family, who have resided there for some 20 years.

More recent students were Norman Worsley, who went into engineering; Don Barton, who recalled how James sang snatches of songs by Gilbert and Sullivan to himself in the office; and Terry Gower, who went to England and San Francisco to complete his architectural studies. Eventually he formed the architectural practice of Micklejohn & Gower in the interior of BC.

The James & Savage firm did not employ a secretary. The partners themselves typed most letters – in a fairly speedy, two-fingered hunt-and-peck method in James's case. Client correspondence was addressed not to "Mr. J.N. Anderson," but to "J.N. Anderson, Esq." For an unmarried lady, James sometimes used the old-fashioned "Mifs" as the form of address, though this had gone out of style early in the 19th century. A public stenographer typed their specifications. A receipt from Miss Kitto shows that for a particularly difficult four-and-half page letter with quadruple copies, she was paid $1.75. Certificates issued for payment to the contractor were hand-written.

The partners used many English Arts & Crafts details in their designs. In the large "manor" houses and the storey-and-a-half semi-bungalows, the outside walls in most cases are stuccoed, only the gables have plain or waney-edged weatherboards in the upper part. "Waney-edged" refers to the de-barked edges of boards, which show irregularities. These impart the feeling of naturalism so important to the Arts & Crafts movement. Some of the houses have Tudor-style half-timbering, others do not. Chimneys are brick or brick finished with stucco up to a tile course, with either a brick or cement cap from which the flues emerge. A metal "S" brace is often an artistic feature on the stucco chimneys. This style of home used a steeper pitch roof than the more generally used 45-degree pitch. In the 1920s and '30s, James and Savage often used a 12-in-10 pitch (a 12 inch vertical rise over a 10 inch horizontal run), which sometimes flared at the bottom to a 10-in-12 fillet, or "bell-cast" turn of the eaves. This flare imparts a lighter look to a roof than having the same pitch down to the eaves. Eaves at gables have minimal or no overhang. The gables have ventilators in the weatherboarding – most are oblong in shape, others are cut-outs in the shape of dovecote holes or triangles – to allow ventilation of the attic area. The soffits under the eaves are fairly narrow and enclosed so that rafter ends are not exposed. A plaster "hood" projects slightly over windows in the gable ends to provide protection from the weather. Savage used this feature routinely, James, only occasionally. In both partners' work a slightly pointed lintel, reflecting Tudor style, is often featured over the main windows, or French doors and entranceways. Where shutters are used they are of a size to cover the windows, for that was their original purpose. In the James & Savage designs, the shutters are usually decorated with a cutout diamond, heart, or firtree. Later designers did not consider the reason for shutters and the proper proportion for shutters was lost in favour of narrower decorative details – a fad which James deplored.

The partners so often used the high 12-in-10 roof pitch, that they had a special triangular set-square made for drawing the elevations. My father mentioned this unusual triangle, but it is not in my possession, so maybe it stayed with Savage when the partnership came to an end. Savage continued into the 1940's designing English Arts & Crafts bungalows and cottages some with the 12-in-10 roof pitch.

In the '20s and '30s, architects visited their construction sites frequently. The tradesmen usually completed their trade apprenticeship in England and came to Canada as experienced artisans whose work could be relied upon. James would consider alternate suggestions from such tradesmen if the results equalled those already specified.

Either partner might visit the jobs, especially those close to where he lived. Jeanne Groos recalled a house for a doctor on Upper Terrace as a "James" house. She lived for a while with Uncle Percy and accompanied him when he went to check on the progress of this house. There is no record of a house designed by James on Upper Terrace. But Savage designed a house for Dr. A.B. Nash at 3515 Upper Terrace in 1930. Jeanne must have gone with James when he checked the progress of the Nash job, while Savage himself was busy elsewhere.

James and Savage designed a number of the early houses in the Uplands. The block bounded by Lansdowne, Uplands Road, Dewdney and a trail that became Somerset Avenue (later Nottingham Road) contained five houses designed by James from 1927 through 1930. Between the houses the original oak meadows were lush in spring with lilies and shooting stars under the delicate snowberry bushes.

One of these five is the residence at 3065 Uplands Road designed for Mr. H.C.V. MacDowall. Dr. and Mrs. Eric Graham lived there in the 1970s and invited me to come and see the house, so little changed over the years. The pantry still had the original sliding glass doors to the cupboards and the breakfast room had its original light fixture. Only another bathroom had been added. On the second floor Mrs. Graham confided their one dissatisfaction with the house and opened a little door that gave onto the narrow dogleg stairs to the attic. "Look, you can't take anything up to the attic." The huge undivided attic has a lovely range of windows. These look out over the Uplands oak trees that totally hide evidence of other houses and give a fine view of the distant sea and mountains. But, short of taking out the windows and hoisting furniture in, there is no way that the attic can be made habitable. Recently a pool table has been introduced to the space. However friends remember playing up there with the MacDowall youngsters. Families really appreciated attics as space to keep school age children out from underfoot in the days before "family rooms" came into fashion.

When I was old enough, my dad sometimes took me on his inspection tours. I loved balancing on the catwalks across the excavations to get into the partially framed buildings. I delighted in marching around between the 2x4 framing instead of going through the framed doorways. Peering up the stairwells, climbing the ladders and judging the location of bathrooms while my father consulted with the contractor, all became part of my "inspections." Sometimes he had me hold the end of the 100-foot tape so he could verify a measurement.

H.C.V. MacDowall, residence, 3065 Uplands Road, Oak Bay, 1930, front view. This ground embracing design reflects C.F.A. Voyseys design concepts. (Photo by author)

Then with a warning not to let the tape twist over, he'd grant me the privilege of winding the varnished linen tape slowly back into its sturdy tan leather case.

Many of the lots were large and rocky. The roads in Uplands and on Gonzales Hill twisted and turned. So the houses could be sited to take the best advantage of any views and not necessarily have their sidewalls parallel to neighbouring houses, or the lot line. The 1926 Hinton and Bird houses are examples of this.

After I wrote an article in the June 30th, 1996 *Islander*, about James's work, I received a phone call from the great-grand- daughter of Mr. A.B. Cotton whose house built in 1928 still stands at 990 Terrace Avenue. She told me that Mr. Cotton had lived in a very similar Georgian house in Kent at Bushey Ruff in the Alkham Valley, near Dover. When Cotton bought property on Terrace Avenue, he asked James for an almost identical house, and may even have supplied some photographs of their home in England. What an unexpected fact to find nearly 70 years and several generations after the construction! The English house had five reception rooms, while 900 Terrace has three and a wonderful entry hall. The staircase winds gracefully round three of the hall walls and under a Palladian window.

At the top of the stairs, an open gallery with balustrade carries out the spacious feeling of the entry hall. The family home in Kent had six windows on the second floor of the main elevation, while the James version in Victoria has five.

The careful detailing on this house included a maroon baize-covered door in the pantry with a four-inch diameter glass window for the staff to check on the progress of the meal in the dining room. The French doors on the terrace are held in place with shutter dogs. The plans specify that these had to be specially made. The hall stairs have 11-inch face to face treads. James mentioned the rule that the sum of tread and riser should

A.B. Cotton 1928 residence 990 Terrace Avenue, Victoria

be 17 or 18 inches, which gives stairs a comfortable "way-of-going," which does not tire the user. The rule works for all steps from ladders to shallow garden steps.

In 1929, within the James & Savage partnership, James did a large addition to the R.H.B. Ker house at 1524 Shasta Place, including a library, new bedrooms and new back stairs.

The same year he designed a Tudor Arts & Crafts home for R.H.B. Ker's mother, Mrs. D.R. Ker at 841 St. Charles Street. with two South facing loggias, one with a glazed wind screen, such as he'd also used in the Taylor house at Sooke. This property backed onto her son's property.

A James house was the earliest house to be given Heritage Designation by the Saanich Municipality. *Miramar*, at 2901 Sea View Road, was designed for Mr. C.L.H. Branson in 1928. The Branson plans show a fine panelled hall and the fanciest newel posts of any James house. Upstairs, two porches are indicated on the filed plan, one for sleeping. The chimney with flues set at 45 degrees to the roof ridge is a specially handsome example of Tudor design. The living room fireplace design used carved caps to columns with strap ornamentation. Mr. Branson requested an unusual feature – a niche for a sculpture near the front door. The Bransons only lived in the house for a short time after it was built in 1928, and for many years it was rented.

Recently new owners have greatly increased the size of the house, gutted the original building and altered the interior substantially. In the planning stages they tried out many ideas and the solution is perhaps as good as it could be. But one can't help question the value of Heritage Designation when Council allows such changes to a designated house – despite firm advice to the contrary by the Heritage Advisory Committee. *Miramar* though gutted had to have its roof dormers kept, and the half-timbering had to be replaced as first designed. It is a great disappointment when owners make alterations damaging to the original concept.

Another James house in the Uplands area dates from 1929. During the tenure of Mr. and Mrs. Charles Gibson, I visited *Little Oaks* built for Mr. K.C. Allen at 3175 Tarn Place. The entrance hall stretched from the dining room across the living room with its panelled inward-opening double doors, as far as

R.H.B. Ker, residence, 1524 Shasta Place, Victoria, 1923, garage 1927
(Photo by author, c 1980s)

Mrs. D.R. Ker 1929 residence, 841 St. Charles Street, Victoria, elevations *(Courtesy of CVPDD)*

the den. This floor plan allows all the major reception rooms to view the ocean, as did the 1925 Taylor house in Sooke.

Each of the bathrooms had different coloured fixtures: dark blue in the downstairs cloak room, maroon in one bathroom, apple green in another. The maids' suite on the third floor contained the only white tub. The Master Bedroom had a rather unusual feature – an electric fireplace.

Mrs. Gibson had a fairly complete list of the various owners. One, a sweepstakes winner, only lived in the house for six months! What a way to blow some of the windfall before settling down.

The Gibsons' son noticed supports for blinds inside his bedroom windows. Later he found the original blinds still stored in the basement. He reinstalled them although they were a little tattered and used them while he lived there. He had a great empathy with the house. He painted a competent watercolour of the house and garden, though he did not consider himself "an artist."

The garage attic contained the changing room for the swimming pool. The pool was certainly one of the earliest Uplands pools – merely part of the foreshore of Flotsam Cove enclosed with concrete walls. The water, captured at high tide, warmed as the climate allowed. In winter, waves often tossed large logs into the pool. These had to be cleared away and no doubt became firewood. The property had extensive landscaping. A large contract in the amount of $4,419 covered the stonework for the driveway, granite walls and terraces along the seafront. The original lot has been subdivided and a part sold. Now the point has a dividing fence that constricts the original expansive view from the property.

A few lots further along Shore Road, Mr. and Mrs. J.E. Semmes had *Robinwood* (now 3155 Beach Drive,) a fine example of English Arts & Crafts designed by James in 1929. This two-and-a-half acre property also had seawall layout, a swimming pool and a tennis court, all part of the architectural design. A subsequent owner has been able to add a large compatible dwelling unit that does not diminish the original house, but is separated from it by a protected walkway.

Mrs. D.R. Ker, 841 St. Charles Street, Victoria, c 1933 terrace
(Photographer unknown - Author's collection - BCA #hp68134)

Left: A recent view of C.L.H. Branson, 1928 residence, 2901 Sea View Road (Photo by D. Robertson - Courtesy of the current owner)

Above: Original East view of C.L.H. Branson residence, Miramar, 2901 Sea View Road, Ten Mile Point, Saanich 1928 (Photo by author c. 1985)

The 10-sheet set of plans for the original 1929 house include the four elevations, the ground and upper floor plans, the basement, sections which show the construction of the chimneys, the plot plan, driveway and gate piers, interior details of fireplaces, doors, stair rail, panelling and kitchen details. Other interior details are drawn at half an inch to a foot. Carved newel posts are shown full size.

Oriental families now own several of the large houses. I spent a most rewarding visit with Dr. David Liang when he lived at *Robinwood*. He was pleased to show me a scale model of the house that an architectural student had made. The roof lifted off to reveal the upper floor correct in every detail – the height of the walls and the closets fascinated me. Then the whole upper floor lifted off to show the main floor with its reception rooms.

Above: K.C. Allen residence, 3175 Tarn Place, Oak Bay, 1929, front view, little changed. (Photo by Savannah - Author's Collection)
Right: Seafront view, recently altered with half-timbering added to second storey replacing the plain stucco and the shingles.
(Photo by H. Knight - Author's Collection - BCA # hp68519)

"I have the original blueprints for the house," Dr. Liang told me. "On the basement plan, there is a room labelled 'Chinaman's Room'." As I covered my embarrassment with a weak smile, he graciously concluded with a delightful tongue-in-cheek comment that gave us both cause to smile broadly, "I think the world has come full circle."

The 1929 bungalow for R.H. Shanks, Esq., assistant manager at the BC Land Company, at 1017 St. Patrick on the corner of McNeil Street, was designed as a modest home for a small family. It featured several bay windows and an unusual dormer roof. Until recently this house had been occupied by only its second owner in 70 years. She reported Mr. Shanks as a great gardening enthusiast, who particularly specialized in roses. The original fence installed by Mr. Shanks has long iron arches to support climbing roses and is still in place along the front and side lot lines. Even today the roses put on a glorious show in early June.

John Anderson, manager of Wm. O'Neil (Victoria) Limited, asked for a simplified version of the Shanks plan to be built at 2000 Beach Drive in 1931. Most of the bay windows were omitted from the Shanks design. Two bedrooms were provided on the main floor, as in the Shanks house, but the stairway to the attic was shut off from the entry hall with a door and the attic left unfinished. Later Anderson finished one room in the attic as his study. A file among the James papers at the BCA confirms that some years later Johnny and Betty Anderson had James design a built-in unit for their bedroom, consisting of drawers and dressing table along the east wall. Their house is on a list James kept indicating his designs among the James & Savage jobs, but the plan is stored in the *Savage Collection* at the CVA, the only one incorrectly filed by the firm that stored all the drawings for years.

My family often visited their great friends, the Andersons, at this house. As they had no family of their own, they acted as very doting "Uncle and Aunt" to many of their friends' children. Although situated on a busy corner, their house had a high fence and shrubbery round the garden, which made it very private. The Andersons so enjoyed their garden that they both wanted their ashes sprinkled in the flowerbeds. This was done in the case of Mr. Anderson, who died first. It is not known whether Mrs. Anderson, who later spent many months in a nursing home, had her wishes followed or not, though the house was not sold until she died.

An elderly English contractor who built one or two houses for speculative investment and sale each year, ("spec houses") liked the Anderson plan and asked James for plans with new elevations. Arthur C. Ham built c.1932 on a corner lot at 2812 Cadboro Bay Road. Later Ham used the plan again without further permission or elevations, but just altered them himself. James did not take "Old Ham" – as he called him – to court, but merely warned him. He knew Ham to be an excellent Old Country workman and felt sorry for him at a time when things were so precarious with the economy. After James returned from England in 1934 and through 1941, Ham continued his requests for small house designs, most of which were built near the corner of Thompson and Cadboro Bay Road.

I attended kindergarten at the old Pemberton House that Norfolk House School used on St. Charles Street, while the school my father designed for 801 Bank Street was being built. A plain half-timbered Tudor style complemented the banks of classroom windows in the new building. Miss Atkins, the head mistress, asked if, in lieu of completing the payment of architectural fees, she could write off several terms for my tuition. On the Board of the school at the time, my father most likely accepted her offer to barter services. George Gibson, the English-trained sculptor from Shawnigan Lake, carved the school motto on a plaque installed in the main hallway.

A number of projects that did not come to completion show up in the papers at the BCA between 1927 and 1930. A group of Union Club members, together with Countess de Suzannet, wanted to develop a country club at Towner Bay on the north shore of Patricia Bay. A plan for the 33-acre subdivision provided for 29 lots and a Clubhouse. The membership entrance fee was to be $100 plus annual dues. We visited the area and had a picnic on the beach with Mr. Scott, a prime member of the steering committee, but the scheme fell victim to the economy of the times. In 1931, James received payment for sketches, working drawings, specification and receipt of tenders.

Other schemes that came to naught at this time include a Malahat hotel, a Marine Drive golfers' hotel at Shoal Bay with a budget of $27,000, and a private school for boys near Sooke.

The first Colwood Clubhouse burned down while Mr. Sayward was on a business trip in Seattle. Several local architects phoned Sayward in Seattle asking to design a replacement for him. He reported the calls from these eager beavers when he called James to consult him about the new building. Apparently he told them he was very happy with Mr. James as his architect and on his return to Victoria intended to commission him for the replacement clubhouse.

With the boom years still inspiring confidence in expansion, the Clubhouse designed in 1929 was much larger. It opened in 1930 and became a Mecca for movie stars and the beautiful people of the golf world.

With the effects of the Depression, the club suffered and membership fell to well under 100 just before the Second World War. There must have been problems just to keep the large building going. During the war the members had a small clubhouse built. For a while the old clubhouse became a Veterans Rehabilitation hospital – a nice place to recover in the gracious rooms that overlooked fairways interspersed with giant oak and richly-scented Douglas fir trees. In those years, the former clubhouse could still be seen as you drove along the Old Island Highway near Langford. But as the trees grew bigger, the view dwindled and eventually it disappeared altogether.

In the early 1950s, Mother Cecilia Mary and the Sisters of the Love of Jesus took the building over as a nursing home. The *Daily Colonist* of June 23rd, 1973 recounted the story of this remarkable woman. She arrived from England in 1921 and was the first Anglican nun in BC. The following year on April 8th, she founded the Sisters of the Love of Jesus, an Anglican community in Vancouver. She made news on July 30, 1937, when she led most of the sisters in the community into the Roman Catholic Church. Sister Cecilia became famous for the animal shelter she ran within the nursing home precinct, which though disapproved of by the church won considerable world-wide support from animal lovers and a lot of local press coverage.

Finally the building became the administration centre for

Royal Colwood Golf Club, 1930 (Photo by Savannah - Author's collection)

The Royal Colwood 1930 clubhouse entrance (Photo by author c. 1985)

Rear view of the Royal Colwood 1930 clubhouse (Photographer unknown – author's collection - BCA #hp68134)

the Juan de Fuca Hospital Society that took over all the care hospitals in the Greater Victoria area. With lack of proper upkeep, the building fell into disrepair. Moss grew on the shingles. Water from the rotting roof ran down the walls of the main stair hall. The plaster decoration of the fireplace in the Mother Superior's room – the Ladies Card Room in the clubhouse days – crumbled from water damage.

In the early 1980s, the Colwood Club considered re-acquiring the clubhouse when they needed more space for their club now grown to 800 members. But only half the membership bothered to turn out for the vote. By a close majority – only four votes – they chose to let the old clubhouse die.

The late Dr. Eric Graham, then Studies Administrator at Royal Roads Services College, spoke before the Colwood hearing when the Juan de Fuca Hospital Society sought to demolish the building. Hoping to convince them of the structural superiority of the building, he declared, "If a Force Nine earthquake hit this area, the Clubhouse building – and the house I live in (the residence designed for H.C.V. MacDowall), also designed by Mr. James, would both be unharmed."

At that final meeting the Hospital Society declared themselves to be "more interested in saving lives, than preserving old buildings." The building was demolished, but the efforts to save it had dragged on and the period for the government grants the society had hoped to receive had lapsed. Someone purchased and has stored the clubhouse windows in the hopes that they may yet be used in some new structures in the area.

With changes in ownership and the economy, some of the bigger houses that James designed have undergone changes over the years, many being divided into accommodation for several families. Two of the largest houses have very different histories.

In 1930, Mr. Sayward (who built the Colwood Golf Club) gave a handsome present to his daughter, Margaret Livingstone Sayward. She married a Mr. Forbes-Wilson in 1927, but soon after they became known as Mr. and Mrs. F. Forbes Sayward-Wilson. For some years they resided at 3125 Beach Drive.

A major example of James's English Arts & Crafts designs, this house had five family bedrooms and a maids' suite with two bedrooms and a sitting room off the kitchen. It featured an English Renaissance plaster ceiling in the living room, a panelled inner stair hall with a flat Tudor-arch fireplace, and stair balusters with carvings by George Gibson. James later undertook a couple of small alterations: the first for Mr. J. Wattie, the man who gave out dollars to children who visited on Halloween when he rented the Bullen house – a habit he continued at 3125 Beach Drive; the second, for Mr. R.W. Mayhew. The plans for these are filed at the CVA in the *P. Leonard James Collection* and are compatible with the original design. In James's lifetime somebody painted all the half-timbering the same colour as the stucco, a choice that did not meet with his approval.

However he has been spared from seeing some of the later "improvements." Recent owners have overridden the intent of the architect with alterations conflicting with the 1930 English

Arts & Crafts concept, and the integrity of the original style has been lost. Lower gables were raised to the level of the main roof saddle. At one point the house became fussy and over-decorated with additional Tudor timbers inserted between those of the original design, plus half-timbering added on the lower floor where none existed originally. Extra painted-on lines accentuated each Tudor plaster panel and achieved a rather Bavarian effect. Until recently Oak Bay has made minimal attempts to protect houses with heritage potential.

Several recent owners have modified the interior. A decorator, who was very proud of the results he had achieved when employed by the former owner, met the next owner at a party. Being unfamiliar with local personalities, the new owner enthusiastically announced, "Of course I'm having the dreadful decorating redone."

I had the opportunity to see through the house when it was on sale for $6,000,000 in the 1980s. The interior decor included many strident touches of gold, green, scarlet and what James

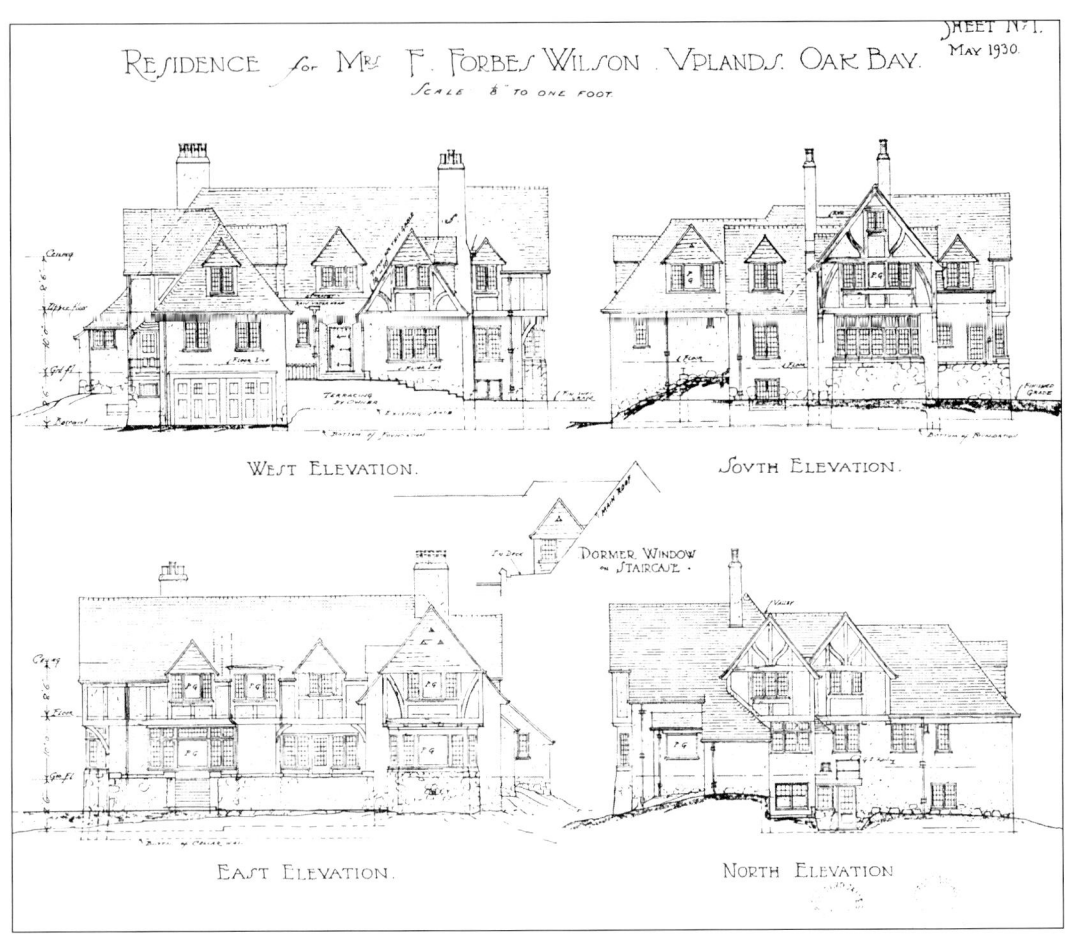

F. Forbes-Wilson, 1930 elevations for residence at 3125 Beach Drive. Oak Bay. This house vastly changed in appearance with raised roof saddles and 1912-style dropped finials, However the beautiful living room Bow window has been retained. *(Courtesy of OBBD)*

might well have called "a mind-numbing delphinium blue." No buyer came forth. The ostentatious stone wall had gold-tipped iron railings with a central niche for a board, announcing as a hotel might, the name, *Eagles Nest*. The board has recently been removed. I could only find the main stairway and hall panelling and possibly the downstairs washroom by the front door in original condition, plus a French door Mr. Mayhew had put in. A Renaissance fireplace of grand proportions complete with columns overwhelmed the living room; the English Renaissance plaster ceiling had been replaced with a grander one of Italian Renaissance design. A Victorian-style fireplace that would be more suitable in Craigdarroch Castle replaced the original Tudor-style Batchelder fireplace in the panelled stair hall and contributed to the unbelievable range of styles.

Of course owners want to alter their own space to reflect their needs, requirements and idiosyncratic sense of style. Indeed, as my mother said more than once, "The only taste some people have is in their mouth." Fortunately most owners and their architects wish to retain the feeling of the original building and do not attempt to turn their houses into a parody of styles.

An owner of this property, advertising it for sale in the *Times-Colonist* on May 29th, 1993, claimed the house had been designed by Sir Percy Leonard James – perhaps an overblown touch of historical snobbery to bolster the vast price!

The house has undergone further drastic renovations. Possibly only the polygonal bay window in the living room remains. Nothing of its original design concept appears to have been saved and bay windows have appeared where there were none before. Perhaps the staircase survived the gutting, but the original front door did not. A pre-First World War design element has been introduced with dropped finials in the gables. So much for a reference to historical design.

In 2003 this residence topped the local market, selling for seven million dollars.

The residence for Capt. and Mrs. W. Hobart Molson is one that has been tastefully turned into apartments yet retains its original architectural integrity. The Molsons lived at 1663 Rockland Avenue from its completion in 1931 until 1950. Their son David has mentioned he felt that growing up in that house influenced his decision to take up architecture. He also mentioned that James used a new method of blocking in the studding that would curtail the spread of fire.

As a six-year-old, I visited the house designed with amenities for the young Molsen family. It fascinated me to learn that a cupboard by the side entrance was for the storage of prams. My father made a point of showing me the elevation drawing which indicated that a special window glass was used for both the day and night nurseries. "Vitaglass" came from England and screened out harmful rays from sunlight – a trivial detail never forgotten.

Quite a lot of special plasterwork was used throughout the house. Mr. Oliver, the plasterer, made the family crest and motto, a crescent moon on its back with wings on either side, "Industria et spe" (By Work and Hope) over the front door and

Capt. W. Hobart Molson 1930 residence, 1663 Rockland Avenue, Victoria, view of terrace (Photographer unknown - Author's collection - BCA #hp68423)

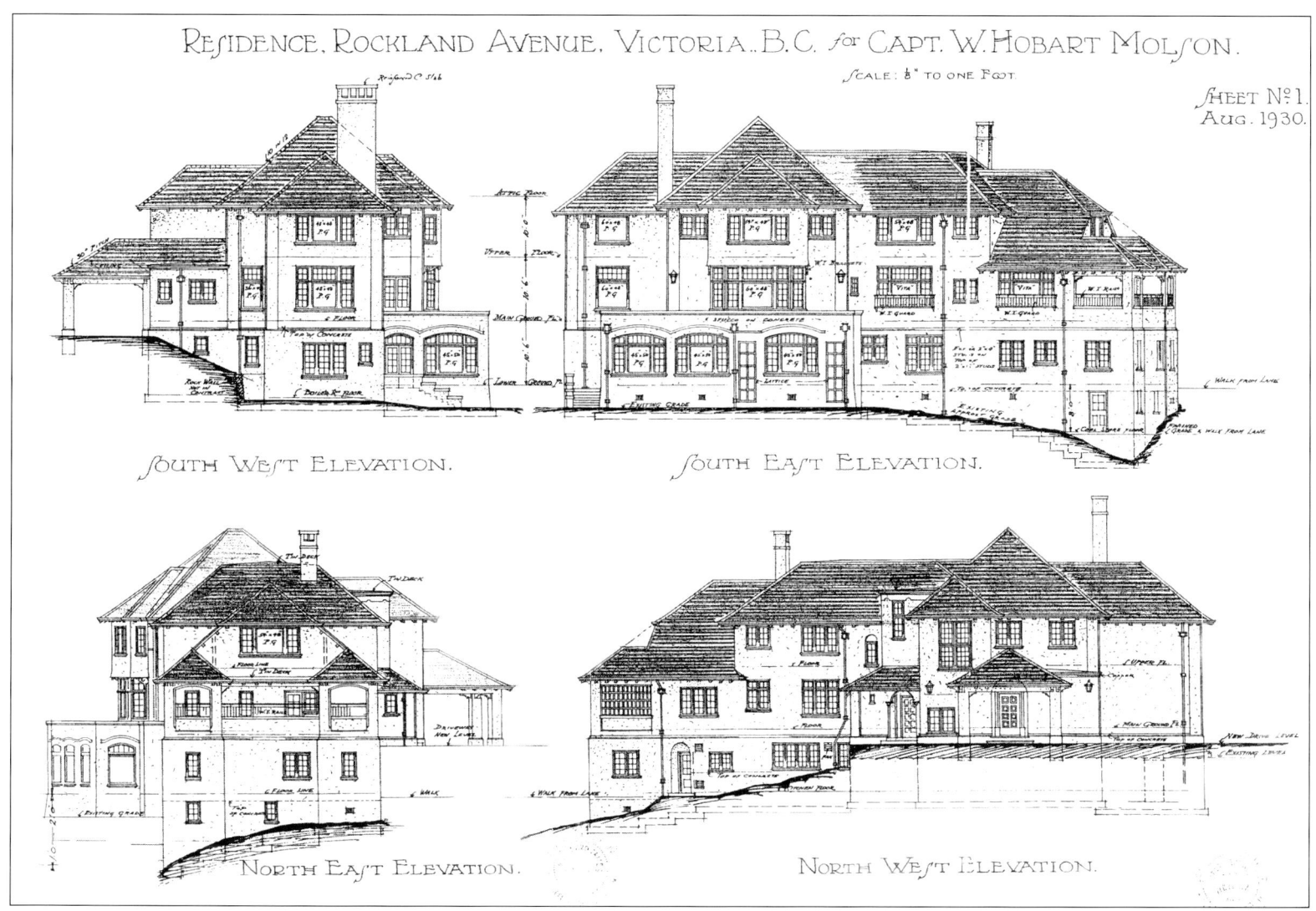

Elevations of Capt. Hobart Molson 1930 residence at 1663 Rockland Avenue *(Courtesy of CVPDD)*

the plasterwork on the living room fireplace to details supplied by the architect. Even in 1930 there must have been catalogues for plaster mouldings, but competent plasterers were trained to carry out such work on the job and the architect had the freedom to interpret cove designs and decorative details to suit the proportions of any particular room.

The City issued Building Permit 6262 for the carpentry portion of the building to Hunter & Halkett . A building inspector (perhaps an inexperienced one, or someone who chaffed against any regulations not devised by himself) took exception to this practice of issuing separate contracts for the major trades. Although noting the standard use of separate contracts under the AIBC rules, on Sept 23rd, 1930 he wrote to James & Savage:

> Contractor assuring us that you as Architects have made some arrangement which requires each sub-trade, Plumbing, Heating and Electrical to take out building permits for their proportion of cost. Above method is entirely unsatisfactory and leads to a false statement of building costs, with the two-fold object of low assessment and permit fees.

On Sept 24th, James replied to this bureaucratic fusspot: he pointed out the impossibility of changing this standard practice and the obvious reasons.

> Neither the Plumbing or Wiring Contracts had been let at that time, so the Contractor could not possibly say what the value of the sub trades would be.

> We shall at all times be glad to co-operate in seeing that true value of contracts are stated.

In the 1980s, some friends had the apartment which contained the original living room – still retained in its full-size glory (20 feet x 31 feet). The indirect lighting trough round the entire room fascinated them and they went out and bought the 58 bulbs needed for all the sockets. With hydro costs in mind, they did not often use them but turned them on so visitors could see the effect. Such a consideration was not a problem in the days of the Molson family and our current need to conserve energy had not been thought of then.

My article on P. Leonard James, published in the *Times-Colonist*, June 30th, 1996, mentioned that he designed the Molson house on Rockland Avenue.

"You are quite wrong," declared a woman a couple of years my senior when I met her at a luncheon soon after the publication of the article , "I used to play in that house when I was a child."

I remonstrated that I remembered the house being built and had run through the rough studding.

"It can only have been an alteration." She declared adamantly.

The Molson file in the James papers at the BCA confirms that the first contract was the complete demolition of the old house on the property. The good lady in question had correctly remembered playing in the earlier house on the property – the demolished Luxton house, designed by Col. Ridgway Wilson in 1914.

The specification for the demolition of the old house on the property the Molsons bought, said: -

> Pull down and cart away from the site the whole of the existing house and sheds and fences attached thereto; also the granite terrace and steps. NOTE The foundation walls alone are to remain and the Contractor shall take care not to injure same.

Maureen Meardon wrote about the 13,000 square foot Molson house for *Boulevard Magazine*, February/March 1996. Her article entitled *A Touch of Tuscany* referred to the apartments now in the house as "elegant suites."

She declared:

> The house resembles a villa. Strong and stalwart, it looks as though it could stand in the company of a Florentine palazzo. Not a house screaming to be recognized. It's a subtle declaration of quality and artistic achievement.

The slight crook in the house, for which there seems to be no reason, intrigued her. She mentioned that the architect went to a great deal of trouble to do it and that it is barely noticeable. She asked if I knew the reason for the crook in the house. Built into the earlier, now demolished, house, it is unlikely that more will be discovered beyond the fact that the crook existed in the original Luxton house foundation, and was retained for the Molson house "footprint." It must have been an excellent foundation for James to have preserved and reused it. The careful camouflage of its existence must be credited to his skill. On one floor the space is filled with an odd-shaped pantry. On the next floor the back staircase has an irregular stairwell opening that is hardly noticeable.

In the houses themselves, a gracious feeling for space is readily apparent, as is an understatement in the detailing which was always appropriate and reflected the current trends in styles. James's innate good taste shows in his designs. His work, whether large or small, used lovely proportions and satisfying space in the interior rooms. Over the years, the buildings have "rolled with the punches": alterations, additions, re-siting to allow subdivion of an original large lot, fires, even some shady doings as well as great pride and satisfaction, all have become part of their history.

CHAPTER TWELVE

A Year Away

By 1933 the Depression had the West Coast of Canada in its grip and building had come to a standstill. Molly received upsetting news about the grave state of her father's health and affairs from his accountant in Scotland. So, P. Leonard James decided to close his office and join us on an extended trip to England and Portugal to sort things out.

On this trip across Canada, my father warned me to be careful on the train. As an adventurous nine-year-old, I was no longer scared of the creaking metal plates where the train coaches joined and was strong enough to open the heavy train doors. I liked to lead the family as we trooped to the end of the train to sit in the Observation Car. Unlike the metal cars that made up the main part of the train, this car was made of wood and could best be described as a giant streetcar with some seats in the open. Mother said, "Don't sit there, you'll get covered with smuts," as she hurried into the enclosed central part of the car. It had windows right up to the car roof to allow a good view of the towering Rockies.

We used to get off the train when it stopped "to stretch our legs." As we walked along the platform admiring the coaches, my dad pointed out the names of cars after some Canadian features. The first class cars had names like *Birch Grove* or *Cape*

Scott. In addition to the Grove- and Cape-class cars, there were also Manor-, Glen-, Chateau- and Mount- class cars. The first-class cars, assembled at the end of the trains, had signs instructing passengers to "Walk forward for meal service" in the dining car. The tourist cars at the front of the train instructed passengers to walk back to the same dining car for meals. The tourist cars had plain single names – no "Manors" or "Chateau" for them – and consisted of cars with plain seat or sleeper sections. The seats in sleeper sections made into an upper and a lower berth at night, heavy green curtains provided privacy along the corridor. First class accommodation offered more variety – from drawing rooms that slept three, compartments for two, as well as sleeper sections. The 1960 "Official Register of Passenger Train Equipment" in *Canadian Pacific Railway* by Patrick C. Dorin gave a full list of car names. He also listed some fifty 48-seat Dining Cars, in use over the years, and indicated crew sleeping quarters for seventeen men were arranged in the baggage car.

"Well I never!" chuckled my father when he spotted a tourist car which seemed most inappropriately named to him as a resident of Victoria, "This car is called *Uplands* – not Second Class surely!" (*The Uplands* is the foremost residential area in Victoria and contained a number of houses that he had designed.)

The big Canadian trains had almost ground level station platforms and steps built into the vestibule ends of each car. A sturdy stool set out by the porter at the bottom of those steps made it easy to reach the first high step on the train and the porter stood nearby to assist anyone who needed help. Father compared this system to the English trains, which always had built-up platforms, so you could easily step on and off the train.

We crossed the Atlantic on the *Antonia* another Cunard "A" liner. (So called because all the ships on this service had names beginning with A and ending with "ia".) White Star ships also served the Montreal to Britain route, but the memory of the terrible *Titanic* disaster lingered with many people, including my father. He preferred not to travel on the line that had once failed to observe proper safety precautions. We left Montreal on Friday, August 25th.

A small liner, the *Antonia* had three classes, Cabin, Second and Third, or "Steerage." The Third Class was accommodated on the lower decks at the stern. They had no access to the upper decks. A door with a "Crew Only" sign, provided the only entry. When father and I took a tour of the ship, we went through this door and saw the Third Class Dining Room with long communal tables. The Second Class Dining Room had a linoleum floor with tables for small groups like the Cabin Class, but did not have the plush chairs, handsome carpet or velvet drapes trimmed with the tassels and tiebacks that were provided in Cabin Class.

The Purser ran a "sweepstake" each day allowing passengers to guess what mileage would be achieved on that day's run, and Dad placed a daily bet.

My parents attended the Fancy Dress Ball and the Ship's Concert, where brave or brash fellow passengers performed. My mother went to the latter with trepidation; with her high musical standard, she hated to hear music "murdered."

We landed at Liverpool after a passage which took six days, seven hours and thirty-five minutes, and made our way to London for the next leg of our journey to Portugal.

Father's notes show we caught the Royal Mail Line's MV *Highland Brigade* on Saturday, September 16th, 1933, from the Tilbury docks on the Thames. After we landed at Lisbon, this ship would complete a return trip to South America in six-weeks. As we proceeded up the Tagus River to Lisbon, my father commented on the many fine villas, with either sparkling white or brightly tinted stucco, some even cobalt blue.

We stayed in a hotel on Praca Dom Pedro IV Square, known locally as "Rossio" and dubbed by the English "Roly Poly Square." In those days the huge black and white tile wave pattern covered a whole city block. Just walking over it made one feel slightly off-balance.

The Scottish accountant had warned Molly that her father was just throwing good money after bad with the old copper mine he had opened in Spain. For every five hundred pounds (Sterling) that he invested in the mine, he earned only one hundred pounds by the time the copper was mined, shipped to England and refined near Bristol. The mine manager had had a freewheeling hand until my mother arrived. She consulted lawyers and had to wait a week or more, until her father's hand became steady enough to sign a document giving her power of attorney. She said, "I was the Managing Director of a mine for one day. Just long enough to stamp and sign everything and close down the business in proper fashion."

Father enjoyed sketching in colourful Lisbon: buildings with Art Deco motifs; boats with high prows painted with seeing-eyes; walls, trellises and pots brilliant with bougainvillea, scarlet and gold cannas, and geraniums. Entire elevations of some of the buildings were decorated with blue, yellow and orange tiles. Flat-roofed International Style buildings were very much in evidence; my father thought them very suitable to the Portuguese climate.

On our return to London, we soon established ourselves in furnished rooms at #107 Inverness Terrace in the Bayswater district. We had two large rooms up one flight of stairs. We shared the bathroom on the landing above our floor with the German-Finnish family on the top floor. A shilling to make the geyser function produced hot water almost immediately. I am not sure of the kitchen location. It might have been combined with the bathroom, or it was on the half-way-down landing – this the most probable, as my mother would have had a fit if she'd had to share a little kitchen with another cook and various bathers! We had seen such arrangements when we hunted for our accommodation.

We lived at Inverness Terrace for 44 weeks and were within easy walking distance of Whiteley's Department store and Kensington Gardens. Selfridge's was only a short bus ride away. All London could be reached by the Underground, or Tube. The first electric subway trains had been running since 1890, so my parents were familiar with such travel. Even so, trips on the tube seemed strange and exciting. Strong drafts and unusual smells filled the stairs and corridors with their poster-covered walls. All sense of surface direction was lost; fortunately, the direction signs were excellent. To passengers waiting on the platform, the deadly third rail seemed to exert a hypnotic attraction. As the trains approached the stations, the people standing on the platform felt a rush of air. After a quick transfer of passengers, the trains disappeared again into the warm dark tunnels, averaging a station every three minutes.

We went several times to exhibitions in the Crystal Palace. Father had attended many shows there when he lived in London. He must have often thought of it when he worked on the Crystal Garden in Victoria.

We saw a spectacular fireworks show there. We had seats on an outside balcony and delighted in a programme of wonderful set pieces, some parts moving on rails in front of the stationary parts. As well there were the rockets – all we ever saw in Canada – and sparkling Catherine Wheels then unknown in Victoria.

Father spent a good deal of time visiting many displays of the latest 1934 developments in housing design and materials. He attended the Ideal Home Exhibition at Olympia, where he noted ideas inspired by the trend setting Bauhaus. He found "Staybrite Steel," the latest thing in stainless steel for sinks and harder than the Monel metal used in Canada. The "Sunspan" house used three-ply wooden doors in the kitchen. He did a sketch of a broom cupboard there and later added a note, "R.J.J. says NBG." Mother, obviously not impressed with the design, commented, "No Bloody Good."

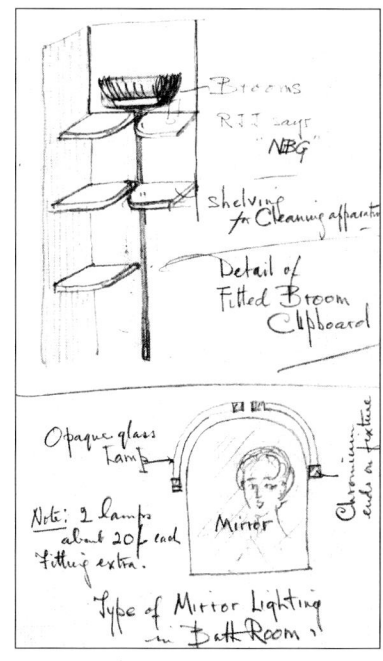

P. Leonard James's English sketch of broom cupboard and early tube lighting, perhaps fluourescent, 1934 **(Authors collection)**

Among his notes, sketches of the new treatment of stairways, without dust collecting banisters, but using partial walls with a plain hardwood capping and handrail above, appeared. This concept delighted my mother who hated the dust catching 1910 banisters at our house. After our return home, we had all our banisters enclosed with plywood on both sides and painted her favourite colour, aqua, with a black handrail. My parents also redecorated their bedroom and included built-in furniture based on the principles of sectional furniture, another new concept he had seen at the displays and which they both liked. They painted the new wooden units silver, which complemented the pale lavender walls and the deep-blue and red-violet curtain material brought home from England.

The Dutch Village, Coulsden, the St. Margaret's Estates, Edgeware and a house in Rugby by the partnership of Erick Mendelsohn and Serge Chermayedd, FRIBA, illustrated many examples of the ideas of Walter Gropius. and the Bauhaus school. The Royal Institute of British Architects offered lectures on the formalism of the new International Style. At Wembley and at British Industries House the plain modern fireplaces and interior details interested him. He found the best kitchen cabinets at British Columbia House. They were made of Douglas fir from BC.

Thirty-five display homes, chosen from 500 plans entered in a competition, made the Modern Homes Exhibition at Gidea Park the largest exhibit. After digesting all these new ideas, father put his impressions of Gidea Park into an article, but I don't know that it was ever published. In part he said:

- Has the perfect small house been discovered at last?

- There is much more in common between the small houses of England and Canada today than was the case a decade or so ago. The open type of plan has been adopted here making available all the space for living purposes, rather than cutting it up into a series of small rooms as formerly. This is all to the good.

- A pamphlet describing these homes claimed they contain features entirely new to this country. I fancy we should find, on investigation, that some of these originated in Canada, so familiar do they appear to the visitor from that portion of the Empire.

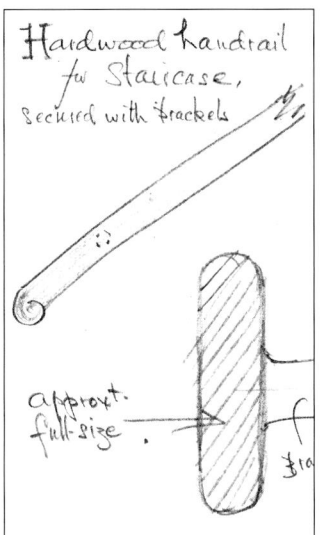

P. Leonard James's English sketch of wall-hung handrail, 1934. Later used in Dr. T.H. John's 1940 residence (Author's collection)

- I venture to think that, in some respects, the Canadian prototype still has the advantage…A few cases in point:

• such narrow staircases, frequently with "winding" steps, would not be tolerated in Canadian homes;

• practically all flooring used in Canada is of the "Tongued-and-grooved" variety in narrow strips, stained and polished. Contrast this with the deal floor boards used regularly in English houses, with joints that hold dust and dirt unless completely covered with carpet or linoleum;

• almost entire absence of clothes cupboards in bedrooms (if provided, they are too narrow to be of real use);

• the kitchen sink invariably has fixed drainer boards a most insanitary arrangement. Drain boards should either be hinged (for ease of cleaning) or made in one piece of a material such as stainless steel;

• unsightly water pipes are conspicuous in some of the houses; I noted one bathroom wall covered with a conglomeration of piping, a lodgment for dust and dirt. All pipes are kept out of sight in Canadian houses.

- The English houses score distinctly with:

- their electric fireplaces,
- and the excellent metal windows of various types which are rarely found in Canadian houses.

In particular, the indirect lighting arrangements often built into the furnishing intrigued him. Short opaque lighting tubes 12 and 20 inches long with chromium ends, and others of a curved shape, were no doubt early fluorescent fixtures. In England they were first manufactured in 1928.

Another novelty at that time, the Pollard's "Invisible Glazing" for shop windows offered no reflection, in fact there appeared to be no glass between the viewer and the display, however if you reached in towards the displayed merchandise, you became aware of the curved glass which created the effect.

Once back in Canada, father designed several houses inspired by various treatments of the new International Style, which my mother, as a great fan of modernist ideas, really liked. These flat roofed buildings became known as Art Moderne.

As a family we made many trips and excursions from London. We visited the London Zoo several times. The chimpanzees sat round a table and had a tea party for the enjoyment of the public, and their antics certainly amused my father. We

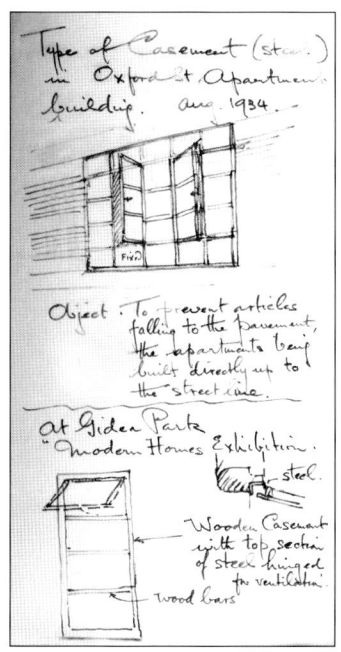

P. Leonard James's English casement window design to prevent objects falling from apartment windows 1934 (Author's collection)

also visited Whipsnade, the recently created "open zoo," a branch of the London Zoo in the country which had only been open since May 1931. The animals appeared to roam in the open. Moated areas kept the animals under control: bars and cages were rarely used.

In March we toured the Cotswold country near Stratford-on-Avon. The new Shakespearian Theatre designed by a woman architect, Elizabeth Scott, had recently been completed and Father was interested to see this warm brick building on the banks of the Avon River. Unfortunately, we were unable to see a play there.

Father's old stamping grounds in Dorset came in for visits too. We hiked the four miles from Swanage to Worth, the village where my father was christened. As with most English footpaths, stiles, which excluded cattle, allowed one to cross the hedges and stone walls at property lines. We saw the leper's window in the village's Norman church. The small window, built on an angle, allowed an afflicted person to stand outside, hear the service and see the altar without infecting the congregation.

Father made sketches wherever we went. Often he just took off for the day by himself. His sketches included the Dorset coastline, Wren churches, the London parks and Thames River. He made notes of the rigging of the Thames barges, the sail-powered workhorse of the London river, still in use in 1934. Today any remaining barges are there only as tourist attractions.

Our travels ended with a couple of historically important events, which I would never have recalled without Father's trip notes. At that time, England's fastest and best trains, "The Royal Scot" and "The Flying Scotsman," made daily express trips to Scotland. After the Second World War, with the cut-backs of the British Rail service and the end of the steam era, these famous and much-loved trains ran no more. But his notes report that we rode the "Royal Scot from Kings Cross Station to Dundee."

Then as we left the British Isles we had a great sight as we passed Clydebank. Father recorded:

"On September 21 departed from South Pier, Princess Dock at 7 p.m. An hour or so later we passed the new Cunarder, No. 534, which is to be launched next Wednesday by the Queen. Had a fine view of the hull. Although night time, it was brightly illuminated as work was still proceeding."

No 534 was named the *Queen Mary* at its launching. But that was not the name the Cunard Company had picked out. The Cunard President went in person to seek the King's approval. "Your Majesty, we want to name this mighty ship after our great Queen." The King forgot the Cunard precedent to use names ending in "ia" and immediately replied,

"Queen Mary would be delighted." So the ship was not named after Queen Victoria as planned.

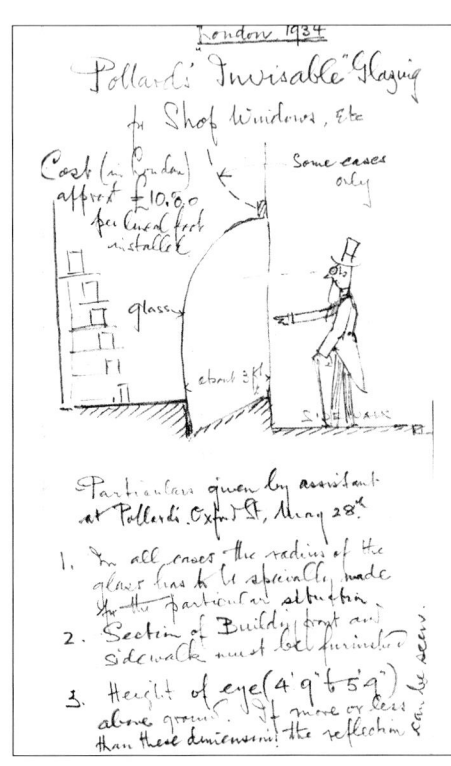

English sketch of invisible shop window, 1934
(Author's collection)

CHAPTER THIRTEEN
The Practice After 1934

James re-opened his office on our return from England in 1934 in the Bridgeman Block on Broughton Street, where James & James had established an early office. There was no staff that year or the next. A telephone arrangement allowed both home and office to use the same number, so that people at home could catch any calls when he went out of the office. Later he shared an office with a surveyor in the Arcade Building and finally set up his practice on the fifth floor of the Royal Trust Building at the corner of Government and View streets.

From this office he enjoyed a fine view of the Juan de Fuca Strait and the Olympic Mountains. Each morning one could observe the garbage scow as it left the harbour with a cloud of following gulls. A few miles beyond the breakwater, it dumped Victoria's garbage into the ocean to the delight of the hundreds of milling seagulls which descended on the flotsam, making off with whatever they could and leaving whatever did not sink to float back onto the beaches.

According to the City of Victoria Archive records the garbage had been dumped in this way since 1892. But in those early days, the scow containing "night soil, swill and filthy and offensive matter dangerous to health" was towed a prescribed two miles out of the harbour at 4 AM by decree of the City Council.

Victorian Victorians, before the age of unions and overtime wages, were saved the indignity of seeing the disposal of their waste. By the 1950's, the scow was towed out about 9:30 in the morning. Perhaps this fascinating but revolting sight eventually brought about the Hartland Dump solution in 1960!

During our year in London, we had observed the heavy traffic controlled efficiently by cheerful policemen on "point duty." They wore very visible white gauntlets. The officers directed London's busy traffic, by waving the complicated lanes of vehicles through squares and round Piccadilly with free-flowing movements that my mother described as "balletic." On their return to Victoria, my parents found local attempts at traffic control exasperating and rather laughable. At busy periods and when the hordes of government workers went home, an officer installed a sign made out of piping at the intersection of Douglas and Fort Streets and possibly there were others at major intersections. A hole in the centre of the road supported the sign, which had small STOP and GO arms at right angles. A stolid officer, looking very pompous, stood beside it, tooting his whistle and turning the sign to offer drivers their right-of-way. The system didn't last very long. On June 27th, 1935 four traffic lights appeared along Douglas Street. Those first lights, installed over the centre of the intersections, had just a red STOP and a green GO, no amber warning light having yet been considered.

The aftermath of the Depression lingered on in Victoria, little development or building occurred until the Second World War, when the housing needs of shipyard workers and training facility requirements had to be met.

The houses built in the Thirties and Forties were generally much smaller. No back stairs for non-existent servants. Pantries, porte-cochères, high ceilings and that Edwardian feature, the sleeping porch, had all gone the way of the dodo. Textured stuccoes now started to replace the old roughcast stucco and a ceiling height of only eight feet became standard in most rooms. James used to talk about rising costs and how every break in the elevations added to the cost. He considered that costs caused the popularity of the ranchhouse-style, low roofs with flat, often uninteresting elevations. Sometimes an enormous Roman brick chimney of a size for five or more flues, but serving only the Living Room fireplace and furnace, became the main decorative feature of a ranchhouse. He felt such a chimney violated good design. Recalling the dictum generally followed by that great Victorian trendsetter and critic John Ruskin, and by the Arts & Crafts Movement, he used to shake his head and say, "Not built in Truth and Beauty."

It is of interest to consider the operation of the one-man office of those days, as compared to the firms of more recent times when several architects band together to keep an office going. One member of such a firm, if qualified, would also handle the engineering end of things; another person would deal with the business end of the operation; the most outgoing member of the firm would seek new clients through whatever connections he might have, such as golf or social clubs; another member might specialize in specification writing; and another would be the main designer for the firm, with all members assisting as needed and taking their share of job inspections.

In the one-man office, the one man did everything. James didn't have time for social clubs, although his regular attendance at church probably brought him some ecclesiastical and domestic commissions.

Just consider the wide knowledge required to complete a house commission. First he met with the client at the site, ascertained the client's wishes, and assessed the grades, landscape, views, neighbours and exposure of the site. He consulted the local authorities about regulations or restrictions on the property, zoning, codes, approvals required for the design and availability of services. He then drew up proposed ⅛ inch scale plan and elevations (where one inch on the drawing equaled eight feet on the building layout) and usually enlivened these drawings with coloured pencil. Based on the building size he made a ballpark estimate of cost for the client to consider. If the client wasn't satisfied another scheme might have to be prepared, and, if the client decided not to carry out the construction of either building, only one set of proposed drawings could be charged. On reaching final approval the architect completed the ¼ inch or ⅛ inch scale working drawings.

He took part in many further discussions of materials, visited suppliers with the client and his wife and also spent time consulting an array of catalogues and meeting with salesmen. A thorough knowledge of construction and local requirements was necessary. He made detail pencil drawings for the millwork, usually ¼ inch scale to show panelling, built-in cupboards and sideboards. He made sectional drawings through the chimney flues and stairways at the same scale. After construction began, he supplied 1 inch to the foot, or other size detail drawings as required, with full-size details of ceiling coves for the plasterer and special mantel and window sections, also full-size, for the millwork.

He interviewed salesmen about specific products with a view to describing special items in the specifications. A public stenographer typed the specifications according to his directions for the specific commission, including some parts of specifications that he routinely used. He had to consider the conditions at the site that might require blasting, or special drainage. He consulted the local authorities for approval of the final design. Local trade papers had to be informed about the opportunity for contractors to submit tenders on commercial work. For domestic work, the architect usually invited tenders from men on his list of proven contractors.

When the tenders were received, the architect advised the client whether or not to accept the lowest bid. Sometimes contractors who missed out complained that the winning man would lose money over the job, however such would usually not be the case. His favourite contractors worked for him again and again. He prepared the contract document consisting of the plans and the specification – sometimes the owner required that his solicitor approve the documents. The signing by owner and contractor took place at the architect's office. Surveyors sited the building according to the architect's plot plan and the ground was broken.

After the work started, almost daily inspections included

checking dimensions on the site and the work of all trades as the building progressed. He brought any discrepancies to the attention of the general contractor. The contractor would ask him to inspect any of the delivered materials, if he perceived a problem. After examining the accounts submitted by the general contractor as the work progressed, the architect prepared certificates of payment for the owner to reimburse the general contractor. Extras that the owner decided upon and meetings with the owner and his wife over colour schemes and such, had to be attended to. James complained, "Some of the ladies take up a great deal more time than others."

Sometimes legal proceedings rose during the course of the work and had to be dealt with. Even stamps and sundries had to be purchased by the lone practitioner. The last person to receive his payment? The architect, of course.

Some years after they bought their old house at 2840 Cadboro Bay Road, the W.B. Pease family consulted James about restoring it. Edgar Dewdney had built this Victorian bungalow. He had commanded the army engineers who surveyed and built the difficult Dewdney Trail inland from Hope. Later, he became the fifth Lieutenant Governor of British Columbia.

The old bungalow had not worn well, suffering a succession of owners and indifferent care. People in the thirties thought of Victorian houses as old-fashioned, and not old enough to be considered historically important and desirable. A great many of them were demolished. People didn't like the high ceilings, the lack of insulation and general draftiness, or the out-of-date bathrooms and kitchens. Originally these houses were heated with only the kitchen range – kept banked down all night – and open fireplaces. It was possible then to hire a girl who would "sleep-in," attend to the family fireplaces and do the general housework.

One of the owners had installed a coal-fired hot air furnace. The Pease family struggled with this unreliable heating system for some years. The furnace required stoking night and morning as well as during the day. Eventually, due to failing health, Mr. Pease had to give up its care. Mrs. Pease also found it too difficult and hated the messy coal dust, some of which infiltrated the house. Since the end of the First World War, it had become almost impossible to hire servants. Owners and architects had to consider new approaches to heating and housing in general.

Dora Crowe, one of the Pease daughters, sent me snapshots of herself and her sister, Mary, outside the old Dewdney house, which they called *Ballybawn* after family property in the Old Country. On January 15, 1992 Dora wrote:

> Here are a few pictures of the old house. Do you remember it at all?
>
> It was long and low – a series of additions, 8 rooms, doors opening from one room to another, lacking a proper passage – and fireplaces in all bedrooms, except the maid's next the kitchen! Also fireplaces in the two sitting rooms.
>
> The furnace was my mother's despair! Temperamental as the British weather. When it did go, it was ungenerous with its

heat. Hence your father called in for advice and I guess he felt like saying if it was a horse, he'd shoot it! He would mean the whole ramshackle house – no insulation – and dry rot setting in.

So the old folks had him design what you see now on that spot. I believe the fireplace tiles were rather special in the old house and I guess they sold to some builder!

In 1938, the Peases demolished the old house and built on the same site. James suggested they retain the old basement foundation, build their compact, textured stucco English Arts & Crafts vernacular-style house on the front section of the foundation and develop the back part as a patio. A hole cut through the concrete made an interesting pond close to the back of the new house. The remainder of the old foundation walls soon supported Mrs. Pease' favourite rambler roses and shrubs. When completed, the new house had an established appearance with the mature trees of the old orchard clustered around it.

Mary Pease, their artistic, unmarried daughter, didn't want to have the view from her bedroom cut up with casement glazing bars that were part of James's design for the rest of the house, so she had full panes of glass in her bedroom windows. Her view looked out over the open fields, known as "the Chinaman's fields," which stretched all the way to Foul Bay Road. Chinese market gardeners worked these fields and supplied great quantities of vegetables to the city markets and to the Chinese vegetable trucks that brought produce to householders' doors.

Today the fields of the Lansdowne slope are covered with houses, most of which have views of the Olympic Mountains. The Peases' large orchard garden has been subdivided and a house tucked in behind the 1938 *Ballybawn.*

In 1938, Mr. F.B. Ward chose an English Arts & Crafts style house with a minimum of half-timbering, to fit into his semi-country site at Christmas Hill. Even after the new Patricia Bay Highway was built below the house, it could hardly be seen from that busy road because of the oak trees. Developers purchased the house in the early 1980s, with plans for a large housing development. Concerned neighbours were assured the house would be retained, upgraded and incorporated in the final development scheme. In the interim, these neighbours found the house had a number of different tenants with varying degrees of desirability. Some littered the garden with old cars and garbage. A religious group, wandering home from their early morning hilltop devotions, helped themselves to firewood from neighbours' piles. Eventually the house stood empty.

Now one dark and stormy night, actually about twilight on Christmas Eve, 1986, a bulldozer chugged up the hill. The neighbours, busy with last-minute Christmas preparations, barely noticed. In the gathering dusk, the bulldozer systematically destroyed the house. Early next morning, although it was Christmas Day, workmen came and burned all that remained of the building. A neighbour whose aunt had lived at the house was distraught about this cloak-and-dagger demolition.

The demolition seriously upset heritage supporters. The Hallmark Society, Victoria's heritage group dedicated to preserving historic and architectural landmarks, had made municipal building departments aware of the need to keep a lookout for late-night activity at empty buildings with heritage value. But Christmas Eve is a difficult time to keep a regular eye on things. It is unrealistic to expect staff to be available, or busy police, to respond to such a call, as the developers were well aware. The property stood as an unkempt lost cause for a decade. Then late in 1997 development of almost identical houses started at a distant corner of the property. The aesthetic value of individuality in designs has been lost in this new era of development schemes.

The largest of James's English Arts & Crafts-style houses from this period is the rectory at 930 Burdett Street in the precinct of Christ Church Cathedral. Always known as *The Deanery*, it served as home to the Dean of the Cathedral for many years. The name of the architect J.C.M. Keith appears as the consulting architect on the working drawings by P. Leonard James, which are stored at The Archives of the Anglican Diocese of British Columbia. James included Keith's name as a courtesy title, for Keith had retired by 1937. But it was a well-deserved mention of his name, as Keith had won the competition for the design of Christ Church Cathedral and continued as the architect for the Anglican Synod until his retirement.

Nearby, Mr. and Mrs. Norman Yarrow had the Chapel of the Peace of God designed by James as a memorial for their son John, killed in a motor accident while returning from Scotland to his college in Cambridge in 1938. The chapel stood next to the Bishop's Palace at the corner of Vancouver Street and Burdett Avenue, and became known as the Bishop's Chapel. The Archives of the Anglican Synod are now attached to this chapel. At the same time, the Synod had James upgrade the Bishop's Palace

The Deanery, 930 Burdett Street, Victoria, 1937
(Photo by author)

with new heating plant and insulation. But that fine old building, designed by architect John Teague for Dr. Pollard, has not survived, despite the upgrading. These days bishops and deans seem to prefer to live a little further away from their workplace.

Other church work now came to James. First, St. John the Baptist Anglican Church for Cobble Hill in 1938, and then St. Peter's Anglican Church at Comox in 1939. The consecration for this latter church took place in September 1939. My father took me up island for this service at which Bishop Sexton officiated. My mother bought me my first suit for this event and warned me to watch out for the Bishop who had a reputation for liking the girls! He did invite a few of the party into the Sacristy to watch him don his vestments before the service, but her concern about possible hanky-panky was unfounded. On our return home we stayed near Big Qualicum and heard the news about the *Athenia* being sunk and learned that war had been declared.

The Cathedral Sunday School at the corner of Niagara and Medana Streets in James Bay offered a chance to use structural brickwork. The pattern he chose is called "English Bond" and consists of alternate courses of headers and stretchers. These form a solid wall unlike the brick veneer more usually seen, which just faced concrete or wood frame construction.

By the mid-1930s Oak Bay felt the need for fire protection within the municipality. They chose the site at 1703 Monterey Avenue as equidistant to South Oak Bay and the Uplands. As a

St. Peters Anglican Church, Comox, 1939 (Photo by Architect)

resident and the architect who had designed the Municipal Hall, James was consulted about this new building. The choice of Tudor style allowed the new building to blend into its residential neighbourhood. Constructed in 1937, it had only two gabled bays. When the department needed to expand, a third half-timbered gable was added. It established the English village-style for municipal service buildings at the site, which is now continued with the design of the much more recent cottage-style police station.

Mrs. Hammersley, new owner of 1989 Crescent Road, required some interior alterations and made a rather unusual request. Her daughter boarded at Miss Gildea's school at Cliffside, Shawnigan Lake, where the Home Economics teacher had greatly impressed Mrs. Hammersley. She asked James to consult this teacher before he completed his plan for her new kitchen. Rather amazed at her request, he laughed when he told my mother and me at lunch one day. He refused to travel to Shawnigan to meet this teacher, but agreed to see her if she came to Victoria. He, no doubt considering the client's unusual request as just one more peculiarity of a lady client, handled it with his customary politeness. But his final design had an island kitchen, a fairly new approach to residential kitchen planning, which was perhaps a result of this consultation.

James continued to design houses in the English Arts & Crafts style with Tudor detailing. Mrs. P.S. Lampman, widowed by 1941, commissioned her third James-designed house. It is a semi-bungalow that stands, with some additions, behind a big hedge at 925 St. Charles Street. This plan, built at ground

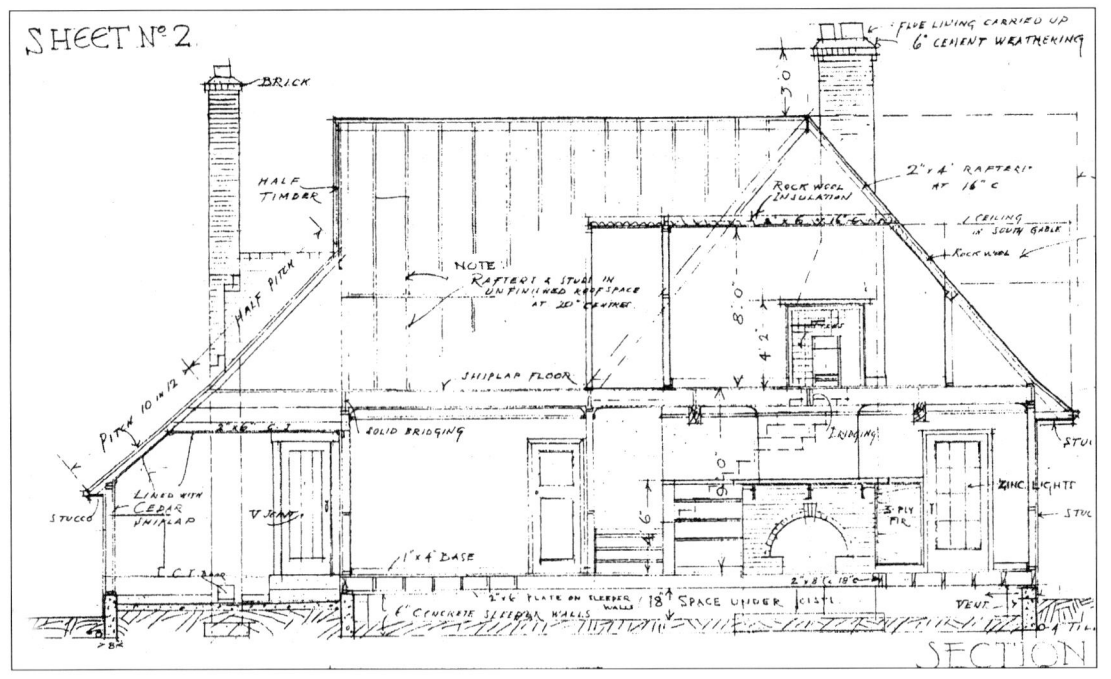

Mrs. P.S. Lampman residence, 925 St. Charles Street, Victoria, 1941, shown in section (Courtesy of CVPDD)

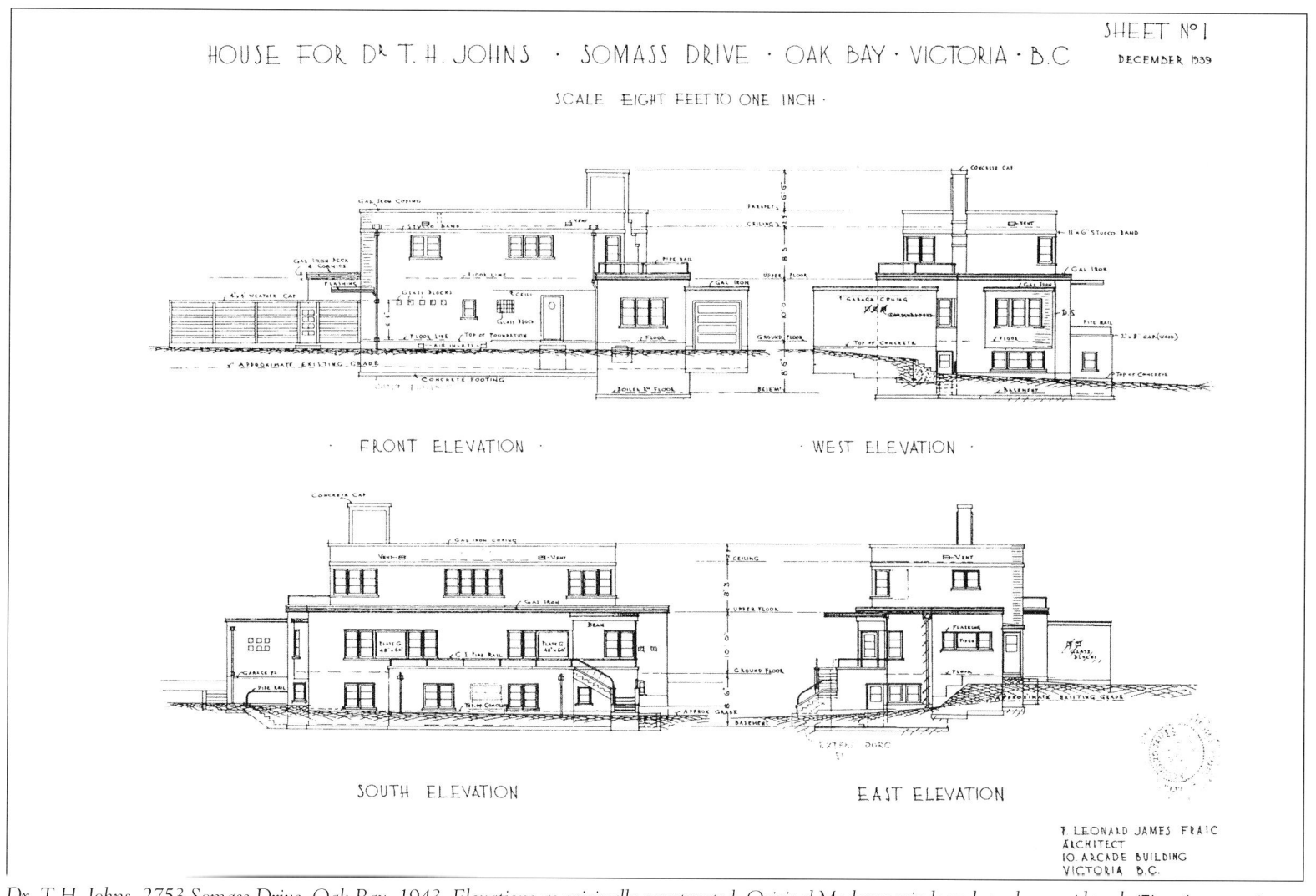

Dr. T.H. Johns, 2753 Somass Drive, Oak Bay, 1943, Elevations as originally constructed. Original Moderne windows have been replaced. (Elevations courtesy of current owners)

level, was a cozy retirement home in contrast to the Lampman's Nottingham Road house, which had many steps and a steep driveway.

At this date smaller houses had only one telephone, usually installed in an arched niche in the hallway; in this Lampman house however, the phone was installed in a shallow cupboard that could be opened from the kitchen or the living room for greater convenience.

A painting of the Lampman bungalow by Edward Goodall, appeared on the cover of the October, 1952 issue of *Western Homes*, which sold for 25 cents.

After long years of acquaintance many friends became clients when their housing needs changed. The family often had Sunday afternoon tea parties that included Arthur and Olive Musgrave. The ladies all wore hats and smart fox-fur neckpieces. Arthur Musgrave was Engineer for the Municipality of Oak Bay. In 1940 the Musgraves asked James to plan their new home. The Tudor-style house at 572 Newport Avenue is the only one he designed with diamond panes in that modern feature, the corner window. The owners, great gardeners, enjoyed viewing their garden through these corner windows.

Inspired by designs and ideas he had seen in London and the many examples of the Bauhaus idiom that appeared in architectural magazines, James branched out with examples of the Modernist style, later to be called Art Moderne. The first house designed with ideas from his observations in Gidea Park was for Edgar W. and Dorothy Griffiths in 1936 at 235 Denison Road.

James's decision to use shiplap siding is quite a departure from the usual stucco treatment of exterior walls. It certainly gives the house an unusually crisp image.

The Streamlined Moderne-style house for Dr. T.H. Johns, the dentist, built at 2753 Somass Drive on the Oak Bay waterfront in 1941, has stucco walls with a semi-circular bay window, some rounded corners and canopies. Glass blocks, then enjoying their first popularity, were used minimally on a curved wall, which was dubbed a "piano wall" to indicate its shape.

Miss B.E. O'Keiffe, a well-known teacher in Victoria, and Miss G. Field, as co-owners, had an Art Moderne-style house built on the hill above Shoal Bay, at 500 Beach Drive, in 1941. The original design has been incorporated in a greatly expanded house with only one window still in its original position.

Plans exist for a small flat-roofed house designed for Victor and Dr. Marion Sherman "at Ten Mile Point." An exhaustive search for the house along Sea View Road, plot plan in hand, disclosed that the site is the back part of the *Miramar* property. The Shermans lived in the big house for a number of years and considered building a smaller, one-level, house for their retirement years on the back part of the large property. Unfortunately, this plan, which might have saved *Miramar* from the devastating expansion imposed by later owners, was never built.

Clients commissioned a number of one-storey bungalows as the 1930s housing market declined. Some people chose a small home drawn up by a draughtsman as a cheaper alternative than hiring an architect. But James believed an architect's fee to be a small investment to ensure sound construction and good design. He condemned the obvious faults of many of these draughtsman-designed houses: bathrooms situated at the end of the hall with the toilet visible to visitors arriving at the front door; lack of proper overhang or porch to protect the visitor awaiting entry to the house; direct entrance into the living room, allowing drafts to sweep in and engulf people sitting in the room; and inadequate closet space. The use of "beer bottle" stucco then so popular for many smaller homes – so named because broken beer bottles were mixed with the sand – offended his taste and was never seen on a James house.

Eventually, his own bungalow designs assumed a simpler, low-roofed appearance. The E.A.M. Williams bungalow built in 1945 on the hillside at 1918 Crescent Road, Oak Bay used wide stucco bands to accentuate its long lines. The planned use of Roman brick for the lower level changed during construction. (Roman brick is a longer and thinner brick that became popular at this time.) A larger window set in regular brickwork with stone surround does not enhance the intended feeling of horizontality. The plain living-room fireplace is in the Art Deco tradition and the interior finish, mantel and door frames are constructed of simple half-round wood, a treatment popular with Frank Lloyd Wright.

Richard Field, an accountant, had his house at 3140 Midland Road, Oak Bay built in 1946. Mrs. Field insisted on a plan with very little circulation, just rooms opening into one another. James had grave concerns as to how well the low chimneys she wanted would draw among the oak trees, but they seem to have performed well enough. Some small alterations have been made, but no major changes spoil the look of the original. The house is enhanced with a splendid garden that is almost hidden from the road by a thicket of native shrubs.

Private building had come to a standstill with the Second World War. However the Wartime Housing schemes to supply housing for shipyard workers provided lots of work. McCarter & Nairne were awarded supervision of this work for Vancouver and the Island. They asked James to undertake the local supervision.

Three hundred houses made up the first contract in Esquimalt. A solid group of these homes built on the hill along Colville Road had part of the sidewalk raised and fenced above the road grade to solve the problem of the different levels. The project filled many vacant lots throughout the municipality. The plans and elevations all came from Ottawa and the same basementless designs can be found all over Canada where war work required a supply of housing. The scheme called for two staff houses at Lockley and Admirals Road and an adjoining dining hall to accommodate single men. Considered temporary structures to be removed after the war, one of the staff houses still exists and the dining hall is now the property of a private club.

The City of Victoria arranged to construct many more Wartime Houses. The sites on available lots spread over several neighbourhoods including Fernwood, Fairfield, James Bay and what is known today as the Sears-Hillside area. The houses are still in use, but now privately owned. By the time the Wartime Houses were built, I was a college student helping my father part-time in the office. We used to make inspection tours to check that the work had reached certain stages, so the contractors could be paid for the work completed: Foundations poured – Framing completed – Roofing installed – Electrical work roughed in – Plumbing roughed-in – Plumbing installed – Drywalling completed (for these buildings were not plastered) – Electrical wiring completed – Painting, interior and exterior – Landscaping, which consisted of levelling the front of the lot and laying sod only on the front part. For checking the paintwork, James carried a small mirror to see that the tops of doors were painted. Also he had a device to check that the window glass was the specified thickness and not the thinner standard glass. Laid against the window, this tester showed the thickness of the glass.

Ottawa tried to impose Eastern Canadian 40-foot lot sizes. Esquimalt, concerned that the houses might become slums after the war, insisted on 50-foot lots. Victoria also stuck to the 50-foot lot size. After the war, veterans eagerly bought these reasonably priced houses in which to raise their families. Today, these lot sizes make the properties quite valuable and they have so far not been included in development plans.

James continued to be associated with McCarter and Nairne for the Grant Block which they designed for Royal Roads in 1944. After the war he worked with them again as their local associate for the Western Match Factory at 754 Fairview Road in Esquimalt in 1945, and in 1946 for the Sidney Roofing plant on the Victoria West side of the harbour. Still plenty of work but not very creative.

Involvement with the professional associations was a continuing responsibility. James represented the Victoria Chapter and often took the night boat over to Vancouver to attend the AIBC meetings. Since his induction into the first Convocation of the College of Fellows of the Royal Architectural Institute of Canada held in Toronto in 1931, he represented BC at some of the RAIC conventions. In 1941 he was elected to the Senate of the College of Fellows of the RAIC. In a letter of congratulations, Norman Yarrow said, "I am quite sure that it is a well merited recognition, and I am glad that the Architects of Canada recognize ability in this manner."

For the February 1946 RAIC Annual Assembly at Quebec City his good friend, the architect L.Wilfrid Hargreaves, persuaded James to borrow the old buffalo coat he'd used in his early days of practice in Winnipeg. Hargreaves was a man of small stature and the coat was so long and heavy that James wondered how Wilfrid had managed to wear it. On the train trip across Canada James was joined by a number of the other Western architects, all bound for Quebec.

The Architectural Training Committee suggested that the four Schools of Architecture (McGill, Toronto, Manitoba and Beaux-Arts) should include Town Planning in their courses.

The professors present were unanimous in their opinion that there was insufficient time to include this subject in the two-year course that students took after their bachelor degree and interested students would have to take it as a post-graduate subject.

James noted a discrepancy in the time students had to serve in different provinces. Ontario students were required to serve only one year before registration, while graduates of the other Schools of Architecture served two years following graduation. "P. Leonard James proposed that students be required to serve <u>two</u> years in an architect's office after graduating from a recognized School of Architecture before becoming eligible for registration in any Province." This motion was carried.

The delegates learned of the government plan to subsidize veterans employed in architects' offices as "learners" with the government paying 2/3 of their salary The example given showed that the Government would pay $16 per week, the employer $8, for a total salary of $24.

Much discussion took place about establishing an RAIC office and Permanent Secretary in Ottawa. Only the Province of Quebec Association was opposed. The final resolution handed to the incoming Council asked them to consider the advisability of establishing such an office and a permanent Secretary by the end of December 1947.

While at the convention, James renewed his acquaintance with Percy Erskine Nobbs of Montreal, and Forsey Page, of Toronto. Returning across Canada with several architectural colleagues, James found his supply of whiskey had run out by the time the train made a 20-minute stop in Calgary. When he asked for directions to the nearest liquor store, the porter said, "It's just at the end of the street, Sir."

Perhaps lumbered with the immense buffalo coat Hargreaves had lent him, he walked to the store. When James was about to complete his purchase, the Alberta liquor store clerk asked for his address. Recalling the time of prohibition in Canada, and different provincial regulations regarding liquor purchases, he wondered if there might be some unusual wartime regulations still in effect regarding an out-of-province purchase. Should he mention BC? (There could conceivably be a waiting period.) Or pretend that he lived in Banff? He decided on a tentative reply, "At present, it's the CPR train down the street." An answer accepted without question.

Percy Nobbs, the architect responsible for the design of Birks stores across Canada, asked James to supervise construction of the first Birks store in Victoria, at 706 Yates Street. The site had formerly been the Poodle Dog Café, a popular haunt and one of the few open after dances at the Crystal Garden finished. Birks remained at the same location for 53 years before moving in May 2001. However the Nobbs elevation on Yates Street was altered some years ago.

People became concerned about the development of Victoria after the long period of the depression followed by the war, when all building projects and street planning had been more or less on hold. In February 1945, James spoke on "*How to Beautify Victoria*" at a Women's Radio Forum. He pointedly remarked, "I firmly believe we shall get nowhere until we have a comprehensive plan of development drawn up under the guidance of a properly appointed Town-Planning Commission. The City of Victoria has the power, under the Town-Planning Act of 1925, to appoint such a Commission."

He called for the union of Victoria, Oak Bay, Esquimalt and Saanich with a Town-Planning Commission to plan for the larger community as one unit. He cited the advantages of town-planning as maintaining the character of each district and the control of districts, to prevent premature sub-dividing with the loss of valuable agricultural land, and to promote the improvement of areas of tourist entry to the city, especially the harbour, which had soapworks, paintworks and many untidy industrial sites. He spoke of a Civic Centre in the vicinity of the present City Hall, the need for a new Arena and Picture Gallery. He also favoured the idea of a canal between Portage Inlet and Esquimalt Harbour, which would clean up the then very dirty inlet water and provide sightseeing for tourists and much pleasure for the local boating families.

The Oak Bay Junior High School (now the Cadboro Bay Road building of the High School) and the Esquimalt High School addition were well underway when the large Federal Building project became a reality. The partnership that survives to this day was formed as James & Polson, and soon took Robert Siddall into the partnership. The latter two partners became responsible for the completion of the schools and other work, so that James was left free to concentrate on his last and largest

The Architect in front of Oak Bay Junior High School, 2101 Cadboro Bay Road, Oak Bay, 1951 (Photo by author)

building. Later the partnership changed to Siddall Dennis Warner and today it continues as Warner James (A. James, not a relation of P.L. James.)

As a newly-trained typist, I started to work full-time for my father. He approved my desire to become an architect, but had doubts about the newly set up School of Architecture at the University of BC. He learned of some omissions in a design by the first Head of the Department and did not approve of the new school for my training. The Manitoba School in Winnipeg was much respected, but far away. He advised me to enrol with the International Correspondence Schools for their courses in Architectural Draughting and Building Procedures. I became an indentured architectural student training in his office, as many others had before me.

As part of the office staff, I saw at first hand how everyone in the building field – contractors, salesmen, draughting staff and clients, especially the doting lady clients – liked and respected my father. I was proud of the respect shown him on every side. I realized that this man, whom I considered a darling, but sometimes annoyingly old-fashioned at home, had earned his position by means of those old-fashioned values. Many times in dealing with local government people who didn't want to make things easy, or with disgruntled sub-contractors and clients unhappy about some part of the work, he calmed and settled dissatisfactions with firm but gentlemanly courtesy.

My father's last major residence was a joy to him. Mrs. Hope Yarrow, one of his favourite clients for whom he had done a

N.A. Yarrow, country home Orchard Gate, Elk Lake, Saanich, 1949 (Photo by author -BCA #hp68550)

number of alterations, wanted a house with really gracious spaces inside, set on a sizable country estate. The butterfly plan design of 1949 embraced a large patio that faced almost due West and overlooked the meadowland. After the many small wartime designs and their cramped plot plans, this commission made a most refreshing change.

For "Orchard Gate," (since renamed "Donnington Farm"), a house exemplifying Voysey's Vernacular Farm style, he used a veneer of old brick from demolished buildings laid up in single Flemish bond. The old bricks lent a soft colouration to the finished walls that could never have been achieved with raw new brick, and allowed the house to fit into its site as if grown from the soil – the old English Arts & Crafts concept.

Mr. Norman Yarrow kept close and knowledgeable watch over the construction and had metal labels stamped out at the Yarrow Shipyard to identify every wire and pipe in the furnace-utility room, which made it look very shipshape. When any discussion of extra costs came up, he used to jokingly warn, "My initials are N.A.Y., you know." The final cost came in at $180,000 so he didn't say "Nay" very often!

CHAPTER FOURTEEN
Glimpses of the Family

Bridge games, golf and gardening were the major pastimes in Victoria. My parents played neither bridge nor golf, but they made up for this lack by their total dedication to gardening. In the late 1920s they designed and developed the beautiful English perennial garden at 2385 Tod Road. They cut up the old lawn tennis court started in 1911, and planted large beds that overflowed with carnations, delphiniums, sneezeworts and tall Michaelmas daisies. One bed became a rose garden. Only a small central oval lawn remained of the old court. An early riser, my father enjoyed checking the garden. Then he took Molly her morning toast and coffee and could report any progress he had noticed before he left for the office.

East of the house, father maintained a large vegetable garden for some years and grew tall English peas, gooseberries and red currants. English families did enjoy their tennis games, and in my teen years he decided to level his vegetable garden and build a clay court. The court had a good foundation of clinkers from the furnace at the Jubilee Hospital. A big steamroller came through a temporary opening made in the fence. It packed the clinkers down and rolled the clay on top. The finished court was marked out with white tape installed with big "U" clips. The surface withstood much punishment, and we had a roller to use when necessary.

Players waiting their turns sat on folding canvas chairs under the weeping willow tree. Molly served homemade ginger beer to the tennis crowd. "Better go out on the court to open it," she would advise. The beer almost exploded out of the bottles. My father liked to tell his story of the dead mouse found in an opaque stone ginger beer bottle. He'd chuckled at his recollection. His guests usually responded with a story to equal or top his.

One day he said, "I've been thinking we should make a pool in the garden."

"Yes I've always wanted a pool," agreed my mother enthusiastically. "In fact this month's gardening magazine has a nice article about pools."

"I must have a look at it," said my father. "Of course we'll want to grow some water lilies."

"They show some beautiful iris growing in a bog garden off the main pool," replied my mother. "I like that idea." They settled on an "L" shaped pool with a bog garden and stocked the pool with water lilies from a nursery and goldfish from Woolworth's. In the spring baby fish could be seen flitting between the lily leaves but we found we had to protect the fish from predatory gulls with a chicken wire screen.

A succession of gardeners employed on a once-a-week basis weeded, cut the lawns and did the edges, but both my parents loved to do most of the work themselves. They rather distrusted most of the gardeners with their treasures, with good reason.

One Chinese gardener asked me if a plant was a weed or not. When I replied a bit uncertainly that it was not a weed, he said firmly "Him weed." And out it went.

Many pets shared our home and garden. At least one dog, a cat, rabbits, bantams and a pair of budgerigars, who had a special cage built into the new extention to the dining room. These birds always chittered when toast burnt in our flip-sided toaster had to be scraped.

My parents devoted each Easter Monday to setting out plants they had bought on Easter Saturday from the old Victoria Market on lower Cormorant Street, where the Civic Square is now situated. They both worked until exhausted. With the Layritz Nursery a regular stopping place, my parents established a fine bed of old-fashioned moss roses in the East garden. Most years they visited Pierre Timp's garden and splurged on 100 bulbs of special new tulips.

While at the market, my father always visited the stall of Mr. Askey, an English fishmonger who wore a boater (straw hat) and a large navy blue-and-white striped apron. There he purchased the kippers he enjoyed so much. He had to cook his own fish because my mother not only didn't like kippers, but claimed that even the smell of them made her "turn green" – perhaps the reason she always stayed in bed until breakfast was over.

Lots of parties took place either at the Savages' home or ours. The Groos cousins lived near us and one of them came over to look after me for the Savage parties. "Looking-after" was an unpaid volunteer job in those days, but with plenty of good eats provided.

The Savages put on fancy dress parties at New Year's for a number of years. As I grew older, it became a tradition to hold a "black tie" – dinner jacket and evening dress – New Year's dance at our house. My mother always insisted on a short Christmas tree, which stood on the closed top of her grand piano to allow plenty of room for our seasonal activities. Records played on our wind-up gramophone supplied music for dancing in the early days.

Father used to mix up a pretty potent punch bowl, which he tasted and tested. To get into the New Year's spirit he followed up the tasting and testing with a first toast to the New Year when it arrived in Halifax at eight in the evening, Victoria time. Newfoundland was not yet part of Canada, so he didn't have to welcome New Year there. As our guests arrived, he joined them in general toasts and they all made a point of celebrating the arrival of New Year in Toronto. After dancing and more convivial drinks New Year's arrived in Winnipeg – another special toast. By the time New Year reached Calgary, my father often succumbed to a queasy head and had to go and lie down. Some years he actually missed the local arrival altogether!

But the best parties were at Christmas time. We played charades, acting-out each syllable with the spoken-word form of the game. Players were encouraged to search the house for suitable costumes for their parts and they contrived quite elaborate scenes. Sometimes bedspreads appeared draped as ball gowns; ostrich feathers or a feather boa rummaged from the costume drawers in the box room were used to create elegant effects; our potato-ricer searched out from its kitchen cupboard, came into play as a microphone for a radio station

My father never forgot the panto routines. In the 1930s, he wrote several pantomimes for our family to perform, full of puns and the old professional tricks he had seen in England. My parents performed a clown act wearing costumes in the Commedie dell'Arte tradition. He "shared" a string of sausages out between himself, and the other clown (Mother), who did not speak at all but did her part in dumb show and carried an umbrella. He would count out to her, "One for you." Then, with a rather calculating look, he'd say, "One – (he'd put one down) – for me **too**." (And he'd slip two more on his own plate.)

"One more for you. And one more for me – *too*." (Slap, slap, slap went the sausages.)

This clown "business" continued until the second clown slowly realized his trickery. After a long process of sharing her mimed confusion with the audience, she then became very indignant and chased him around the room, beating him with her umbrella.

Preparing for the Christmas season mother made puddings in November, and rich dark Christmas cakes, one of which was always saved for Dad's birthday the next December. Dad started his preparations early, gathering Oregon Grape berries when ripe and soaking them for months in gin and sugar. He called the resulting rich red liqueur "Gone Gin" or "Oreygin."

My father became interested in philately when Grandfather Johnston died and a large old collection came to the family. He and his friend, John Anderson both belonged to the local Philatelic Society. In 1936 John was President and my father took his turn as President the following year. The society met once a month at the Empress Hotel; the manager, Mr. Hodges, was also a member of the society. Members with stamps for sale could assemble them in trading books and circulate them among the members. Stamps could be bought or sold via these "stamp circuits." With a world collection to start with my father decided to specialize in the British Empire. His collection won first prize in the Centenary Philatelic show in 1943 which celebrated 100 years since the postal service started in Britain. He developed friends worldwide who collected. They exchanged first day covers, long before the marvelous printed envelopes that match the new stamp designs became available.

During the Second World War air-letter forms became popular, one thin blue page that came ready to be folded into an envelope along printed lines. These air-letters required more expensive franking than letters that travelled by land and sea. Canada issued a beautiful blue 7-cent airmail stamp for use on these form letters.

On winter evenings at home my parents would read aloud in front of the fire until my bedtime. A chapter at a time, they built up my appreciation of *Ivanhoe*, the Robert Louis Stevenson books and other classics. My father often retired to the dining room to go over office accounts or to browse the latest stamp circuit from the Philatelic Society, while my mother sat and knitted, enjoying *Gang Busters* and other favourite crime programmes on the radio. But many evenings my father read to her, sharing articles he had found to be of interest in *Punch* or *The Listener*.

For the Royal Visit in 1939, Oak Bay Municipality constructed bleachers outside the Municipal Hall at Hampshire Road and Oak Bay Avenue. The family purchased tickets to sit there and watch the monarchs pass. The city and each municipality wanted King George VI and Queen Elizabeth to visit them. The resulting Royal Tour was a long one and the crowds along the route very thin in places. Our gardener of that time, Bill Butler, and his sisters drove frantically from one part of the route to another, to wave their union jacks. They wondered if the King and Queen eventually recognized them. One of the sisters insisted that the Queen nudged King George and made him wave to the family on their third curbside appearance.

As a member of the Royal Visit Committee, my father had designed the banners used along the Oak Bay part of the route and my parents were invited to the Council Chamber at Victoria City Hall to see the King and Queen sign the Visitors' Book. Father received a commemorative medal for being on the Royal Visit Committee.

When the Second World War started, an interned German ship, the *Wesser*, arrived in Esquimalt. A neighbour's son worked as a watchman at the dock where the ship was tied up. He brought home a young cat from the ship. It was a real hunter and chose our garden as a good place to catch birds. Not a popular sport in our books – and an "enemy" cat at that! My father nicknamed this animal "The Nasty Nazi." Repeated sprayings with the hose did not deter this cat. We finally caught him and gave him a thorough dunking in the lily pool. He ran off and did not bother us again.

During the war, cars could not travel with headlights on, just parking lights, or special shields that only allowed a small crack of light. To blackout the city from any perceived Japanese threat, the whole city went without streetlights and all houses had to have blackout curtains. Only beyond Royal Oak could full headlights be used.

My father volunteered for service in Oak Bay as an ARP; (Air Raid Precautions) warden. The government issued him a gas mask, a tool and a khaki coverall; his major responsibility was a gas main on nearby Musgrave Street. In case of an air raid or bombing he was to use the tool to turn off the main with 37 turns of the handle. After the war, he used the coverall for dirty jobs in the garden for many years, but the gas mask atrophied on a beam in our basement.

CHAPTER FIFTEEN
Crowning Glory

When approached to take on designing the new Federal Building and Post Office in 1947, James was nearly 70 and seriously considering retirement. However, everyone felt the commission would be the crowning glory to his long career. His good friend Jack McCarter of McCarter & Nairne, who at the time had the commission for the Vancouver Post Office building, as well as C. Gustave Brault, Chief Architect of the Department of Public Works in Ottawa, and Fred Dawson, Chief Architect for BC, were all most persuasive. The Honourable R.W. Mayhew who represented Victoria and was the Minister of Fisheries – and who lived in a James house – insisted that he accept this honour.

Finally he agreed, but only if his brother, Douglas, joined him to undertake the work in a revival of the James & James partnership. For this the largest commission he had ever undertaken, my father no longer felt up to taking sole responsibility. Douglas agreed. They set up an office in the old Campbell building to produce the working drawings. They had a fine English draughtsman, Stan Collings, to assist with the work. The James, Polson & Siddall partnership continued to work out of the Royal Trust building office. They took over the Oak Bay and Esquimalt school jobs he had under construction.

Victoria Federal Building and Post Office at Yates and Government Streets
(Photographer George Simpson - Author's collection - BCA #hp68170)

Completing the drawings for the large five-storey Federal Building and letting the contracts for the construction took the brothers a whole year. At the end of that year, Douglas, ever the laid-back younger brother, announced, "I've just turned 60 and I'm going to retire." And he did, leaving full responsibility for the erection of the building on his older brother's shoulders. He accepted this great disappointment rather stoically, but my mother was furious at Douglas' desertion which left my father with almost four more years of work completing the $2,500,000 contract. He had the help of a good clerk of works and staff, but the senior James brother had always taken his responsibilities very seriously and he felt the pressure, which he had hoped to avoid.

Government of Canada buildings had to be constructed of Canadian materials. Haddington Island stone faced the reinforced concrete structure. The marble in the lobby came from Quebec; its gray patterning is quite striking, but the only coloured veins are greenish. Canadian marbles lack the dramatic colouring that can be found further south in Vermont and other states. Queen Victoria's crown, an artifact from the demolished first Victoria Post Office, which had been on part of the site, is incorporated in stonework near the main lobby doors.

Originally some discussion took place about using the whole block from Yates to View Street for the new building. Perhaps this scheme would have been too expensive, but James also felt the little Rattenbury bank was worth saving.

The new building contained an intriguing requirement for the postal service, an observation passage built in the ceiling over the perimeter of the whole postal area. An inspector could watch workers below, unobserved through a continuous slit window. The passage was only used if dishonesty was suspected among the employees. Measurements of this passage showed headroom of only five feet under a major beam. Anyone doing an inspection in the passage needed to be careful as they passed this low spot lighted only by whatever light came in through the observation slit. This passage ran through both the men's and the women's toilet areas as well as the main postal area. His partner Bob Siddall recalls that a control in the passage could stop the flushing action of the toilets.

James's nephew, Harold Groos, took a great interest in the building. He had studied architecture while at sea during the Second World War and went into the real estate business after the war. He took his small son, Charles, to see the job and talked to him about everything that Uncle Percy had to plan and consider for the Post Office. Charles, impressed by all he learned about Uncle Percy, said seriously – as only a four-year-old can, "But Auntie Molly helps him too," – a quote that lives on in the family.

After those years of responsibility, the opening made a fitting

The opening of the Federal Building and Post Office, Victoria, by Prime Minister Louis St. Laurent, P. Leonard James on the right, 1952
(Photographer George Simpson - Author's collection - BCA # hp68133)

honour and a very special day for P. Leonard James, the architect. He joined the group by the front entrance of the Post Office and Federal Building with the Honourable Mr. Mayhew and local politicians. Prime Minister Louis St. Laurent came to Victoria for this official opening on September 5th, 1952.

In the 1990s, the James name would become more noticably associated with the building. Forty years after the Federal Building and Post Office opened, the introduction of new safety standards required that Government buildings be earthquake proofed. Privatization and the new Canada Post Office service did not require the large downtown Postal Lobby. The former postal area was altered into space for six shops that opened onto Government Street. The Federal Government undertook seismic upgrading, with concrete and steel pilings to bedrock and steel bands around the top of the five-storey building, at a cost of $10,000,000. In effect the building had to be gutted to bring it up to the new safety standards. They planned to retain the use of the top three floors for Federal Departments and, to allow one floor for private office use.

As it was no longer to be used as the Federal Building and Post Office, the Government Services and Public Works Department ran an advertisement in the *Times Colonist* asking local people to suggest suitable names. "The name should have some significance to the City of Victoria. The name of a person may be offered, if that person made a contribution to the well-being of Canada or the community and is no longer living."

I did not see the notice, but my son, James, fortunately, did and he phoned me.

"What about it, mother?"

I think we were allowed a six-week period to submit suggestions. Family and friends rallied round. The cousins laughed and said they always called it "Uncle Percy's Post Office," a name that was never a contender! People wanted to use different versions of the name P. Leonard James, some wanted "Percy James," others "Leonard James," even "Percy Leonard James." Too long a name would just become the "James Building," which would have been confused with James Bay already so well-known in Victoria. So I picked *P.L. James Place* as definitive, yet with an alliterative flow of words. Many groups received photo-copies of the name forms from the paper. A sign-up sheet for a well-attended event one day produced 140 names. I complained to my son who was also busy collecting: "This seems like overkill."

"That's what you have to do," he said.

Eventually the Department informed me that 48 suggestions had been received and so it seemed that our "overkill" ought to win out. Nevertheless we harboured some concern that the government might have already decided on the name of someone in the political field. I did not really believe in our success the whole year we waited for the decision. Then, in confidence, we learned that "P. L. James Place" had been chosen with 85 percent of the 521 suggestions for the use of that name. The architect of the building would be honoured.

The family had to wait another year with this secret, as the minister of the day, a man elected in an Eastern riding, was unwilling to fit in a trip to Western Canada. However after a change of ministers, Madame Diane Marleau , who also represented an Easten riding, arranged a trip to the West and invitations were sent out. When I met Madame Marleau, she said, "I am so pleased you gathered so many names supporting your father's name. Often when we advertise for a name, three suggestions come in, each with three votes and we don't know what to do."

Madame Marleau, David Anderson and Mayor Cross attended a small reception arranged in the Lobby. The current chairman and a past chairman of the Hallmark Society both attended. My daughter, Janet, and I were picked up and chauffeured to this event in a Government Services and Public Works vehicle. Madame Marleau and I unveiled the bronze plaque with inscriptions in French and English soon after eleven o'clock on June 24th, 1996. At the time the bronze letters saying "Federal Building" were still in place over the lobby entrance doors, but soon these were replaced with bronze letters proclaiming *P.L. James Place*. Before we went upstairs to take part in cutting a large cake with white icing emblazoned "P.L. James Place" in red and blue, with touches of yellow, the programme allowed me to say a few words to the guests and family members who were present. It was my chance to admit that I had been the last James of the family and the surname has died out. However I named my elder son "James," and he and his wife have used the name for their son. I took the chance to acknowledge that, if it hadn't been for my son noticing the advertisement, we might not all be there basking in the reflected glory of P.L. James. My grandson, six-year-old Brian James Alan Cross, wondered why I choked up and could barely continue, as I spoke of the great respect my father had always been shown. It was a touching, special day for us all.

CHAPTER SIXTEEN

Retirement Years

At last James earned a period of retirement. He thought about returning to England to live, but my mother was firm. "We can't possibly," she said. "Rosemary is a Canadian working in Toronto and about to marry another Canadian. It would be too difficult. Anyway, we missed the war living in the comfort of Canada and would never fit in again in England."

Soon after, grandchildren arrived. Though James kept saying he had had his "three score and ten" years as allotted in the Bible, he wanted to see his grandchildren as often as possible. In addition to keeping up a good correspondence, we visited from East to West and vice versa year about. He had to admit that he found these visits rather intense, tiring affairs and declared: "I'm glad to see you arrive and I'm glad to see you leave again for your own home."

In his retirement years the AIBC and the RAIC conferred Honorary Memberships in 1956 and 1967 respectively. Hope Yarrow, now Lady Stuart Taylor persuaded him, in view of their long time association, to undertake alterations and a garden gate at her newly purchased Lansdowne home.

Through the 1960s, my parents continued to enjoy their house and garden, although with more help than before. My mother diligently bottled and preserved enough fruit and jams to fill every shelf in the pantry and made the house redolent with her *pot-pourri*.

Father enjoyed much better health than she did. In his later years, he felt the cold on his pate, and wore a beret round home and at table. But in his late 80s, he became more and more senile. My mother would not acknowledge his senility, or that anything was wrong. So she never hired a proper live-in helper which might have ameliorated their problems. Having suffered several *petit mal* attacks herself, she had lost her ability to smile, to be resilient and to be cheerful. No longer totally reasonable, she made up for it by sheer determination. Her pronouncements sounded very abrupt. "Oh, he's just tired all the time," she said, rather crossly. "He's not the same nice man I married 55 years ago. He is often *most* disagreeable."

On my visits, I found him to be his usual polite self, if a little fuzzy-minded. He could still accurately remember facts about his architectural practice and could quote the correct price of a contract from 40 years before. At the same time he would ask, "Where's my cup of tea, dear?" as he held it in his hand.

The fact that I lived on the Prairies threw a great deal more responsibility on the cousins who lived nearby and who had always loved my parents. They devoted much time and care to Uncle Percy and Auntie Molly, but when events seemed to impinge on financial concerns, they would contact me. I carried on with family life in Saskatoon, upset to be so far from my parents and dreading every phone call. In their final year I had to make six flying trips to the coast.

They behaved much as usual on my arrival and things appeared to be quite normal. Mother would casually announce, "I've just baked some cookies for you, dear, they're in the biscuit box." The cousins and helper said, "Yes, she utterly exhausted herself. She hasn't been near the kitchen in months. After the baking episode, she took to her bed for the rest of the day!"

Father always seemed worried about money. After he finally relinquished the handling of his accounts to his trust company, he still telephoned them, every day. He announced quite seriously that he planned to take a job as an architect being offered in India – though he felt he was really too old for it. He was 90! It distressed all of us to see his nagging concern about his quite adequate finances.

I used to refer facetiously to the major dangers of old age, as the Three F's: "Falls, Fire and Famine." One or other of these dangers often seemed about to overtake my father in his last years. Every morning during one of my visits, I observed that, on rising, he turned up the thermostat. Next he turned the electric stove on HIGH to boil his kettle. Then feeling cold, although he had just cranked up the furnace thermostat, he teetered off down our dog-leg basement stair to ascertain if the oil furnace had indeed come on, for his deafness did not permit him to hear the roar of the awakened furnace. Quite often after this basement visit, he forgot completely about the kettle heating for his tea. The helper who arrived at nine o'clock said he had burnt out five kettles in almost as many weeks.

It is most probable that "Famine" took its toll. Really thin, he might have benefitted from a longer mealtime. The helper always gave them a hot lunch, and washed their dishes before she left. Father ate very slowly in his final years, but no doubt tried to accommodate the helper so she could catch her bus. He had always been used to the larger meal at night and, probably, still expected it.

I and my great friend Joan Considine, who was like a second daughter to my parents, took him to town and got him a new hat to replace the shabby one with stained sweatband that he habitually wore. Family members were all concerned to see the drabness of age overtaking Uncle Percy's dapper image. We went to lunch after this purchase to a restaurant in Bastion Square and he seemed to enjoy himself immensely. He took to singing some old music hall songs with a twinkle in his eye. Conducting with rhythmic, but careful flourishes of his soup spoon, much to the amusement of the young business lunchers at surrounding tables, he regaled us with such songs as, "She could pass for 43 in the dark with the light behind her" and "You could see all the way to Wembley, if it wasn't for the chimbleys in between." When we left the restaurant he insisted, new hat in hand, on ushering several of the young businesswomen through the door with gentlemanly courtesy. Regarding the purchase of the hat, Mother commented flatly, "Unnecessary! A waste of money."

As I lived in Saskatoon, the cousins came in for the responsibility of looking after Uncle Percy, when Auntie Molly had to go to hospital. Mother left saying confidently, "Now, Jimmy, there's everything you need in the larder and the fridge and Mrs. Treadaway (a rather emaciated senior who came in for the half day), will be here in the morning."

During her hospital stay in early December 1969 my cousin, Harold Groos phoned me in Saskatoon and said a change must be made. I got hold of her doctor and told him he had to keep my mother in hospital until I could get out to Victoria and arrange for my father to be moved into a private care hospital. The doctor waffled: "I don't know that the hospital will allow it," he said. To which I replied firmly, "You *must* arrange it." And he did.

I did not realize when I set out on the first available flight that I would be away from my young family over the entire Christmas holiday period. After consultations with doctors, the trust company manager and lawyers, getting my father into the Sandringham Hospital at a moment's notice was comparatively easy.

My days became full of hospital visits to my parents. First I headed for a visit at the private hospital, where I would find my father strapped into a chair with a restraining jacket. Because he didn't want to be there, he had headed off home through one of the "alarm" exit doors, only to be recaptured near Foul Bay Road. The staff couldn't believe he had gone so far so quickly.

Then I stopped at the Jubilee to see mother and reassured her with the whopping white lie; "Father is comfortably settled in the Sandringham." Finally, I would drag myself in the door of the empty family home and head for a badly needed booster shot from my dad's drink cupboard.

Mother came home a few days later. I stayed on over Christmas. Joan and Mike Considine came to our Christmas dinner.

Father had by then settled down well enough to be allowed out of the Sandringham to visit for the meal. Mother insisted that a cooked half-turkey from the delicatessen be ordered. Joan worked hard with her charm and her delightful stories, raising a smile from my father. Her magic kept everyone cheerful at our time-honoured family table.

By the time I went home on New Year's Eve, I had procured a live-in housekeeper for mother and it seemed possible that father might be able to return home. But on January 3rd, 1970, he died, a short while after Harold Groos, visited him. Harold reported that Uncle Percy had recalled the early days of music hall on that visit and entertained him with some verses of: "I can't get away to marry you today, my wife won't let me!" By the time Harold returned home that afternoon, there was a call to say Percy Leonard James had passed peacefully away. I thanked God for this gentle end to his life in his 92nd year. Mother directed that he be buried with a single red rose laid by him in his coffin.

Only six months later his wife, Rose Jesurun, known as "Molly," died in the 87th year of her age on June 11th, 1970.

CHAPTER SEVENTEEN
The Legacy

Percy Leonard James had a guiding hand in the development of the profession of architecture in Canada. On his arrival in 1906 he became a Member of the newly formed Alberta Association of Architects. Always concerned about standards for the practice of architecture, in 1906 the year of its formation, he became a Charter Member of the National body, called the Architectural Institute of Canda. Within a year it became the Royal Architectural Institute of Canada. After moving to BC he took the position of treasurer in the local Society of Architects and worked towards the formation of a proper provincial Institute. When the Institute was constituted in 1920 he became Charter Member #31 of the Architectural Institute of British Columbia and for many years represented the Victoria Chapter at meetings in Vancouver. Over the years the RAIC honoured him with the first Fellowship awarded in British Columbia and later with a seat on the Senate.

When I cleared out the family home of sixty years in 1970, it seemed at first that the record I had of his work was pitifully small. It included some old progress photos of the Crystal Garden, the Royal Jubilee Hospital and the Federal Building. Among the stored possessions in the basement, I had rather expected to find trunks of old working drawings. However these had all disappeared and at the time it was a relief not to have to worry about them.

On my return to Saskatoon, I realized I had only a small book with photos of my father's residential commissions. The houses had been standing for 30-odd years, when my mother suggested that he should take pictures showing them in their mature gardens. She felt it a good project to occupy some of his retirement days, and they had fun doing it together. The current owners, wondering who these two old dears were, often came out to talk to them. Mother with her stick, but wearing a stylish hat of course, no doubt made suggestions as he aimed their aged box camera, which took fairly good photographs. On learning they were the architect of the house and his wife, an invitation to come in for a cup of tea invariably followed and some of his memories about the construction and prices of the house could be brought to light and shared.

It wasn't until I moved back to Victoria in 1978 that I learned that all the existing working drawings had been given by my father to the surviving partnership, Siddall, Dennis & Warner. R.W. Siddall arranged to store these plans and he installed a sign in the office: "In continuous practice since 1909." The plans of Hubert Savage were also given into his safekeeping. In August 1996 these drawings went to the City of Victoria Archives (CVA), where they are stored as the *P. Leonard James Collection* and the *Hubert Savage Collection*. They represent a fine record of many of their buildings and give definitive information. Although the plans of the partnership have both names on them, the collections at the CVA indicate which jobs each partner designed.

Then a former neighbour of my parents said, "You know all your father's papers are safe: they are in the BCA." These papers had been kept in our box room, but when the upstairs was made into an apartment after I married, the box room became its kitchen and my father had to find a new home for his papers. I should have been aware things might still be stored in the attic, because as a teenager I had helped him put old issues of architectural magazines up there. I used to tease him, "How many houses in Victoria are insulated with old *Architectural Records*, *Pencil Points* and *Architectural Journals*?" But as the apartment upstairs was rented when my parents died, it seemed nothing to do with the remainder of our family home, and I forgot about those magazines as I dealt with the many other family things.

It turned out that Chad Evans, an art historian who as a small boy lived next door to my parents, rented the apartment at 2385 Tod Road when he got married. One day, he became curious about the access panel to the attic in the upstairs corridor ceiling and climbed up to see what was there. He found boxes and boxes of my father's office records. And being an historian he knew what should be done with them. But when he suggested they should go to the British Columbia Archives (BCA), his landlord did not agree, and claimed them as his property. So there was an anxious waiting period until the landlord eventually sold the house, and told Evans he could do what he wanted with the papers. He donated the James personal papers to the BCA in 1976. I am certainly grateful to him for his curiosity, for without it the papers, which have supplied so much information about the jobs of P. Leonard James, might still be in the attic of the old family home or even destroyed.

The records are filed under Add.MSS 502. This wealth of material dates from 1920 through 1940 and discloses some commissions for which there are no other records. These papers make James probably the best-documented architect of the period in Victoria. This collection takes up two metres of shelf space at the BCA. The material is varied. In some cases only a sketch plan or a specification has been saved; in others, letters, notes and prices are recorded. There are six boxes on residential work, three on general commercial jobs – including the two Colwood Clubhouses and the CPR commissions, five boxes on the Provincial Royal Jubilee Hospital, and a couple of boxes with mixed notebooks and miscellaneous loose items including the rules for the Jubilee hospital competition.

These records show the entire range of commissions of a practicing architect. I have not concentrated only on major commissions, for he dealt with buildings large and small depending on his clients' needs, and also with buildings that clients wanted altered.

Having typed for my father in later years, I knew his habit of noting on specifications for certain trades, "take from Such-and-such spec," which would point to a job for the "Such-and-suches," even if the drawings had been lost. Checking the name in directories, an address could be found. Then, with luck, blueprints of the plans at a municipal building department would confirm the find. Occasionally the present owners would still have the original owner's set of blueprints, and at least one owner had these framed. However it was a challenge to locate some houses with the address given only as "Uplands," "Thetis Island," "Ten Mile Point" or some street that has suffered a name change.

Aside from this great trove of information and the many buildings that survive, one needs to look at his plans. The titles, the printing and the working drawings mostly came from his own hand and are examples of the English training of the period. It was not in his nature to be flamboyant. One can see his art and feel his empathy with the styles, his concern with details that are always suitable, lightened with the application of his own ideas; he never interpreted the styles in an over-decorated manner, as some architects did. His work represents the flowering of the pre-war Tudor Revival style and the English Arts & Crafts style that replaced it in Canada just after the First World War. The Tudor influence has never left, but with time the renderings have become ever weaker and more watered down in the hands of diverse practitioners. After his last visit to England inspired by International Style examples he used the style for schools and designed several houses in what became known as Art Moderne or Streamlined Moderne. James's last and largest building – the Victoria Federal Building and Post Office on the southwest corner of Government and Yates Streets – is in the Moderne tradition and is considered an example of the Stripped Classicism style.

Clusters of P. Leonard James's residences can be found in the Rockland-St. Charles-Pemberton area., and throughout Oak

Bay and the Uplands.

Credit is due to Percy Leonard James for the only heated salt-water pool under glass in the world. He placed the building under the largest area of glass on the continent. And it was his concept to float the Crystal Garden on a concrete raft.

For the CPR Marine Terminal he made the first use in Canada of cast stone, a new, more reasonably priced material than stone that had been used by several leading architects in the States.

The Jubilee Hospital South Wing had the strength to allow an additional floor to be added in later years. In it and in all his work his designs incorporated the originality, good taste, appreciation of design, and the sound knowledge of construction that his first boss in London had foreseen.

My father believed that an architect should consider his client's wishes first and foremost, but be open to new ideas as they came along. He intuitively used a wide range of design possibilities and always considered the suitability of the design to the site and the neighbourhood.

His facile mastery of the medium, adept handling of space, and his ability to combine elements of different styles have made a major and lasting contribution to the extensive and diverse range of architecture in Victoria.

Appendix

Lists Of Commissions 1909 – 1954
by P. Leonard James FRAIC, MAIBC

Information from indicated Archives, with updating from City of Victoria Residential Building Plans database being compiled by the Victoria Heritage Foundation, and Building Permits, the Oak Bay database compiled by Larry McCann, and from other sources as mentioned.

Partnerships are indicated where they apply. The commissions of the James & Savage partnership are credited where the authorship is known from the drawing collections at City of Victoria Archives. Costs where given, include contractor's quote with extras, and plumbing and heating prices.

1909 Mrs. J.W. Lysle - Residence *Stonehenge Park* (Extant)
    1179 Munro Street, Esquimalt
    Contractor: William A. Gleason
    Cost: $7,000
    Esquimalt Archives / Esquimalt Assessment Rolls

1909 Senator G.H. Barnard - Alterations to 1462 Rockland Avenue, Victoria   TOH / CVPDD

c.1909 Mrs. Johnston - Bungalow (Extant)
    2279 Lincoln Street, possibly moved from 2358 Beach Drive, Oak Bay
    Madge Wolfenden Hamilton / Article with photograph

1910 Judge William Galliher - Residence, *Bannavern* 15 rooms (Extant as condominiums)
    914 St. Charles Street, Victoria
    Contractor: N. Benneck & Sons
    Cost: $14,000   BP#1915 / CVPDD
    BCA / CVA

1910 Hannah James - Residence *Durleston* (Extant, additions)
    2385 Tod Road, Oak Bay
    Cost: $3,500
    OBBD [later became P. Leonard James's own residence]

1910 Duncan Ross - Residence (Extant)
    1560 Rockland Avenue, Victoria
    Cost: $10,000   BP#02145 / CVPDD

1910 W.S. Drewry - Residence (Extant)
    727 Linden Avenue, Victoria
    Cost: $5000   BP#1886 / CVPDD

JAMES & JAMES PARTNERSHIP FORMED IN 1910

1910 Oak Bay Municipal Hall (Demolished)
    Oak Bay Avenue, corner of Hampshire, Oak Bay
    Photo dated 1910
    Cost $14,000
    Detail of Notice Board, dated 1912 (ORB)
    Architects: James & James
    CVA / Photos, family knowledge

1910 Algernon H. Pease - Residence later named *Drummadoon* (Extant)
    off Sinclair Road, moved and now University of Victoria Medical Services, Saanich
    Architects: James & James
    Article by Geoffrey Castle / Madge Wolfenden Hamilton

1910 A.W. Bridgman Commercial Building - Alterations and new façade with Art Nouveau motifs at 604 Broughton Street, Victoria (Extant)
    Architects: James & James
    CVPDD / *This Week* June 1912.

1911 Arthur E. Haynes - Building two storey brick (Demolished)
    731-1/2 Fort Street, Victoria
    Architects: James & James
    CVA – P.L. James Collection

1911 Deans Block - commercial building (Extant)
777 Fort Street, Victoria
Architects: James & James
CVA – P.L. James Collection

1911 Francis F. Hedges - Residence (Extant with some alteration into triplex)
1327 Arm Street, Victoria
Cost: $3,500   BP#2832 / CVPDD
Architects: James & James

1911 J.E. Shenk - Residence (Demolished)
512 Selkirk Avenue, Victoria Arm, Victoria
Contractor: J.E. Shenk
Cost: $4000   BP#3011 / CVPDD
Architects: James & James

c.1911 Railway Station - not built
Architects: Rattenbury, James & James
BCA plan on file

1911 Hewitt & Hinton - Residence (Extant)
Probably a speculative house
1334 Minto Street
Cost: $2,160 BP#3350 / CVPDD
Architects: James & James

1911 Hewitt & Hinton - Residence (Extant)
Probably a speculative house
1338 Minto Street, Victoria
Cost: $2,160 BP#3350 / CVPDD
Architects: James & James

1911 Hewitt & Hinton - Residence (Extant)
Probably a speculative house
1344 Minto St.
Cost: $2,800 BP#3349 / CVPDD
Architects: James & James

1911 St. Mary's Anglican Church (Demolished)
Elgin Street, Oak Bay
Cost: $6,332 (seating for 250)
Architects: James & James
BCA *History of St. Mary's Church, Oak Bay, Victoria* by Percy James / CVA / photos

1912 Balmoral Hotel (Demolished)
1107-9 Douglas Street, Victoria
Contractor Thomas Catterall
Cost: $7,000
Architects: James & James
Architect, Builder & Engineer, August 15, 1912 / *This Week*, June 1, 1912 / ORB

1912 C.S. Baxter - Residence (Extant, now two apartments)
1790 Beach Drive, (formerly 2685 Cranmore Road) Oak Bay
Contractor: Palmer
Architects: James & James
Blueprints filed at OBBD / ORB

1912 Frank Burrell - Residence (Extant, now apartments)
1064 Beverley Place, Victoria
Contractor: J.E. Shenk
Cost: $9,000 BCA / ORB / CVPDD
Architects: James & James

1912 G.H.S. Edwards - Residence (Demolished by 1965)
1312 Beach Drive, Oak Bay
Cost: $8,880 ORB / Photo
Architects: James & James

1912 Frank W.H. Giolma - Residence (Extant)
35 Olympia Avenue, Victoria
Cost: $3,600 ORB / Madge Wolfenden Hamilton
Architects: James & James

1912 E.H. Harrison - Residence (Extant, with addition)
50 Highland, renamed King George Terrace, Oak Bay
Cost: $4000 ORB
Architects: James & James

1912 Dr. J.D. Helmcken - Residence (Extant, now apartments)
1015 Moss Street, Victoria
Contractor: J.E. Shenk
Cost: $14,800 ORB / CVPDD
Architects: James & James

1912 Herbert F. Hewett - Residence and Hall
1535 Davie Street, Victoria
Residence on Clara Street in City Directory (Extant, altered)
BCA
Hall at 1602 Redfern Street, on rear of same lot when lot was larger (Extant, altered into a residence)
Architects: James & James
ORB / Madge Wolfenden Hamilton

1912 H.S. Lott - Residence (Extant, porte-cochère added by Maclure with other alterations about 1915)
1220 Transit Road, (formerly St James Street) Oak Bay
Architects: James & James
Madge Wolfenden Hamilton / Isla Terry

1912 D.M. Malin - Residence (Extant, alterations)
1324 St. David Street, Oak Bay
Contractor: F. Wood
Architects: James & James
ORB

1912 J.W. Morris - Residence (Extant, now apartments)
1558 Beach Drive, Oak Bay
Contractor: A.H. Mitchell
Cost: $25,000 CVA / Coloured perspective drawing in BCA
Architects: James & James

1912 Oak Bay Grocery (Extant with added "Tudorizing" now The Blethering Place)
2252 Oak Bay Avenue, Oak Bay
Contractor: F. Wood
Architects: James & James
ORB / OBHB

1912 Oak Bay Five Room Wooden Elementary School at Willows, Oak Bay (Demolished 1956)
Contractor: Eli Hume
Architects: James & James
Architect, Builder & Engineer July 1913, p.13

1912 Oak Bay Four Room Wooden School and Manual Training Department (Demolished)

Oak Bay Avenue (site of present Municipal Hall)
Architects: James & James
ORB / BCA photo

1912 J.T. Reid - Residence (Extant)
1393 Rockland Avenue, Victoria
Contractor: A.H. Mitchell ORB / CVPDD
Cost: $13,600
Architects: James & James

1912 Richardson & Stephens - Alterations (store)
Architects: James & James
ORB (No details)

1912 Duncan Ross - Garage (No details)
Architects: James & James
ORB

1912 Salt Spring Island Trading Coy. (No details)
ORB

1912 Surrey Building - Alterations to store fronts (Altered)
1217-1243 Broad Street / 631-637 Yates Street
Architects: James & James

1912 Arthur Small - Residence
St. Patrick Street, Oak Bay (not found)
Contractor: probably C.G. Hurrell
BCA Box 1/8 Bullen specification copied from Arthur Small specification / Madge Wolfenden Hamilton

1912 Beveridge - Demolished
2248 Oak Bay Avenue, Oak Bay
Architects: James & James
McCann Database

c.1913 Rev. Wm. Barton of St. Mary's - Bungalow (Extant, altered, enlarged)
2422 Esplanade Avenue, Oak Bay
Madge Wolfenden Hamilton

1913 Mrs. Elizabeth L. Watts - Residence (Extant)
1025 Joan Crescent, Victoria
Contractor: Eli Hume
Cost: $6,750   BP#5967 ORB / CVPDD
Architects: James & James
ORB / CVPDD

1913 St. Mary's Church - addition, North and South aisles, (seating increased to 400) West end and Vestry (Demolished)
Elgin Road, Oak Bay
Cost: $5,000
James & James

n.d. St. Mary's Church - North aisle addition - another 100 seats
Elgin Street, Oak Bay
Cost: $1,100
James & James

1914 Capt. H. Jarvis - Residence (Extant)
1050 St. Patrick Street, Oak Bay
Contractor: George Calder
Cost: $3,600 OBBD
Architects: James & James
n.d. Weston "Plans and specifications supplied"

1913 Directory E.E. Weston (contractor) a resident of the Balmoral Hotel.
Architects: James & James
ORB

n.d. C.R. Davidson - Four Bungalows (Demolished)
1847 Crescent Road, Victoria
CVA 1-0420

JAMES & JAMES PARTNERSHIP ENDS IN 1914

1919 Oak Bay Golf Club - Proposed
ORB

1919 Malcolm Henderson - Residence (Extant)
Grand Forks, BC
ORB

1919 R. Henderson - Alterations to *Kenilworth* (Demolished)
338 Foul Bay Road, Victoria
Cost: $5,000   BP#959 / BCA / ORB

1919 Mrs. Hannah James - Bungalow (Extant with additions)
2776 Cadboro Bay Road, Oak Bay
Contractor: Fairhurst Bros.
Cost: $2,000 OBBD Permit #1112

1919 St. Mary's Church Hall (Extant with 1927 extension)
Yale Street, Oak Bay, 1600 Block
Contractor: G.F. Lowe
Assessed value $14,000
BCA / CVA [27-7]

1919 C.P. Lesley Pearson - Bungalow (Extant with addition)
2714 Lincoln Road, formerly Seagull Avenue, Oak Bay
Contractor: Fairhurst Construction
Cost: $3,400 OBBD

1920 H.F. Bullen - Residence (Extant as condominiums)
906 St. Charles Street, Victoria
Contractor: Peter McKechnie
Cost: $60,000 BP#8533 / CVPDD
BCA / CVA [23-2]

1920 Bamfield - A job handed over by F.M. Rattenbury (not located)
BCA 8/18

1920 J.A. Rithet - Sun Room Addition
1299 Rockland Avenue, Victoria
Contractor: G.F. Lowe
Photo

c.1920 David T. Forbes - Semi-Bungalow (Extant, altered)
362 Sunset Avenue, Oak Bay
OBBD plan unsigned / Madge Wolfenden Hamilton

1921 Major F.V. Longstaff - Alterations and Addition of Study (Extant)
50 King George Terrace, *Seabank*, Oak Bay
CVA [21-4]

1921 J. Gilbert Phillips - Bungalow (Extant but turned 90 degrees on its site.)
2376 Central Avenue, Oak Bay
Contractor: G.F. Lowe
BCA

1921 E.D. Grierson - Addition to drawing room
906 Pemberton Road, Victoria
Contractor: Hunter & Halkett
BCA

1921 H.H. Boyle - Bungalow under Soldiers Settlement Scheme (Extant)
1320 Franklin Terrace, Victoria
Cost: $4,489   BP#1054 / CVPDD / BCA

1921 Royal Jubilee Hospital (Extant with added floor on top by others)
Fort Street at Richmond Road, Victoria
Contractor: Parfitt Brothers
Architect: P. Leonard James
Associate Architect: Major K.B. Spurgin.
BCA / CVA [21-3]– 56 plans

1922 Sunroom for the T.B. Ward
Provincial Royal Jubilee Hospital (Demolished)
CVPDD

1922 Addition to 1912 Oak Bay High School (Demolished)
Oak Bay Avenue (site of current Municipal Hall) Oak Bay
ORB

1922 St. Mary's Anglican Church - Addition (Demolished)
North Aisle (100 more seats)
CVA [27-7]

1922 Colwood Golf Club (Burned down) Cost: $15,000
Addition of Lockers (1925) and Lounge (1926)
BCA

1922 Judge P.S. Lampman - Residence (Extant, additions)
820 Pemberton Road, Victoria
Contractor: Thomas Ashe   BP#1500
Cost: $9,632
BCA / CVA / CVPDD

1923 Mrs. S. McLure - Bungalow (Extant)
1812 St. Anne Street, Oak Bay
Cost: $5,000
BCA / ORB / OBBD

1923 Canadian Pacific Railway - Marine Terminal Building (Extant as Wax Museum), Victoria
Cost: $171,024
Architects: F.M. Rattenbury & P.L. James
BCA / CVA [23-1]

1923 Miss H. Nation - Residence (Extant)
1524 Shasta Place, Victoria
Cost: $12,126
BCA / CVA.[23-3] / CVPDD

1923 W.E. Oliver - Bungalow (Extant)
1368 Craigdarroch Road, Victoria
Contractor: Thomas Grayson
Cost: $6,000   BP#2003 / CVPDD
BCA / CVA [23-4]

1924 Canadian Pacific Railway - Crystal Garden (Extant, altered)
713 Douglas Street, Victoria
Contractor: Luney Bros.
Architects: F.M. Rattenbury & P.L. James
BCA / CVA [24-1]

1924 Canadian Pacific Railway - Alterations to Government Street Office (Extant)

Contractor: Luney Bros.
Architects F.M. Rattenbury & P.L. James
BCA

1925 Canadian Pacific Wharf, Victoria - Covered Way (Demolished)
Contractor: Luney Bros.
Cost: $3155 BCA
Architect: P. Leonard James

1925 Canadian Pacific Railway - Swimming Pool (Altered and endangered)
Lake Louise, Alberta
BCA / Plans discarded
Architect: P. Leonard James

c.1925 Canadian Pacific Railway - Swimming Pool (Extant)
Digby Pines Hotel, Nova Scotia
A direct copy of the Lake Louise pool

1925 P.W. deP. Taylor - Residence *Deerlepe* (Extant)
7107 Deerlepe Road, Sooke
Contractor: George Calder
Cost: $9,812
BCA / PLJ perspective at BCA / CVA [25-2]

1925 J.A. Sayward - Interior Alterations, new porte-cochère (Demolished)
1301 Rockland Avenue, Victoria
Contractor: Luney Bros. Ltd.
Cost: $13,150 BP#2565 / BCA

1925 Goodwin - Alterations and additions
1655 Hampshire Road, Oak Bay
Contractor: George Calder
BCA

1925 Stores at Douglas, Humbolt and Burdett streets, Victoria
SDW recorded and discarded plans

1926 Mrs. E. Alexander - Inn (Extant, additions)
near Palmer Station, 5 miles from Victoria
BCA

1926 E.H. Bird - Semi-Bungalow (Extant)
6 Sylvan Lane, Oak Bay
Contractor: Eli Hume
Cost: $8,543
BCA / CVA [26-1]

1926 H.J. Hinton - Semi-Bungalow (Extant)
20 Sylvan Lane, Oak Bay
Contractor: Eli Hume
Cost: $7,800
BCA / CVA [26-2] / OBBD / Madge Wolfenden Hamilton

1926 Alfred Carmichael & Co. - Shops (Extant altered)
718 Fort Street, Victoria
Contractor: Luney Bros.
Cost: $10,000 BCA

1926 F.P. Walker - Bungalow (Demolished)
204 Superior Street at Michigan, Victoria
Tenders: $5680 – $7235
BCA

1926 Gordon's - (Extant, alterations)
739 Yates Street, Victoria
BCA [8-25]

1927 H. Burt-Smith - Semi-Bungalow (Extant)
1193 Beach Drive, Oak Bay
Contractor: Morry, Chamberlain & Alton
Cost Permit for $5,800   Final cost: $11,000
BCA / CVA [27-2]

1927 Mrs. R.H. Hall - Residence (Extant, addition)
1354 St. David Street, Oak Bay (Original plan specified stucco without any timbering which was added later.)
Contractor: Eli Hume
Cost: $6,738
CVA [27-3]

1927 R. Henderson - further Alterations
Irving Road, Victoria
BCA

1927 Hans Hunter - Country House (Extant, alterations as Capernwray Harbour Bible School)
Thetis Island, BC, by the Ferry dock
Contractor: George Calder
BCA / CVA [27-6]

1927 Mrs. M.I. Hutchinson - Semi-Bungalow (Extant)
3029 Uplands Road, Oak Bay
Contractor: Eli Hume
Cost: $12,000
BCA / CVA [27-1] / OBBD

1927 W. and L.D. White - Semi-bungalow (Extant, apartments)
1661 Hollywood Crescent and Wildwood Avenue, Victoria
Cost: $5,947   BP#4401 / CVPDD
BCA / CVA [27-4]

1927 J.A. Sayward - Greenhouse Additions to gardener's cottage
1301 Rockland Avenue, Victoria
Contractor: Morry, Chamberlain & Alton
BCA

1927 A.D. MacFarlane - Alterations
1906 St. Anne Street, Oak Bay
Contractor: Thomas Ashe
Cost: $3,130
BCA

1927 R.H.B. Ker - Garage (Extant)
1524 Shasta Place, Victoria
Contractor: Eli Hume
Cost: $1,450
BCA

1927 C.H. Carpenter - Residence (Extant)
2595 Lansdowne Road, Oak Bay
Minimalist Classical Revival
Contractor: P. McKechnie
Architect P. Leonard James of James & Savage
BCA / OBBD

1927 J. Allen - Bungalow with porte-cochère (Extant 2nd storey added)
1280 Dallas Road, Victoria
Cost: $3,500   BP#4172
Architects: James & Savage

1927 Malahat Hotel - Proposed
BCA

1928 Malcolm McBean Bell-Irving (married Nora Jones) - Residence (Extant)
572 Linkleas Avenue, Oak Bay (Sited on four-acre lot)
In 1998 moved to 588 Linkleas Avenue (Sited on one third of its original four acre lot, and turned 90 degrees from original.)
Contractor: Lambie & Kidd   Cost: $10,553
Architect P. Leonard James of James & Savage
BCA hp068410 / CVA [28-1] / OBBD BP#1995

1928 C.L. Branson - Residence *Miramar*, (Extant, large addition)
2901 Seaview Road, Saanich
Contractor: W.E. Tapley
Cost: $20,090
Architect: P. Leonard James of James & Savage
BCA / CVA [28-5] / Heritage Designation

1928 A.B. Cotton - Residence (Extant, alterations)
990 Terrace Avenue, Victoria
Contractor: Ernest T. Day & Co.
Cost: $16,200
Architect P. Leonard James of James & Savage
CVA [28-4]

1928 D.L. Gillespie - Alterations to *Stoneyhurst*
1365 Rockland Avenue, Victoria
Cost: $13,900
BCA

1928 R.H.B. Ker - Summer Residence (Extant)
2282 Arbutus Road, Saanich
Contractor: Eli Hume
Cost: $8,970
Architect P. Leonard James of James & Savage
BCA / CVA [27-5]

1928 Judge P.E. Lampman - Residence (Extant)
2570 Nottingham Road, Oak Bay
Contractor: J.W. Green
Cost: $13,300
Architect P. Leonard James of James & Savage
CVA [28-2]

1928 Allies Hotel, Victoria - proposed alterations and repairs
BCA

1928 Alcock, Downing & Wright - Measuring and preparing valuation of warehouse, 544 Yates Street, Victoria
BCA

1928 Marine Drive Proposed Hotel
Shoal Bay, Oak Bay
BCA

1928 Proposed Private School, Sooke
BCA

1929 K.C. Allen - Residence, *Little Oaks* (Extant, half-tim-

bering replaces shingled upper storey on ocean elevation)
3175 Tarn Place, Oak Bay
Contractor W.E. Tapley
Cost: $37,200 BCA / CVA [29-1] / OBBD
Architect: P. Leonard James of James & Savage

1929 B.C. Land & Investment Co. - Stores (Extant)
1223 – 1235 Government Street, Victoria
Contractor: H. Catterall
Cost: $18,695
Architects James & Savage
BCA James file / CVA (Savage Collection)

1929 Dugald S. Gillespie - Extension and Sunroom (Extant)
1021 Moss Street, Victoria
Contractor: Chamberlain & Alton
Cost: $3,500 BCA

1929 Major W. Garrard - Residence *Rook's Nest* (Extant)
Tod Inlet 20 acre property, now part of
The Butcharts Gardens
Contractor: E.A. Higgs
Architect P. Leonard James of James & Savage
BCA / CVA [29-4]

1929 Johnston Coffee Shop - Interior design (No longer exists)
1223 Government Street, Victoria
BCA.

1929 Mrs. D.R. Ker - Residence (Extant)
841 St.Charles Street, Victoria
Contractor: Eli Hume
Cost: $30,040 BP#5415 / CVA [29-3]
Architect P. Leonard James of James & Savage

1929 R.H.B. Ker - Addition (Extant)
1524 Shasta Place, Victoria
Contractor: Eli Hume
Cost: $10,000
Architect P. Leonard James of James & Savage
CVA [23-3, 27-5]

1929 John E. Semmes - Residence *Robinwood* Seawall, Tennis Court and Swimming pool (Extant, some alteration and large separate addition)
3155 Beach Drive, (formerly Shore Road) Oak Bay
Contractor: Morry, Chamberlain & Alton
Cost: $20,000
Architect P. Leonard James of James & Savage
BCA / CVA [29-5]

1929 R.H. Shanks - Bungalow (Extant)
1017 St. Patrick Street, Oak Bay
Architect P. Leonard James of James & Savage
BCA

1929 Maj.-Gen. P.E. Thacker - Residence (Extant, altered)
2575 Lansdowne Road, Oak Bay
Contractor: Lambie & Kidd
Cost: $15,300 BCA / CVA [29-6]
Architect P. Leonard James of James & Savage

c.1929 P.Leonard James - Dining Room Extension
2385 Tod Road, Oak Bay
Cost: $2,410

1930 Mrs. C.F. Armstrong - Alterations to residence
      1630 York Place, Oak Bay.
      Contractor: Hunter & Halkett
      Cost: $5,775   BCA

1930 Colwood Golf Club - New Clubhouse (Demolished).
      (Old) Island Highway, or Goldstream Road
      Contractor: Hunter & Halkett
      Cost: $63,760 BCA / CVA [29-2]
      Architect P. Leonard James of James & Savage

1930 Forbes-Wilson - Residence *Eagles Nest* (Extant, much altered)
      3125 Beach Drive, Oak Bay
      Contractor: Hunter & Halkett
      Cost: $35,200
      Architect P. Leonard James of James & Savage
      BCA / CVA [30-5]

1930 Mrs. E.C. Hart - Addition to Residence
      Laurel Lane, Victoria
      BCA

1930 H.C.V. MacDowall - Residence (Extant)
      3065 Uplands Road, Oak Bay
      Contractor: Eli Hume & A. McKinty
      Cost: $15,000
      Architect: P. Leonard James of James & Savage
      BCA / CVA [30-2] / OBBD

1930 Capt. W. Hobart Molson - Residence, *Gavignol* 22 rooms. (Extant, converted to 7 suites)
      1663 Rockland Avenue , Victoria
      Contractor: Hunter & Halkett
      Cost: $55,600   BP#6262
      Architect: P. Leonard James of James & Savage
      BCA / CVA.[30-4] 22 drawings

1930 Norfolk House School - (Extant, enlarged)
      801 Bank Street, Victoria
      Contractor: Williams, Trerise & Williams
      Cost: $12,594
      Architect: P. Leonard James of James & Savage
      BCA / CVA [32-1] / CVPDD

1930 Col. E. Pepler - Addition to Residence (Extant)
      333 Denison Road, Oak Bay
      Contractor: Hunter & Halkett
      Cost: $1,463   BP#5957
      Architect P. Leonard James of James & Savage
      BCA / CVA {30-1]

1930 Judge P.S. Lampman - Addition to Residence, dining room (Extant)
      1630 York Place, Oak Bay
      Architect P. Leonard James of James & Savage
      Oak Bay's Heritage Buildings Stuart Stark

1931 J.N. Anderson - Bungalow (Extant)
      2000 Beach Drive, Oak Bay
      Contractor: E.J. Hunter
      Architect: P. Leonard James, of James & Savage
      (A list in author's possession shows this as James job.)
      BCA / CVA [filed in Savage Coll.] / OBBD

1931 Four Mile House - Alterations (Extant)
(Old) Island Highway, View Royal
Architect P. Leonard James of James & Savage
CVA [31-2]

1931 G.H. Harman - Residence (Extant, somewhat altered)
1586 York Place, Oak Bay
Contractor: Eli Hume
Architect P. Leonard James of James & Savage
BCA / CVA [31-1]

1931 P. Leonard James - Bungalow (Demolished by fire)
20 Laburnum Gardens, became 2397 Tod Road, Oak Bay
Cost: $3000
Architect P. Leonard James of James & Savage
OBBD / BP#1863

1931 Mrs. O.M. Jones - Alterations and Addition to Residence
599 Island Road, Oak Bay
Contractor: W.E. Tapley
BCA

1931 Holland (Demolished)
1959 Hampshire Road, Oak Bay
Architects: James & Savage
L. McCann, UVic Database

1931 Towner Bay Club House and Subdivision - (Proposed)
Architect: P. Leonard James of James & Savage
BCA

1931 Canadian Legion Hall, Pro Patria Club Rooms - Alterations (Demolished)
625 Courtney Street, Victoria
Cost: $3,500
CVA 2-1224, 2-1225

c.1932 Major G. Boyer - Proposed Bungalow, Pender Island
BCA

c.1932 Christian Science - Proposed Church (Extant, different design or altered)
Kelowna, BC
Architect: P. Leonard James of James & Savage
BCA

c.1932 Mr. A.C. Ham - Bungalow (Extant)
Built as a speculative house
2812 Cadboro Bay Road and West Thompson, now Neil Street, Oak Bay
Contractor: A.C. Ham
Architect P. Leonard James of James & Savage
OBBD

1932 Mrs. G.J. Whetham - Alterations to Residence.
St Louis Street, Oak Bay
BCA

1932 Mrs. G.J. Whetham - Proposed Farmhouse, Patricia Bay
BCA

1932 L.C. Ogilvie - Addition of sunporch and lych gate to Residence (Extant)
1339 Lansdowne Road, Oak Bay BCA

1932 Mrs. R. Pendry - Proposed house sketches
BCA

1932 Miss K.A. Hall - Alterations to Residence
2625 Lansdowne Road, Oak Bay
Contractor: Lambie
BCA

1932 R.P. Butchart - Design for new mantle in Residence
Letter in author's collection.

c.1932 N.A. Yarrow - Alterations to Residence
925 Foul Bay Road, Oak Bay
Author's recollection

1932 Norfolk House School - Gymnasium (Extant)
Cost: $3,376
Architect: P. Leonard James of James & Savage
BCA / CVA [32-1]

1933 Mrs. Mabel Groos - Cottage (Extant with additions)
1971 Watson Street, Saanich
Contractor: Joseph Browning
Cost: $1,665
Supervising Architect P. Leonard James, design believed adapted from the "Suffolk" house by Douglas James.
BCA

1934 A.C. Ham - Bungalow (Extant)
Built as a speculative house Davidson listed as first owner
2270 Neil Street, Oak Bay
Contractor: A.C. Ham
OBBD

1934 A.C. Ham - Bungalow (Extant)
Built as a speculative house
2276 Neil Street, Oak Bay
Contractor: A.C. Ham
OBBD

c.1935 Daily Colonist - Alterations to Editorial Department,
Broad Street, Victoria
Author's recollection Plans discarded

1935 J. McMillan - Residence (Proposed ? unable to locate)
Saanich, BC
Recorded by SDW [35-1] drawings now lost

c.1936 G. Wellburn - Residence (Extant)
4905 Indian Road, Deerholme (Duncan) BC
Author's and Wellburn family's recollections

1936 James A. Wattie - Alterations to the Forbes-Wilson house (ground floor bedroom and bathroom)
3125 Beach Drive, Oak Bay
BCA / CVA [30-5]

1937 The Deanery - Residence in Christ Church Cathedral Close (Extant)
930 Burdett Avenue, Victoria
Contractor: Parfitt Bros. Ltd.
Cost: $10,000   BP#10486
Architect P. Leonard James, (Consulting Architect) J.C.M. Keith
CVA [38-4] / originals in The Archives of the Anglican Diocese of BC

1937 A.C. Ham - Bungalow (Extant)
Built as a speculative house

2768 Cadboro Bay Road, Oak Bay,
Contractor: A.C. Ham
OBBD

1938 A.C. Ham - Bungalow (Extant)
Built as a speculative house
2269 Neil Street, Oak Bay
Contractor: A.C. Ham
OBBD

1937 Oak Bay - Fire Hall, original two bays (Extant, plus addition)
1703 Monterey Avenue, Oak Bay
BCA / CVA [37-1] / OBBD

1938 Mrs. E. Smith - Residence (Extant)
2608 Cavendish Avenue, Oak Bay
Contractor: Parfitt Bros.
OBBD

1938 Bishop's Palace - Remodelling (Demolished)
Corner Quadra Street and Burdett Avenue, Victoria
Article with photo 1938 saved by architect, date and source unknown

1938 Chapel in memory of John Yarrow (Extant, with Archive added)
Corner Quadra Street and Burdett Avenue, Victoria
Plans in The Archives of the Anglican Diocese of BC / SDW {38-1}

1938 St. John's Anglican Church (Extant with alterations)
Cobble Hill, BC
BCA Specification / The Archives of the Anglican Diocese of BC

1938 E.W. Griffiths - Residence (Extant)
235 Dennison Road, Oak Bay
Contractor: E.J. Hunter
Cost: $8,500
BCA / CVA [39-1]

1938 Mrs. H.F. Hammersley - Kitchen alterations to Residence
1989 Crescent Road, Oak Bay
BCA

1938 George P. Napier - Bungalow (Demolished or enlarged)
Deep Cove, Saanich Peninsula
BCA / CVA [38-2]

1938 W.B. Pease - Residence *Ballybawn* (Extant)
2840 Cadboro Bay Road, Oak Bay
Letter to author from daughter, Mrs. D.A.S. Crowe

1938 Commander J.D. Prentice - Alterations and Additions to Residence
2028 Runnymede Road, Oak Bay
BCA

1938 Miss F. Uren - Frame and stucco Bungalow
Ladysmith, BC (Not located)
BCA

1938 F.B. Ward - Residence (Demolished)
Christmas Hill, Saanich
CVA [38-3]

1939 Cathedral Sunday School (Extant as school)
Niagara Street at Medana, Victoria

Contractor: Williams Trerise & Williams
Cost: $9,000. BP#211172
The Archives of the Anglican Diocese of BC

1939 St. Peter's Anglican Church (Extant)
Comox, BC
The Archives of the Anglican Diocese of BC

1939 A.C. Ham - Bungalow (Extant)
Built as a speculative house
2957 Foul Bay Road, Oak Bay
Contractor: A.C. Ham
OBBD

1940 Mrs. J.I. Cassie - Bungalow (Extant)
1354 Monterey Avenue, Oak Bay
BCA / CVA [40-5] / OBBD

1940 Arthur V. Danby - Bungalow (Extant)
1549 Despard Avenue, Victoria
BCA

1940 Dr. T.H. Johns - Residence (Extant)
2753 Somass Drive, Oak Bay
Contractor: L.G. Scott
BCA / CVA [40-1]

1940 A.S.G. Musgrave - Residence (Extant)
572 Newport Avenue, Oak Bay
BCA / CVA [40-2]

1940 H. Rive - Bungalow (not located)
Roberts Bay, Sidney CVA [40-4]

1940 F.B. Ward - Billiard room added (House Demolished)
Christmas Hill, Saanich
BCA

1940 T.H. Woolson - Semi-Bungalow (Extant)
2989 Foul Bay Road, Oak Bay
CVA [40-3]

1940 Bapco Paint Warehouse and Pump House (Demolished)
200 Belleville Street, Victoria
CVA 2/0839

1941 A.C. Ham - Bungalow (Extant)
Built as a speculative house
2257 Neil Street, Oak Bay
Contractor: A.C. Ham
OBBD

1941 Gilbert G. Fraser - Residence (Extant with addition)
513 Transit Road, Oak Bay
BCA / CVA [41-3]

1941 Harold Johnston - Bungalow (Extant)
1561 Despard Avenue, Victoria
Contractor: D.A. Wallace   Cost: $4,750
BP#213450 / CVA [41-1] / CVPDD

1941 Mrs. P.S. Lampman - Semi-Bungalow (Extant with addition)
925 St. Charles Street, Victoria
Contractor: A. Middleton
Cost: $7,000 BP#213218
BCA / CVA [41-2]

1941 R.W. Mayhew - Alterations sunroom and library (The Forbes-Wilson house)

3125 Beach Drive, Oak Bay
BCA / CVA [30-5]

1941 Miss B.E. O'Keiffe & Miss G. Field - International Style Bungalow (Extant much enlarged)
500 Beach Drive, Oak Bay
Contractor: T. Lambie
BCA / CVA [41-4]

1941 Yarrows Shipyard No. 2 (Demolished)
Records discarded (SDW 41-5) CVA 2-0110

1941 Victoria Machinery Depot Plate Shop (Demolished)
CVA 2-0110

1942 J.V. Cook - Semi-bungalow (Extant)
2561 Queenswood Drive, Saanich
Contractor: E.J. Hunter
BCA / CVA [42-2]

1942 Dr. Thomas Mercer - Alterations
2750 Tudor Road, Saanich
CVA [42-1]

1943-45 Wartime Housing, Esquimalt and Victoria (Extant)
Designs from Ottawa of houses for war workers, and two temporary two-storey staff houses – one Demolished (Cost: $29,000 each) and a dining hall (Extant) (Cost: $33,000) for single workers at Lockley Street and Admirals Road
Architects: McCarter & Nairne
Associate architect: P. Leonard James

1944 Cadet Block, the *Grant Block* at Royal Roads, Colwood (Extant)
Architects McCarter & Nairne,
Associate Architect P. Leonard James

1944 A. Campbell - Store and alteration to Residence (Extant)
1779 Lillian Road, Victoria
BCA / CVA [44-3]

1944 Canadian Legion - Britannia Branch No 7, alterations (Demolished)
780 Cormorant Street, Victoria
BCA CVA [44-7]

1944 A.S. Denny - Alterations to Cottage Brentwood Bay, BC (Not located)
CVA [44-6]

1944 H. Gaunt - Bungalow (Tudor style)
Shawnigan Lake, BC (Not located)
CVA [44-1]

1944 Harold Husband - Interior alterations to Residence
3150 Rutland Road, Oak Bay
CVA [44-4]

1944 J.R. Murray - Alterations
501 Newport Avenue, Oak Bay
BCA / CVA [44-2]

1944 *The Daily Colonist* - Commercial Printing office (Demolished)
Broad Street, Victoria
BCA

1944 Island Farms - Alterations
608 Broughton Street, Victoria
BCA

1945 E.A.M. Williams - Residence (Extant)

1918 Crescent Road, Oak Bay
CVA [45-1]
1945 Wartime Housing - Plot Plans
CVA [45-2]
1945 Western Match Company (Extant)
754 Fairview Road, Esquimalt
Cost: $200,000
Architects: McCarter & Nairne, Vancouver
Associate Architect: P. Leonard James
CVA [45-3]
1946 Buckerfield's Ltd. - New Premises (Extant)
2101 Douglas Street, NE corner of Douglas & Pembroke streets, Victoria
CVA [46-6]
1946 Church of the Blessed Sacrament (Father Bradley)
Admirals Road, Esquimalt
BCA – Box 7 file 15
1946 Richard C. Field - Bungalow (Extant, slightly enlarged)
3140 Midland Road, Oak Bay
CVA [46-2]
1946 E. Hill - Concrete store (Art Deco style)
Quadra and View streets, Victoria
BCA / CVA [46-1]
1946 James H. Hill - Addition to Residence
2741 Dalhousie Street, Oak Bay   BCA
1946 Knights of Pythias - Remodelling
Plans noted and discarded SDW
1946 Mrs. I. McPherson - Residence (Extant)
3250 Weald Road, Oak Bay
CVA [46-5]
1946 Pantorium Dye Works - Addition
905 Fort Street, Victoria
BCA / CVA [46-3]
1946 Sidney Roofing, Victoria West (Demolished)
Architects: McCarter & Nairne, Vancouver
Associate Architect: P. Leonard James.
Plans noted and discarded SDW
1946 H. Wallace - Alterations & Additions to Residence
3175 Beach Drive, Oak Bay
BCA / CVA [46-4]
1947 F.G. Aldous - Bungalow (Extant)
2915 Tudor Road at Sea View Road, Saanich
CVA [47-3]
1947 Mrs. H.J. Crane - Alterations to Residence
1554 Prospect Place, Oak Bay
CVA [47-1]
1947 Alterations to building
Herald Street, Victoria
CVA [47-4]
1947 Henry Birks & Sons (B.C.) Ltd - Store (altered)
706 Yates Street, Victoria
Architects: Nobbs & Valentine, Montreal
P. Leonard James, Resident Architect
CVA [47-2]
1948 Two-Storey Warehouse at Laurel Point for British American Paint Company (Demolished)
200 Belleville Street, Victoria
CVA [49-3]

1948 C. Cowan - Proposed Apartment
Plans noted and discarded by SDW

1948 Davis Motors - Plans noted and discarded by SDW

c.1948 Col. Stuart Morgan - Proposed log house
Parry Road, Metchosin
Stan Colling's and Author's recollections

1948 Ralph Dumbleton - Bungalow (Extant)
2275 Lansdowne Road, Oak Bay
CVA [48-3]

1948 Dr. M.N. Sherman - Residence (Not built)
Sea View Road, Saanich
CVA [48-4]

1948 Federal Building & Post Office (Extant, seismically upgraded in 1995-6)
South-west corner of Government and Yates streets, Victoria.
Renamed P. L. JAMES PLACE in 1996
Architects: James & James
Cost: $2,500,000
CVA [48-5 – 135 plans]

1949 Wm. N. O'Neil (Victoria) Ltd. (Demolished)
551 Yates Street, Victoria
Plans noted and discarded by SDW [49-1]

1949 N.A. Yarrow, Residence *Orchard Gate* (Former entrance on Pat Bay highway no longer used)
(Extant, sympathetically enlarged as *Donnington Farm*)
691 Donnington Place at Brookleigh Avenue, Saanich
Cost: $180,000
CVA [49-2]

1950 Esquimalt High School - Extensions and Additions S.D.#61 (Extant with additions as L'Ecole Victor-Brodeur S.D. #93
637 Head Street, Esquimalt
Architect: P. Leonard James of James, Polson & Siddall
CVA [50-4]

1951 Oak Bay Junior High School S.D.#61 (Extant as part of High School)
Cadboro Bay Road, opposite Epworth Street, Oak Bay
Architect: P. Leonard James of James & Polson
CVA [51-5]

1951 Canadian Red Cross, Victoria Branch - Addition to Building (Extant)
1046 Fort Street, Victoria
Architects: James, Polson & Siddall
CVA [51-1]

c. 1951 W.B. Malkin - Warehouse alteration
916 Yates Street, Victoria
BCA Box 9

1951 C.J. Williams - Residence   3034 Larkdowne Road, Oak Bay (Extant)
Architects: James & Polson
CVA [51-2]

1952 George Jay School S.D.#61 - Alterations and Additions
Architects: James, Polson & Siddall
CVA [52-1]

1952 Willows School S.D.#61 - Alterations & Additions

Architects: James, Polson & Siddall
CVA [52-1]

1952 Doncaster School S.D.#61 - Alterations & Additions
Architects: James, Polson & Siddall, Associate Architect Hubert Savage
CVA [52-1]

1952 Strawbarry Vale Elementary School S.D.#61 - Alterations and Additions
Architects: James, Polson & Siddall, Associate Architect Hubert Savage
CVA [52-2]

1952 Oaklands School S.D.#61 - Alterations & Additions
Architects: James, Polson & Siddall
CVA [52-3]

1952 Willows Elementary School S.D.#61 - Proposed Ten-Classroom Addition
Architects: James, Polson & Siddall
CVA [52-4]

1952 Doncaster School S.D.#61 - Alterations & Additions
Architects: James, Polson & Siddall
Associate Architect Hubert Savage
CVA [52-5]

1952 Mount Douglas School S.D.#61 - Alterations & Additions

Architects: James, Polson & Siddall
Associate Architect Hubert Savage
CVA [52-8]

1952 Titerie, J & Co.
225 Gorge Road
Cost: $45,500 BP#29772 / CVPDD
Architects: James, Polson & Siddall

1953 P. Leonard James - Alteration of residence into two apartments
2385 Tod Road, Oak Bay
Architect: P. Leonard James
Author's recollection

1954 Sir Eric and Lady Stuart-Taylor - Alterations and Garden Gate for Residence (Extant)
2875 Lansdowne Road, Oak Bay
Architect: P. Leonard James
Author, photos.

Map by the Geography Department, University of Victoria, shows the locations of these houses – courtesy of Dr. Larry McCann

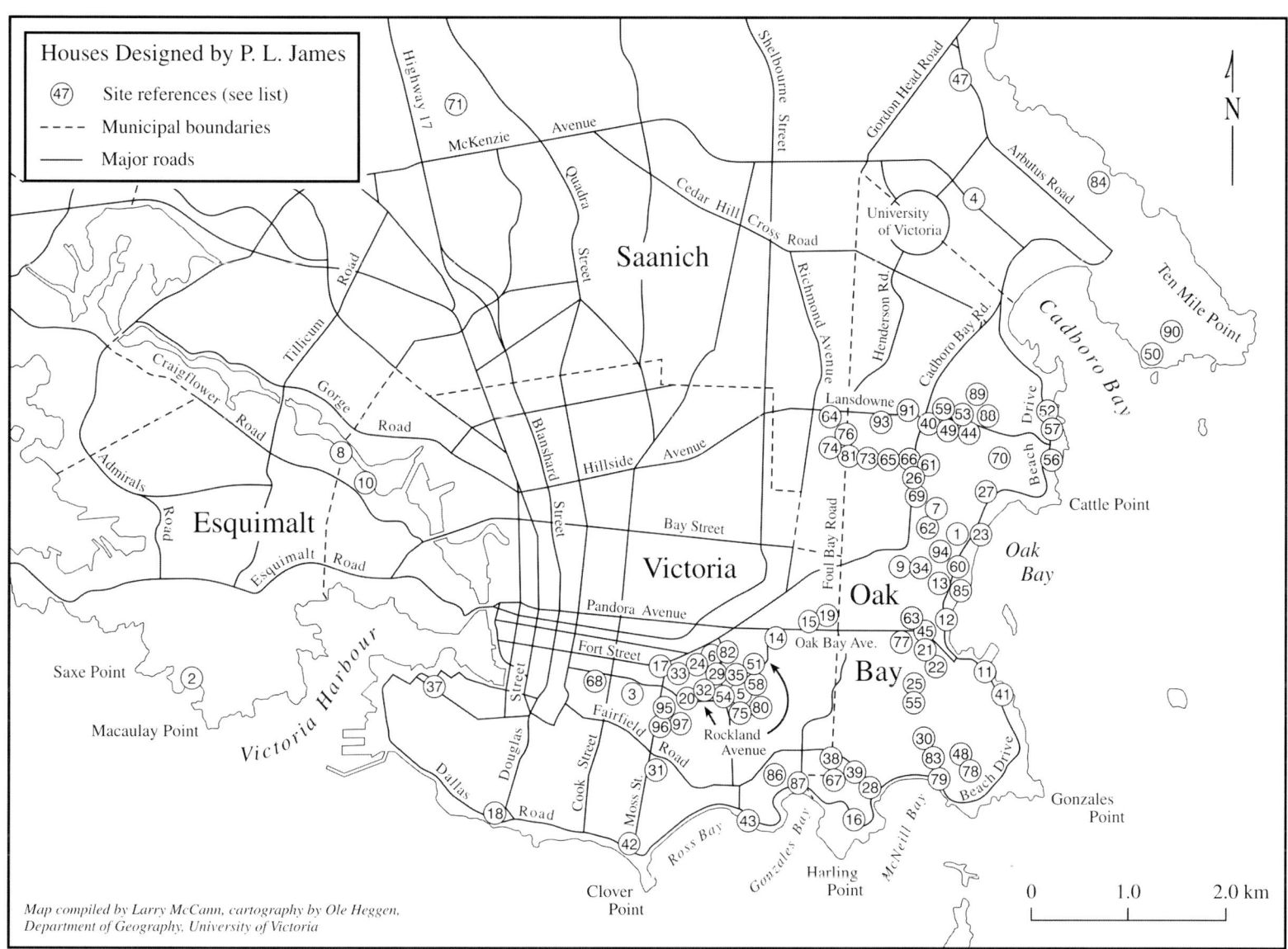

Appendix – P. Leonard James Houses

P. Leonard James Houses Listed by Street Address with map numbers included

#	Address	Client - Year
1	2279 Lincoln Rd. O.B.	Mrs. Johnston - 1909
2	1179 Munro St. Esq	Mrs J.W. Lysle - 1909
3	729 Linden Ave. Vict	W.S. Drewry - 1910
4	Sinclair Rd. Saan	Algernon Pease - 1910
5	1560 Rockland Ave. Vict	Duncan Ross - 1910
6	914 St. Charles St. Vict	Hon. Mr Justice Galliher - 1909
7	2385 Tod Rd. O.B.	Mrs H. James - 1910
8	1327 Arm St., Vic West	Hedges, Francis F. - 1911
9	2361 Cranmore Rd. O.B.	Mrs. F.C. Wolfenden - 1911
10	512 Selkirk Ave. Vic W	J.E Shenk. - 1911 Demo
11	1312 Beach Dr. O.B.	G.H.S. Edwards - 1912 Demo
12	1558 Beach Dr. O.B	John W. Morris - 1912
13	1790 Beach Dr. O.B.	Baxter, C.S. - 1912
14	1064 Beverley Pl. Vict	Frank Burrell - 1912
15	1535 Davie St. Vict	H. Hewett - 1912
16	50 King George Tce. O.B.	H. Harrison - 1912
17	1015 Moss St. Vict	Dr. J.D. Helmcken - 1912
18	35 Olympia Ave. Vict	Frank W.H. Giolma - 1912
19	1602 Redfern St. Vict	H. Hewett (Hall) - 1912
20	1393 Rockland Ave. Vict	J.T. Reid - 1912
21	1324 St. David St. O.B.	Donald A. Malin - 1912
22	1220 Transit Rd. O.B.	Herbert. S Lott. - 1912
23	2422 Esplanade, O.B.	Rev. Wm. Barton. - c.1913
24	1025 Joan Cres. Vict	Mrs. E.L. Watts - 1913
25	1050 St. Patrick St. O.B.	Capt. H. Jarvis - 1914
26	2776 Cadboro Bay Rd. O.B.	Mrs. Hannah James - 1919
27	2714 Lincoln Rd. O.B.	L. Pearson - 1919
28	362 Sunset Ave. O.B.	David T. Forbes - 1919
29	906 St. Charles St. Vict	Harry Fenwick Bullen - 1920
30	2376 Central Ave. O.B.	J. Gilbert Phillips - 1921
31	1320 Franklin Tce. Vict	H.H. Boyle - 1922
32	820 Pemberton Rd. Vict	Judge P.S. Lampman - 1922
33	1368 Craigdarroch Rd. Vict	W.E. Oliver - 1923
34	1812 St. Ann St. O.B.	Mrs. S. McLure - 1923
35	1524 Shasta Pl. Vict	Miss H.M. Nation - 1923
37	204 Superior St.	F.P. Walker - 1926
38	6 Sylvan Ln. O.B.	Ernest H. Bird - 1926
39	20 Sylvan Ln. O.B	H.J. Hinton - 1926
40	3029 Uplands Rd. O.B.	Mrs. M.I. Hutchinson - 1926
41	1193 Beach Dr. O.B.	Henry Burt-Smith - 1927
42	1280 Dallas Rd. Vict	J. Allen - 1927

43	1661 Hollywood Cres. Vict	W. and Lilian Daisy White - 1927
44	2595 Lansdowne Rd. O.B.	C. Carpenter - 1927
45	1354 St. David St. O.B.	Mrs. R.H. Hall - 1927
47	2274 Arbutus Road Saan.	R.H.B.Ker - 1928
48	572 Linkleas Ave. O.B.	M. Bell-Irving - 1928
49	2570 Nottingham Rd. O.B.	Judge P.S. Lampman - 1928
50	2901 Sea View Rd. Saan.	C.L.H. Branson - 1928
51	990 Terrace Ave. Vict	A.B. Cotton, - 1928
52	3155 Beach Dr. O.B.	J.E. Semmes - 1929
53	2575 Lansdowne Rd. O.B.	Major-General P.E. Thacker - 1929
54	841 St. Charles St. Vict	Mrs. D.R. Ker - 1929
55	1017 St. Patrick St. O.B.	R.H. Shanks - 1929
56	3175 Tarn Pl. O.B.	K.C. Allen - 1929
57	3125 Beach Dr. O.B.	F. Forbes-Wilson - 1930
58	1663 Rockland Ave. Vict	Capt. W. Hobart Molson - 1930
59	3065 Uplands Rd. O.B.	H.C.V. MacDowall - 1930
60	2000 Beach Dr. O.B.	John N. Anderson - 1931
61	2812 Cadboro Bay Rd. O.B.	Ham, AC. (1st owner, Felton) - 1931
62	20 Laburnum Gdns. O.B.	P.L. James - 1931
63	1586 York Place O.B.	G.H. Harman - 1931
64	1971 Watson St. Saan.	Mrs. M.M. Groos - 1933
65	2270 Neil St. O.B.	A.C. Ham - 1934
66	2276 Neil St. O.B.	A.C. Ham - 1934
67	235 Denison Rd. O.B.	E.W. Griffiths - 1936
68	930 Burdett Ave.	Anglican Synod - 1937
69	2768 Cadboro Bay Rd. O.B.	A.C. Ham - 1937
70	2840 Cadboro Bay Rd. O.B.	W.B. Pease - 1938
71	Christmas Hill, Saan	F.B. Ward - 1938 Demo
72	Deep Cove North Saan	George P. Napier - 1938 Demo
73	2269 Neil St. O.B.	A.C .Ham - 1938
74	2957 Foul Bay Rd. O.B.	A.C. Ham - 1939
75	1549 Despard Ave. Vict	Arthur V. Danby - 1940
76	2989 Foul Bay Rd. O.B.	T.H. Woolson - 1940
77	1354 Monterey Ave. O.B.	Mrs. J I. Cassie - 1940
78	572 Newport Ave. O.B.	A.S.G. Musgrave - 1940
79	500 Beach Dr. O.B.	Miss B.E. O'Keiffe - 1941
80	1561 Despard Ave. Vict	H. Johnson - 1941
81	2256 Neil St. O.B.	A.C. Ham - 1941
82	925 St. Charles St. Vict	Mrs. P.S. Lampman - 1941
83	513 Transit Rd. O.B.	Gilbert G. Fraser - 1941
84	2561 Queenswood Dr. Saan.	J.V. Cook - 1942
85	2753 Somass Dr. O.B.	Dr. T.H. Johns - 1943
86	1779 Lillian Rd. Vict	A .Campbell - 1944
87	1915 Crescent Rd. O.B.	E.A.M. Williams - 1945
88	3140 Midland Rd. O.B.	Richard C. Field - 1946
89	3250 Weald Rd. O.B.	Mrs. I. McPherson - 1946
90	2915 Tudor Ave. Saan	F.G. Aldous - 1947
91	2275 Lansdowne Rd. O. B.	R. Dumbleton - 1948
92	691 Donnington Pl. Saan.	N.A. Yarrow - 1949

93	3034 Larkdowne Rd. O.B.	C.W. Williams - 1951
94	2608 Cavendish Avenue, O.B	Mrs. E. Smith - 1938
95	1334 Minto St. Vict	Hewitt & Hinton - 1911
96	1338 Minto St. Vict	Hewitt & Hinton - 1911
97	1344 Minto St. Vict	Hewitt & Hinton - 1911

4905 Indian Rd. Deerholme, BC Gerry Wellburn - c.1936

7000 Deerlepe Rd. Sooke P.W.deP. Taylor - 1925

Grand Forks, BC Malcolm Henderson - 1919

Ladysmith, BC Not located Miss F. Uren - 1938

Roberts Bay, Sidney Not located H. Rive

Shawnigan Lake, BC Not located H. Gaunt - 1944

Thetis Island, BC Hans Hunter - 1927
(Now Capernwray Harbour Bible School)

Tod Inlet, Brentwood Bay, BC Major W. Garrard - 1927
(house and property now part of The Butchart Gardens)

Commissions By Douglas James, MAIBC (1888 - 1962)

1907 Arrived in Victoria as a fully qualified architect from London, England.

1907 Employed as draughtsman by Samuel Maclure for Dunsmuir's Hatley Park.
Much of his practice centred on Duncan. The collected information about his jobs comes from many sources and is far from complete. Would anyone with further information please contact the author at 1-250-384-2461, dbrutus@shaw.ca.

1910 Formed partnership with his brother, P. Leonard James. For **James & James** jobs, see the P. Leonard James List. 1910 – 1914

1911 Mrs. F.C Wolfenden - Bungalow *Arkholme* (Extant)
2361 Cranmore Road, Oak Bay
Cost: $3,500
Architect: Douglas James of James & James
ORB / Madge Wolfenden Hamilton

1918-20 Agricultural Hall - Alterations Duncan
Hallmark Society file from Dr. Gibson, SFU *C-L* Dec. 4, 1919

1919 Col. Roome - Residence, Duncan (Demolished by fire)
ORB, Oct 15, 1919 2 sets of blueprints sent to Douglas James by P. Leonard James

1919 H.R. Burroughs, Preliminary sketches for house, Cowichan Lake
ORB

1922 D. James - First Residence designed for his own use [Extant]
1033 Herd Road, Maple Bay *Stagstones*
C-L May 14. 1925 / Hamish Mutter
(Present owner, T.M. Varty believes Douglas built his boat *Radiant* at this site.)

1922 C.B. Mains - two storey Building with Butcher Store, Residence and two-car garage (Extant with alterations)
70 Government Street, Duncan
C-L May 25, 1922

1922 Harold Fairfax Prevost - Store (Extant)
Craig Street next to Bank of Commerce, Duncan
C-L Sept 14, 1922

1922 Cowichan Guide Hall (Extant)
Cairnsmore Street, Duncan
CVM

1922 C.F. Davie - Residence (Extant) and garage
363 Beech Avenue, Duncan
C-L Feb. 23, 1922 and May 25, 1922

1922 Capt. L.W. Huntingdon - Extensive Additions
Lamborne Estate (Burnt down only a 1920 cottage remains)
1265 Cherry Point Road, Cowichan Bay
CVM / CG

1923 Gore-Langton - Garage (Demolished)
Government St., Duncan

C-L. Nov. 15, 1923
1923 New Fire Hall & Police Court, 2nd floor living quarters, Duncan (Demolished)
C-L. July 12, 1923

1924 Nanaimo Motors Ltd. - Building
20 Front Street, Nanaimo
Nanaimo Heritage Gateways

1924 D. James - Second Residence designed for his own use (Extant with addition)
811 Wharncliffe Rd, Duncan
C-L. Dec 25, 1924, Jan 22, 1925

1925 Capital Theatre - (Extant altered to shopping complex)
123 Station Street, Duncan
Contractor: E.W. Lee
C-L July 23, 1925 [A horseshoe in the sidewalk indicates the earlier location of the blacksmith at this site]

1925 School (80' x 60') (Extant)
540 Cairnsmore Street (opposite High School), Duncan
C-L Feb. 19. 1925

1926 Carlton Stone - Residence *Stonehaven* (Extant 1997)
3069 Gibbins Road, Duncan
Blueprint exists

c.1926 Residence (Extant)
Built on Ypres Street - moved to Swansnest Subdivision off Indian Road South, Duncan
CVM

1926 Shawnigan Lake Boys' School (rebuilt after fire)
Central Block (Extant), Chapel (Extant but tower entry added), Hobby Block (Demolished and rebuilt on nearby site) Shawnigan Lake School Archives

1926 E. Garside - Residence in *The Essex* style (Extant)
1625 Davie Street, Victoria
Cost: $5500 BP#17660

1927 Maj. H.T.S. (Sherwell) Anderson - Residence (Extant)
Herd Road, Somenos Lake, Duncan
Contractor: E.W. Lee
C-L May 12, 1927

1927 Col. H.A.H. Rice - Acme Motors Garage (1927-1931)
Duncan (Demolished)
C-L May 12, 1927

1927 Cowichan Merchants - Interior Alterations (H.N. Whittaker, Manager)
Duncan
C-L June 16, 1927

1927 Print Shop for *Cowichan-Leader* (Extant)
132 Kenneth Street, Duncan (First ferro-concrete building in Duncan)
C-L Nov 24, 1927

1927 St. Edwards Catholic Church (Extant as funeral home)
Coronation Avenue at Brae Road, Duncan
C-L Oct. 20, 1927

1927 Mr. Totty - 5 Room (EA&C) Bungalow (Extant, enlarged)
1187 Hampshire Road, Oak Bay
OBBD / Family history

1928 Claude and Edna Green - Residence (Extant)

733 Wharncliffe Road, Duncan
C-L Jan. 26, 1928
1928 J.C. Wragg - Store with apartments over,
Craig and Kenneth streets, Duncan (Extant) Half-timbered EA&C
CVM
c.1928 Douglas James - Cottage (Demolished by fire)
Third Residence designed for his own use
Part of 6392 Lakes Road property, Duncan
English Arts & Crafts with half-timbering
Family history and photos
1928 J.C. Sanderson - Bungalow (Extant)
1503 Maple Bay Road at Daykin Road, Quamichan Lake
C-L Jan 26, 1928 p.1
C-L Dec. 28, 1929 reported partnership with Eric Clarkson
1929 G.E. Pritchard - Residence (Extant much altered and enlarged)
1834 Stamps Road, Duncan
EA&C original style C-L Feb 14, 1929
1929 E.W. Paitson - 9 room Residence (Extant)
3385 Upper Terrace, Oak Bay
Contractor: Peter McKechnie
OBBD
1929 *Cowichan Leader* - New Office Duncan (Extant)
C-L Feb 14, 1929
1930 Knights of Pythias - New Hall (Extant)
Brae Street, Duncan
C-L April 30, 1930
1930 P.G. Pearson - Semi-bungalow (Extant)
6899 Norcross Road, Duncan
Owner has blueprints, now given to CVM
c.1928 Admiral R. Nugent property from Col. de Labilliere - Residence (Extant with some alteration)
6685 Norcross Road, Duncan
Contractor: E.W. Lee
Hamish Mutter C-L April 19, 1928, pg. 1
1931 Hugh Charter - Farm Residence (Extant large compatible addition)
3104 Cowichan Valley Highway
Hamish Mutter
1931 Bernard F. Burrows - Residence (Extant)
2893 Sherman Road, Duncan
Hamish Mutter
c.1931 Mr. George Andrews - Residence (Extant)
1089 Nagle Street, Duncan
Listed by CVM
C-L Mar 23, 1932 reported Douglas James of CEF 88 Battalion planned to motor across the States to New York and "will reside in England." Author remembers the car as a Nash
1933 Mrs. C.M. Lamb - 5-Room Residence (Extant)
221 Trunk Road at Ypres, Duncan
Contractor E.W. Lee
Cost: $3,000
C-L Mar 23, 1933

c.1934 Douglas James - Fourth Residence designed for his own use, (Extant, enlarged)
6392 Lakes Road, Duncan
Family history and photos

1935 High School Gymnasium (Extant)
Cairnsmore Street, Duncan
C-L Mar 14, 1935

1936 Elks Building (Extant, altered)
Duncan
CVM

1936 Fairbridge Farms [Douglas James took over supervision of construction after the death of the architect, Major K.B. Spurgin]

1938 H.L. Whittaker - Residence (Extant)
2159 Quamichan Park Road, Duncan
Plan at CVM

1945 Douglas James - Fifth Residence designed for his own use (Extant)
1414 Monterey Avenue, Victoria
Contractor: L.G. Scott
OBBD Permit #5047

1948 Memorial Arena (Demolished)
Architect: Douglas James in partnership with Hubert Savage and D.C. Frame

1946-7 Imperial Bank (Extant)
1301 Government Street, Victoria
Architects: D.C. Frame & Douglas James
Plans at City Hall

1946-8 Federal Building and Post Office, Victoria (Extant)
SW corner of Government and Yates streets, Victoria
Architects: James & James
CVA

c.1950 Douglas James - Sixth Residence designed for his own use Chisholm Trail, Maple Bay (If extant, very much enlarged)
Hamish Mutter and family records

c.1955 Douglas James - Seventh Residence designed for his own use, Verdier Avenue, Brentwood Bay (If extant, very much enlarged)

Commissions By Hubert Savage, ARIBA, MAIBC (1884-1955)

Residential Jobs

c.1913 Burdick - Alterations to Residence
    Oliver Street, Oak Bay
    AIBC Dead File

1913 T.M. Burdick - Alterations to Residence
    Wilmot Road, Oak Bay
    Dr. Gibson, SFU

c.1913 Gardner - Alterations to Residence
    Robertson Street, Victoria
    AIBC Dead Files

c.1913 S. Greenwood - Alterations to Residence
    631 Harbinger Street, Victoria
    AIBC Dead Files

c.1913 Nichols - Residence (Demolished)
    3910 Cedar Hill Road, Saanich
    Cost: $10,000 *Architect, Builder & Engineer*

1913 Hubert Savage (own Residence) (Extant)
    3862 Grange Road, Saanich (formerly Blackwood Road)
    EA&C, chalet with half-timbering
    Author recalls visiting

c.1913 James Fulford - Residence (Extant)
    11 Eaton Road, Saanich
    Chalet style
    Dr. Gibson, SFU / AIBC Dead Files

c.1913 Harvey - Residence on Knapp Island (Extant)
    45 degree wings, three gables with wide eaves
    Hallmark Society records

1913 F.S. Fillmore - Residence
    1828 Crescent Road, Victoria
    Cost: $4,200 BP#6130 / CVPDD

1914 William C. Poole - Residence (Extant)
    520 St. Charles Street, Victoria EA&C
    Cost: $4,600 BP#6379 / CVPDD

c.1925 1020 Burnside Road, Saanich (Extant) [One of several speculative houses Savage built in Marigold area, for which no plans exist. They consistently use his stylistic details] EA&C bungalow
    Joy Barth (Savage's daughter)

c.1925 1050 Jasmine Avenue, Saanich (Extant)
    (Another of the speculative houses.)
    EA&C bungalow

1925 Cato - Bungalow (Extant)
    10950 Madrona Drive, Sidney
    EA&C bungalow
    Blueprint with present owner

1926 S. Greenwood - Residence (Extant)
    1372 Craigdarroch Road, Victoria EA&C
    Cost: $7,500 CVPDD / BP#3170

1926 Thomas Watt - Semi-Bungalow (Extant)
    2529 Bowker Avenue, Oak Bay EA&C
    CVA Savage Collection

1927 E.J. Farmer - Residence (Extant)
601 Transit Road, Oak Bay
EA&C with half-timbering
CVA Savage Collection

1927 Hugh Ferguson - Residence (Extant)
614 Foul Bay Road, Victoria
EA&C with half-timbering
Cost: $8,000 BP#3697 / CVPDD
CVA Savage Collection

1927 1020 Iris Street - *Sylvan Lodge* Residence
A.T.T. Roberts (Extant)
EA&C bungalow
(Plans do not exist. One of the speculative houses)
Author's surmise confirmed by owner's recollection.

1928 Mrs. J.C. Ciceri - Residence (Extant)
679 Island Road, Oak Bay
EA&C with half-timbering
CVA Savage Collection

1928 H.M. Archibald - Residence (Extant)
3415 Cadboro Bay Road, Oak Bay
EA&C with half-timbering
Architect: Hubert Savage of James & Savage
CVA Savage Collection / OBBD

1929 H. Allan - Proposed Residence
Corner Deal and Margate Streets, Oak Bay
CVA Savage Collection - filed plan not built
[Existing house by M.B. Browne / OBBD]

1929 Mrs. Mabel E.C. Dring - Alterations (Extant)
2417 Cadboro Bay Road, Oak Bay
EA&C addition to Colonial Bungalow
Architect: Hubert Savage of James & Savage
CVA Savage Collection

1929 A.C. Johnstone - Residence (Extant)
2629 Tsouhalem Road, Duncan
EA&C with half-timbering
Architect: Hubert Savage of James & Savage
Supervision by Douglas James
CVA Savage Collection

1929 J.A. Merrick - Residence (Extant)
3000 Uplands Road, Oak Bay
EA&C with half-timbering
Architect: Hubert Savage of James & Savage
CVA Savage Collection

1929 Butler - Residence
1315 Coventry Avenue, Victoria
Cost $3,000 BP#5173 / CVPDD

1929 W. Swire Mitchell - Residence (Extant)
15 Beach Drive at Denison Road, Oak Bay
EA&C with half-timbering
Architect: Hubert Savage of James & Savage
CVA Savage Collection

1929 O.W. Pauline - Residence (Extant)
934 Foul Bay Road, Victoria
EA&C with half-timbering
Architect: Hubert Savage of James & Savage
CVA Savage Collection

1929 N.W. Whittaker - Residence (Extant)
    3305 Weald Road, Oak Bay
    EA&C with half-timbering
    Architect: Hubert Savage of James & Savage
    CVA Savage Collection - 2 versions of the design

c.1930 T.W. Hall - Bungalow *Stranton Lodge* (Extant)
    1248 Burnside Road, Saanich
    EA&C bungalow
    Architect: Hubert Savage of James & Savage
    Heritage designation within Knockan Park

1930 Lt-Col. Henry W.L. and Mrs. Grace Margaret Laws - Residence (Extant, some alterations)
    2451 Queenswood Drive, Saanich
    EA&C with half-timbering, "butterfly design"
    Architect: Hubert Savage of James & Savage
    CVA Savage Collection

1930 Dr. Nash - Residence (Extant)
    3515 Upper Terrace, Oak Bay EA&C with half-timbering
    Architect: Hubert Savage of James & Savage
    CVA Savage Collection

1930 H.G. Ogden - Residence (Extant)
    679 Mount Joy Avenue, Oak Bay
    EA&C with half-timbering
    Architect: Hubert Savage of James & Savage
    CVA Savage Collection

1931 A.H. Bennet - Residence (Extant)
    915 Terrace Avenue, Victoria
    EA&C with half-timbering
    Architect: Hubert Savage of James & Savage
    CVA Savage Collection

1931 R.O. John - 7-room Bungalow (Demolished)
    413 Simcoe Street, Victoria
    Contractor: W. Pridham
    Cost: $3,500
    Architects: James & Savage
    Blueprint in City Hall

c.1931 Col. F. Sharland - Residence (Demolished by fire)
    Queenswood
    2494 Arbutus Road, Saanich
    EA&C with half-timbering
    Architect: Hubert Savage of James & Savage
    Print from newspaper in author's collection

c.1931 Col. F. Sharland - Gamekeeper's Cottage (Extant)
    2330 Queenswood Drive, Saanich
    EA&C Bungalow
    Architect: Hubert Savage of James & Savage
    Author recalls the estate and enclosure for deer

1933 T.G. Denny - Residence and 1937 Addition (Extant)
    149 Barkley Avenue, Oak Bay
    EA&C with half-timbering
    Architect: Hubert Savage of James & Savage
    CVA Savage Collection

1934 Herbert Warren - Bungalow (Extant)
    1270 Montrose Avenue, Victoria
    EA&C

Cost: $2,200 BP#8762 / CVPDD
Present owner has blueprints, name not specified

1935 Reginald Genn (Agent) Residence (Extant with additions)
721 Moss Street, Victoria   EA&C
Contractor: E.J. Hunter
Cost: $3,200 EA&C BP#9194 / CVPDD

1936 A. Stuart Bleakney - Residence (Extant)
514 Newport Avenue, Oak Bay
EA&C with half-timbering
CVA Savage Collection

1936 Garage designed for Residence on Island Road [not located]
CVA Savage Collection

1936 Garnet G. Gibson - Residence (Extant)
3435 Cadboro Bay Road, Oak Bay
EA&C with half-timbering, ashlar stone front
CVA Savage Collection

1937 Charles A.O. Clement, - Garden Room Addition (Extant)
679 Island Road, Oak Bay
CVA Savage Collection

1937 Dr. H.G. Chisholm - Residence (Extant)
1398 Oliver Street, Oak Bay
EA&C with half-timbering
CVA in Savage Collection

1937 Hubert Knight - Residence (Extant)
1955 Waterloo Road, Saanich
EA&C bungalow with half-timbering
Owner has framed signed blueprint

1937 W.A. Patterson - Residence (Extant)
2580 Cotswold Road at Weald, Oak Bay
EA&C bungalow with half-timbering
CVA Savage Collection (two versions for this design)

1937 Sir Ernest W. Petter - Residence *The Fort* (Extant, altered)
At Comox, now part of North Island College
EA&C with half-timbering
CVA Savage Collection

1937 Miss Stuart - Bungalow, (Extant)
The Sheiling 2525 Beauford Drive, Sidney
EA&C
Attributed to Hubert Savage Plans not on file.

1938 E. Colclough - Bungalow (Extant, enlarged)
1057 St. David Street, Oak Bay
EA&C with half-timbering
Owner has signed blueprint and architect's signboard

1938 George C. Harris - Residence (Extant, perhaps altered)
3820 Miramontes, Saanich
EA&C
CVA Savage Collection

1938 A.G. Strugnell - Bungalow (Extant)
540 Selkirk Avenue, Victoria
Contractor: Green Bros. Cost: $4,000
BP#210612 / CVPDD

1938 Mrs. A. Everest - Residence (Extant)

3670 Quadra Street, Saanich
EA&C with half-timbering
Owner has signed blueprint

c.1939 Mrs. M.E.C. Dring - Residence (Extant much enlarged)
330 Kinver Street, Esquimalt
Plans not on file Joy Barth recalls

1939 Eric H. Garman - Small Residence
936 Heywood Avenue, Victoria
Cost: $4,000 BP#211442 / CVPDD

1939 Colin and Florence M. Forest, Royal Oak - Restaurant
4509 West Saanich Road, Saanich
(Became first Maltwood Museum)
CVA Savage Collection

1939 J.A. Birnie - Residence (Extant)
2596 Empire Street, Victoria
Contractor: R.W. Payne
Cost: $3,000 BP#211069 / CVPDD

1939 Albert J. Sommer - Residence (Extant)
Beach Drive at Mount Joy Avenue, Oak Bay
EA&C with half-timbering
CVA Savage Collection

1940 R. Halls - Bungalow
31 Lotus Street, Victoria
Contractor: W.B. Dillabough
Cost: $2,800
BP#211864 / CVPDD

1940 George F. Booth - Residence (Extant)
420 Victoria Avenue, Oak Bay
EA&C with half-timbering
CVA Savage Collection

1940 Hollywood Estates One and Two bedroom row-house development with garages behind (Extant, now *Montague Court*)
1715-1739 Fairfield Road and Beechwood Avenue, Victoria
EA&C with half-timbering
CVA Savage Collection

1940 Sir Ernest Petter - Stores (Extant)
1720-22 Lillian Road
Contractor: Green Bros.
Cost: 25,000 BP#212084 / CVPDD
(Similar to Carmichael Stores, 1926, by James & Savage)

1940 F.I. and M. Jardine - Residence (Extant)
1540 Despard Avenue, Victoria
Contractor: Green Bros EA&C
Cost $10,000 BP#212573 / CVPDD

c.1940 Sir Ernest W. Petter - Proposed Annex
Comox EA&C
Architect: Hubert Savage

1941 Mrs. Bailey - Chinoiserie-Style Residence (Extant)
To house oriental collection
528 Goldstream Avenue at Vantilberg, Colwood
CVA Savage Collection

1941 Mrs. Belcher - Residence, (Extant, apartments)

211 Cook Street, Victoria
Contractor: E J. Hunter
Cost: $10,000 BP#212698 / CVPDD

1941 C.S. Henley and Jessie M. Kipling - Residence (Extant, enlarged)
1311 Rockland Avenue, Victoria
Contractor: T. Lambie
Cost: $2,875 CVPDD

1944 W.C. Woodward - Garage and Living Quarters (Extant)
7764 West Saanich Road, Brentwood Bay
EA&C
CVA Savage Collection

1944 L.C. Wakeman - Bungalow (Extant)
1411 Fairfield Road, Victoria
Contractor: J. Wakeman
Cost: $6,250 BP#215424 / CVPDD

c.1944 Alterations to Residence (Ectant)
3455 Cadboro Bay Road, Oak Bay
(Original design by Johnson & Stockdill)
Blueprint filed at OBBD
CVA Savage Collection

1945 D. McConachie - Bungalow (Extant, perhaps altered)
1425 Fairfield Road, Victoria
Contractor: J. Wakeman
Cost: $5,800 BP#216379 / CVPDD

1946 Sir Ernest Petter - Alterations and Addition to *The Haven* (Extant)
1472 Beach Drive, Oak Bay
CVA Savage Collection
EA&C

1950 Mrs. L. Todd-Turner, Residence
Henderson Point, Saanich
EARC eyebrow dormers, herringbone panels
Hubert Savage Commission
CVA Savage Collection

1951 R.E Smith - Residence (Extant)
Henderson Point (only address) Saanich
CVA Savage Collection
Duplex Residence - Joan Crescent, Victoria
CVA Savage Collection

1951 J.H. Todd - Residence
Newport Avenue, Oak Bay
EA&C
CVA Savage Collection

General Commissions

c.1925 War Memorial - Esquimalt (Extant)
Esquimalt Archives

1926 Queen Alexandra Solarium, Mill Bay (Demolished)
Architects: Samuel Maclure & Hubert Savage
CVA Savage Collection

1929 Cridge Memorial Hall, Victoria (Extant altered)
Architects: Samuel Maclure & Hubert Savage
CVA Savage Collection

1935 Drill Hall - RCN Barracks Esquimalt
CVA Savage Collection

1935 Office Block - RCN Esquimalt
CVA Savage Collection

1943 James Bay Hotel - Alterations (Extant)
270 Government Street, Victoria
CVA Savage Collection

1941-2 Windsor Auto Court (Demolished)
Gorge Road, Victoria
CVA Savage Collection

1943 Anderson's Garage - Alterations
Johnson Street, Victoria
Plans recorded by SDW and discarded

1944 Ritz Apartment Hotel - Alteration
Fort Street, Victoria
Plans recorded by SDW and discarded

1945 Creamery
Plans recorded by SDW and discarded

1946 Kyoquot Trollers Company Offices
Plans recorded by SDW and discarded

1946 Switzer's Lockers
Plans recorded by SDW and discarded

1948 Apartment building
Rockland Avenue, Victoria
Plans recorded by SDW and discarded

1948 Memorial Arena (Demolished)
1925 Blanchard Street, Victoria
Architects: H. Savage, D.C. Frame & Douglas James
[Designing partner]
CVA Savage Collection

1948 Royal Dairy Limited
Plans recorded by SDW and discarded

1948 Pure Foods Distributing Limited
Plans recorded by SDW and discarded

1949 Community Hall, Cordova Bay, Saanich
Plans recorded by SDW and discarded

1949 Apartment Belcher Avenue, Victoria
Plans recorded by SDW and discarded

1950 Memorial Hall, Mount Newton, Saanich
Plans recorded by SDW and discarded

1951 Wiring drawing
Plans recorded by SDW and discarded

Schools Designed By Hubert Savage

1921 Cloverdale School addition, Saanich
   CVA Savage Collection

1921-29 Tillicum School and alterations, Saanich
   CVA Savage Collection

1922 Royal Oak - Frame School, Saanich
   CVA Savage Collection

1925 Gordon Head - Frame School, Saanich
   CVA Savage Collection

1931 Mount Newton High School (Mount Douglas) Saanich
   CVA Savage Collection

1945 Mount View Technical Workshop, Saanich
   CVA Savage Collection

1945-6 Tolmie School, Saanich
   CVA Savage Collection

1945-6 Cowichan Lake High School - Auditorium, Home
   Economics Room, Boiler Room
   Lake Cowichan, BC
   Plans recorded by SDW and discarded

1946 Duncan Junior High School - Addition
   Duncan, BC
   Plans recorded by SDW and discarded

1948 Elementary School Industrial Arts Building
   Plans recorded by SDW and discarded

1949 Duncan High School - Preliminary WD, electrical, details, etc
   Duncan, BC
   Plans recorded by SDW and discarded

1948 One Room School
   Plans recorded by SDW and discarded

1949 Courtney Senior High School, Courtney, BC
   Plans recorded by SDW and discarded

1949 Youbou Elementary - Addition
   Youbou, BC
   Plans recorded by SDW and discarded

1952 Mount View High School, Saanich
   CVA Savage Collection (also 1931 drawings)

Hubert Savage Demolished Buildings In Victoria

715 Sea Terrace CVA 1-0057
200 - 202 Belleville Street CVA 2-0840
670 Montreal Avenue CVA 2-0840
821 Burdett Avenue CVA 2-0362
2640 Cook Street CVA 2-1035
319 Government Street CVA 2-1018
356 Simcoe Street (EA&C)
CVA 2-0354

Abreviations Used In Job Lists

AB&E - *Architect, Builder & Engineer*
AIBC - Architectural Institute of BC
ARIBA - Associate of the Royal Institute of British Architects
BCA - British Columbia Archives in Victoria, formerly BC Provincial Archives
BC - British Columbia
BP - Building Permit
C-L - *Cowichan - Leader*
CVA - City of Victoria Archives
CVPDD - City of Victoria Planning & Development Dept.
CVRBP - City of Victoria Residential Building Plans
CVM - Cowichan Valley Museum
Esq - Esquimalt
FRAIC - Fellow of the Royal Architectural Institute of Canada
MAIBC - Member of the Architectural Institute of BC
OB - Oak Bay
OBBD - Oak Bay Building Department
ORB - Old *Records* book of James & James, 1912 – 1920
Saan - Saanich
SDW - Siddall Dennis Warner, Architects
SFU - Simon Fraser University. Architectural history class notes
TOH - *This Old House* published by City of Victoria
Vict - Victoria

Bibliography

Barrett, Anthony A.& Rhodri Windsor Liscombe. *Francis Rattenbury and British Columbia: Architecture and Challenge in the Imperial Age.* University of British Columbia Press, Vancouver: 1983.

Bucher, Ward. *Dictionary of Building Preservation*, edited by Ward Bucher. John Wiley & Sons, Inc. New York: 1996.

Building the West: The Early Architects of British Columbia. Edited by Donald Luxton, Talon Books, Vancouver: 2003.

Carley, Rachel. *The Visual Dictionary of American Domestic Architecture.* Henry Holt & Company, New York: 1994.

City of Victoria Heritage Advisory Committee. *This Old House: An Inventory of Residential Heritage.* Victoria, BC: 1978.

Clarks, Ann Brewster. *Wade Hampton Pipes: Arts and Crafts Architect in Portland, Oregon.* Binford & Mort Publishing, Portland: 1985.

The Crystal Gardens: West Coast Pleasure Palace. Published by the Crystal Gardens Preservation Society, Victoria, BC: 1977.

Davey, Peter. *Arts & Crafts Architecture*, Phaidon. London: 1995.

The Decorative Designs of C.F.A. Voysey. Rizzoli International Publishers Inc. New York: 1991.

Dorin, Patrick C. *Canadian Pacific Railway*, Hancock House Publishers, Saanichton, BC: 1974.

Durant, Stuart. *Architectural Monograph No. 19 C.F.A. Voysey.* Academy Editions / St. Martin's Press, London: 1992.

Ewart, Henry. *Victoria's Streetcar Era.* Sono Nis Press, Victoria, BC: 1992.

Hawkes, Dean. Editor *Modern Country homes in England: The Arts and Crafts Architecture of Barry Parker.* Cambridge University Press, Cambridge: 1986.

Hayward Gallery. *Lutyens: The Work of the English Architect Sir Edwin Lutyens (1869-1944)* London: 18 November 1981 - 31 January 1982.

Hitchmough, Wendy. *C F.A. Voysey.* Phaidon, London: 1995.

Jackson, Frank. *Architects in Perspective Series: Sir Raymond Unwin, Architect, Planner and Visionary.* A. Zwemmer Ltd., London: 1985.

James, Percy. *History of St. Mary's Church, Oak Bay.* Victoria, BC: 1931.

Luxton, Donald. *Taming the West: the Thirty Year Struggle to Regulate the Architectural Profession in British Columbia.* Society for the Study of Architecture in Canada Journal, Vol. 22, No. 4, 1998, pp.108-123.

Mackey, Ellen. *Places of Worship in the Cowichan and Chemainus Valleys.* Sono Nis Press, Victoria, BC: 1991.

Morris, Jan. *The Spectacle of Empire*. Faber & Faber, London Boston: 1982.

Only in Oak Bay: Oak Bay Municipality 1906-1981. Published by Corporation of the District of Oak Bay: 1981.

Orrell, John. *Fallen Empires: Lost Theatres in Edmonton, 1881-1914.* NeWest Press, Edmonton: 1981. Ramsey, C.G, AIA and Sleeper, H.R., FAIA

Architectural Graphic Standards. Published by John Wiley & Sons, New York: 1951.

Reksten, Terry. *Rattenbury*. Sono Nis Press, Victoria, BC: 1978.

Rubens, Godfrey. *William Richard Lethaby His Life and Work 1857-1931.* The Architectural Press, London: 1986.

Service, Alastair. *London 1900*. Granada Publishing, London: 1979.

Shaw Sparrow, W., editor. *The Modern Home: A book of British Domestic Architecture for Modest Incomes*. A.C. Armstrong & Sons, New York: 1904.

Shaw Sparrow, W., editor. *The British Home of Today: A book of Modern Domestic Architecture & the Applied Arts*. A.C. Armstrong & Sons, New York: c.1905.

Stark, Stuart. *Oak Bay's Heritage Buildings: More than just bricks and boards.* Published by the Corporation of the District of Oak Bay, 1986.

Weaver, Lawrence, Editor *The House and Its Equipment.* Country Life, London: n.d. (circa 1914)

Unpublished Manuscripts:

Haegart, Joseph. Unpublished manuscript. BCA n.d.
James & James. *Old Record Book*. 1912 - 1926.
James, P. Leonard. *Early Days*. 1965.

Glossary

Balustrade - See Banisters

Banisters - uprights supporting stair handrail between newel posts. Carved or turned banisters may be called balusters.

Bargeboard - One of a pair of sloped boards at the edge of a projecting eave at the gable end. Also called a gableboard.

Bellcast - Roofs that flare from one pitch to a lesser pitch near the eaves. A flared or splayed roof gives the building a feeling of lightness.

Belt course see **String Course.**

Bungalow - A one-storey house with gabled or hipped roof. The name originated in India where such houses had verandahs.

Casement - A window that is hinged on one side, and opens by swinging out (sometimes in.)

Clear-run timber - wood without knots or defects.

Cottage - Usually a one-storey house with hipped roof. Also used in England and Eastern USA for quite a large house, c.f. the H. James Cottage, a house with two full storeys.

Double-hung windows - Two sashes that slide past each other vertically. Earlier examples use cords, pulleys and counterweight in the mullions and window framing.

Eaves - The projection of the roof beyond the wall below. The eaves may be open to show the rafter ends, or closed in with a flat soffit.

Finial - A wooden member inserted where the barge boards meet at the peak of the roof. These may be pointed, capped or carved. A **drop finial** hangs below the barge boards. Many finials extend both above and below the roof peak.

Half-hipped roof - A gable construction the top part of which is hipped. Sometimes called a jerkinhead gable.

Integral porch - EA&C used a porch within the outer walls of the house, American A & C used a porch design that extended beyond the walls of the house.

Jerkinhead gable - A gable that is finished with a partial hip at the top. Also known as half-hipped. When jettied this roof called a Dutch half-hip.

Jerry-built - Hastily constructed. Most often of substandard materials and methods.

Jettied storey - a storey that overhangs the lower storey.

Lintel - A beam spanning a door or window opening, or an architectural detail representing such a beam.

Lintel course see **String course.**

Mansard roof - A two-pitched roof with lower slope the steepest.

Modillion - horizontal projecting brackets, carved or plain, under soffit. These often line up with the half-timbering if it is used on the wall below.

Mullion - vertical bar dividing two windows or doors.

Muntin - The small molding or bar that separates the individual panes of a multipaned window sash.

Newel - Vertical post that terminates a run of stair railing or balustrade..

Oriel - Projection from main wall in the form of a bay window that starts above ground level, may be supported by corbels (stepped out masonry), brackets or a flared-out support.

Palladian - Neo-classical style popularized by Andrea Palladio (16th Century Italian architect) In residential work this style is most often seen in three-part windows, where the central arched one is flanked by two rectangular windows. Versions of this can be seen in the roof line of a dormer window (as in the William Galliher house); and in the top line of glazed doors and panel doors (as in the Frank Burrell house).

Perspective - a drawing that shows a three-dimensional view of a building.

Pilaster - A rectangular or round column not free standing but attached to or engaged in the wall.

Pitch - Roof slope. Specified as the ratio of vertical inches to horizontal inches, or in degrees.

Porte-cochère - Roofed passage for vehicles past the front entrance, or through house to courtyard.

Roman brick - A long thin brick that became popular in the 1940s. Dimensions 12″x 4″ x 1⅝″

Roughcast stucco - Usually three-coat work consisting of scratch coat, brown coat and a pebble dash coat. Half-timbering is put in place before the wall is stuccoed.

Semi-bungalow - A house with rooms finished upstairs, but with roof extending down to the second floor joist level. Most of the upstairs rooms have partially sloped ceilings and some form of storage space in the half-walls.

Sill - The horizontal course that rests on the foundation, the bottom of a doorway, or a window.

Soffit - Flat surface under enclosed eaves.

String course - A horizontal molding separating parts of a wall surface. Can also be called a **belt course**, or more specifically a **lintel course** or a **sill course** to indicate the level at which it occurs. Also a **water table.**

Two to the weather - Designates use of double shingles, probably an English term for "double-coursed." (Harrison house)

Wainscoting - A wood covering of an interior wall, usually panelling.

Waney-edged - An irregular, rounded edge on sawn timber that was part of the original outside curve of the log.

Watertable - Moulding encircling building above foundation level to shed water.

Weatherboard - Horizontal boards used as exterior wall covering. These may or may not have waney-edges. Often used only in the gable.

Winder - A step with a tread that is wider at one end. A stair made with winders can turn a corner without a landing, and is referred to as a winding stair.

Index

A

Affiliations
  Alberta Assoc. of Architects, 1906, 14
  Architectural Institute of BC
    Charter Member, 1920, 50
    Honorary Member, 167
  Charter Member, Architectural Institute of Canada, 30
  Royal Architectural Institute of Canada
    Charter Member of AIC, 1906, 30
    College of Fellows, 1931, 113
    Honorary Member, 1967, 167
    Senate of The College, 1941, 152
  Society of Architects, Treasurer 1911-1913, 29
Alexander, Mrs. E., 65
Allen, K. C., 119
Amusement Centre See Crystal Garden, 94 - 95, 105
Anderson, J. N., 115, 124
Architectural Institute of BC, 95
Architectural Styles
  Art Moderne, 79, 150
  Classical, 77
  English Arts & Crafts, 76 - 79
  Georgian Revival or Classical, 77
  International Style, 79
  Stripped Classicism, 173
  Tudor, 38, 77
  Tudor Revival, 38, 76

Archives
  BC Archives and Record Service, 113
  City of Victoria Archives (CVA), 113
  Edmonton City Archives, 12
  The Archives of the Anglican Diocese of BC, 146

B

Baillie Scott, M. H., 78, 84
Bannavern, 24
Barrett, David and Shirley, 22
Barton, Don, 115
Barton, Rev. William, 37
Bauhaus, The, 137
Baxter, C. S., 38
Beckton, Herbert S., 108
Better Housing Act, 49
Bird, E. H., 67
Birley, Patrick, 29
Bishop's Palace, 146
Bovey, John, 20
Boyle, H. H., 65
Branson, C. L., 119
Brault, C. Gustave, Chief Architect DPW, 162
Bridgman, A.W., 28
British Industries House, 138
Brown, O. C., 73
Bullen, H. F., 51, 102
Burchell family, 63

Burrell, Frank, 39
Burt-Smith, H., 67
Byng, Governor General Baron, 100

C

Cameron, Alexander W., 12
Campbell, Clive, 115
Canadian Homes and Gardens July, 1933
  "In the Swim Across Canada", 110
Carefree Cottages, 73
Carpenter, C. H., 112
Carr, Emily, 18
Cassie, Mrs. J.I., 58
Cathedral Sunday School, 147
Chermayedd, Serge, 137
Churches
  Chapel of the Peace of God, 146
  St. John the Baptist Anglican, Cobble Hill, 147
  St. Mary's Anglican, Oak Bay, 34
  St. Peter's Anglican, Comox, 147
Clarkson, Eric, 92
Clarkson, John C., 92
Collections
  Hubert Savage drawings, 172
  MS 502 collection, 173
  P. Leonard James drawings, 28, 127, 172
Colwood 1922 clubhouse, 63, 125
Colwood 1929 Clubhouse, 125
Competitions
  Bexhill School, 9

Royal Alexandra Hospital, 13
Royal Jubilee Hospital, 53
Strathcona Hospital, 13
Winnipeg City Hall, 31
Compton Wynyates, 15
Cotton, A. B., 118
Cowichan Valley Museum, 71
CPR
   Crystal Garden See Crystal Garden, 98
   Depot See Marine Terminal, 102
   Digby Pines Pool, 110
   Lake Louise Swimming Pool, 108
   Marine Terminal, 96
Crowe, Dora, 144
Crystal Garden, 92, 95, 104, 153, 171, 181
Crystal Palace, 137

D

Danby, Arthur V., 79
Dawson, Fred, 162
Deans Block, 28
Deerlepe, 58
Dewdney, Edgar, 144
Durleston, 16, 23
Durlston Head, 2
Dutch Village, Coulsden, 137

E

Early Days, 3, 6
Edmonton
   Hospitals, 13
   Lyceum Theatre, 13
Edmonton Bulletin, 12
Edmonton Journal, 12

Edwards, G. H. S., 38
Elford, John, 8
English Arts & Crafts details, 116
Evans and Deacon, 7
Evans, Chad, 172

F

Federal Building, 171
Federal Building and Post Office, 162
Field, Richard, 151
Fire Hall, Oak Bay, 147
Forbes-Wilson, Mrs. See also Sayward-Wilson, 51
Frame, D. C., 74

G

Gaitskill, Dudley, 62
Gaitskill, G. H., 62
Galliher, Judge Wm. A, 24
Garden City Town Planning, 78
Gardom, Basil, 104 - 105, 107 - 108
Gibson, George, 96, 125, 127
Gidea Park, 150
   Exhibition, 138
Glenclova, 79
Gower, Terry, 115
Graham, Mortimore, 23
Green, Claude, 72
Griffiths, E. W., 79, 150
Groos, David, 17
Groos, Everard and Mabel, 17
Groos, Harold, 17, 164, 170
Groos, Jeanne, 17
Groos, Mabel, 11

Gropius, Walter, 137

H

Hallmark Society, 67, 146, 165
Ham, A.C., 189 - 190
Ham, Arthur C., 124
Hamilton, Madge Wolfenden, 34, 36 - 37
Hammersley, Mrs., 148
Hampstead, 2
Hampstead Garden Suburb, 16
Hardie, David, 106
Hargreaves, Wilfrid, 152
Harrison, E. H., 53
Hatley Park Castle, 15, 18
Hayward, Mayor R., 106
Helmcken, Dr. J. D., 31
Henderson, Malcolm, Grand Forks, 50
Henderson, Mr. and Mrs. R., 50
Heritage Designation - *Miramar*, 119
Highgate, 2
Hinton, H. C., 67
History of St. Mary's Church, Oak Bay, Victoria, BC, 34
Honeyman, John J., 66
Hopkins, Edward Colis, 13
Hospitals
   East Sussex, Hastings, England, 42
   Royal Alexandra, Edmonton, Alta, 14
   Royal Jubilee, Victoria, BC, 53
   Strathcona, Alta., 14
Hunter & Halkett, 132
Hunter, H., 62

I

Ideal Home Exhibition at Olympia, 137
Island Arts & Crafts Society, 18

J

James & James, 28, 162
James & Savage, 112
James and Jarvis Navigation School, 15
James Ballroom, 111
James, Douglas, 1, 15, 72, 74, 79, 87
  Radiant, 71
James, Hannah, 14, 16, 45
James, Harold, 1, 11, 14 - 15, 17, 34
James, Mabel Mary, 1
James, P. L.
  Comments on Gidea Park, 138
  Suggestions for post war industrial housing, 43
James, P. Leonard, 13, 20, 49, 103 - 104, 107, 129, 155, 166
James, Percy, 34, 36
James, Polson & Siddall, 154, 162
James, Samuel, 1, 14, 16
Johns, Dr. T. H., 79, 150
Johnson, H., 79

K

Keith, J. C. M., 20, 49, 146
Ker, Mrs. D. R., 61
Ker, R. H. B., 58, 81

L

Laburnum Gardens, 16
Lake Louise, Alta., 108
Lampman, Judge P. S., 56, 79
Lampman, Mrs. P. S., 148
Lee, E. W., 72
Longstaff, Major F. V., 51, 53
Lott, Herbert S., 37
Luney Brothers, 54, 104
Lutyens, Edwin, 85

M

MacDowall, H. C. V., 78, 117, 127
Maclure, Samuel, 15, 18, 20, 38, 50, 77
Magoon, Herbert Alton, 13
Marleau, Madame Diane, 165
Mayhew, R. W., 162
McCarter & Nairne, 151 - 152
McCarter, J. Y., 115, 162
Meardon, Maureen Licata, 133
Memorial Hall for St. Mary's Oak Bay, 48
Mendelsohn, Erick, 137
Merston, Capt. W. C., 66
Miramar, 119, 150
Molson, Capt. W. Hobart, 51, 129
Molson, David, 129
Morris, J. W., 31, 38
Morris, William, 31
Mother Cecilia Mary, 125
Mrs. Forbes-Wilson See Sayward-Wilson, 127
Municipal Hall, Oak Bay, 34
Musgrave, Arthur and Olive, 150
Mutter, Hamish and Daphne, 79

N

Natatorium at Alki Point, Seattle, 110
Nation, Miss H., 58, 79
Nesbitt, James, 20
Nobbs, Percy Erskine, 153

O

O'Keiffe, Miss B. E. and Miss G. Field, 150
Oak Bay Golf Club, 47
Oak Bay Grocery, 39
Orrell, John, 13

P

P. L. James Place, 165 - 166
Page, Forsey, 153
Page, L. E. Godfrey, 14
Page, L.E. Godfrey, 10
Pakenham, Alma, 107
Parfitt Brothers, 54
Pearson, L. P. G., 50
Pease, Algernon and Letitia, 36
Pease, Freddie, 115
Pease, W. B., 144
Pipes, Wade Hampon, 92
Pleasure Palace See Crystal Garden, 95
Pollard's Invisible Glazing, 139

R

Rattenbury, 107
Rattenbury & James, 95, 106 - 107
Rattenbury, F. M., 47, 51, 94 - 95, 103, 105 - 107
Rattenbury, James & James, 95
Regent Street Polytechnic, 14, 40
Reksten, Terry, 107
Rexford, Loring, 53

Robinson, Heath, 29
Robinwood, 121
Royal Jubilee Hospital, 171
Ruskin, John, 142

S

Savage, Hubert, 29, 39, 47, 74, 78, 81, 112 - 113, 115, 172
Saxon Snell, 8 - 9, 11
Saxon Snell & Son, 92
Sayward, J. A., 63, 125, 127
Sayward-Wilson, 127
Schools
    Cathedral Sunday School, 147
    Esquimalt High School addition, 80, 154
    Norfolk House, 124
    Oak Bay Avenue School, 31
    Oak Bay Junior High, 80, 154
    Willows, 31
Scott, Elizabeth, 139
Sechelt, 16 - 17
Semmes, J. E., 121
Shanks, R. H., 123
Shaw, Richard Norman, 76
Sherman, Victor and Dr. Marion, 150
Siddall Dennis & Warner, 172
Signor Clerici, 42
Slater, John, 14
Soldiers' Settlement Scheme, 49, 66

Spurgin, Major K. B., 53, 73
St. Laurent, Prime Minister Louis, 164
St. Margaret's Estates, Edgeware, 137
Staybrite Steel, 137
Stone, Carlton, 79
Stonehaven, 79
Stonehenge Park, 21
Stuart-Taylor, Lady, 167
Sunspan house, 137
Swanage, 2
Swimming Pools
    Crystal Garden, 95
    Digby Pines, NS, 110
    Lake Louise, 108

T

Tang O'Sea, 74, 79
Taylor, P. W. deP,, 58
Teague, John, 146
Thacker, Major General P. E., 61
The Daily Chronicle, 43
The Deanery, 146
Thetis Island, 61
Tod, John, 16
Tomlinson, R. W., 108, 115
Town Planning Commission, 154
Troup, Capt. J. W., 96

U

Unwin, Raymond, 16

V

Victoria Architecturally, 23
Voysey, Charles F. A., 77, 92

W

War service
    12th London Regiment, 43
    ARP warden WW2, 161
    Artist' Rifles Regiment, 43
    Disability certificate, 43
    Royal Engineer Corps, 43
Ward, F, B., 145
Wartime Housing, 151
Wattie, James A., 51
Weismuller, Johnny, 108
Williams, E. A. M., 151
Womens' Radio Forum, 153
Worsley, Norman, 115
Worth Matravers, 2

Y

Yarrow, John, 146
Yarrow, Mr. and Mrs. Norman, 146
Yarrow, Mrs. Hope, 155
Yarrow, Norman, 152, 156